THE ABSOLUTE BASICS OF CHRISTIANITY

The Absolute Basics of Christianity

A fresh look at the basics for all believers

A–Z

PETE PAWELEK

Next Generation Disciples is a two-fold ministry centered first on the development and equipping of the church, directing believers through the three stages of spiritual growth from being a "New Believer" to a "Young Christian" to a "Mature Disciple." The second part of the ministry is worship—and mission-driven, focusing on "Mature Disciples." Believers who have reached this stage should have already been mobilized to fulfill what every believer has been instructed to do repeatedly: to be a witness, "in Jerusalem (the local community), in all Judea (your state or country), Samaria (your outer and surrounding regions), and to the ends of the earth." We aim to work and walk with you through your spiritual growth and to help you achieve what God has planned in your life. Learn more at **www.nextgenerationdisciples.com.**

© 2010 by Pete Pawelek

ISBN-10 0982937229

ISBN-13 9780982937228

Cover design by **David Wickersham**.
   David may be contacted through the author's website, **www.pastorpete.org.**

Book design by **Arc Manor**
   Visit their website at **www.arcmanor.com**

Additional copies of this work and other books by Pete Pawelek may be purchased at
www.pastorpete.org

Special Thanks

I'd like to say thank you to:

My wife Abby and our children, who make each day of my life better then the day before. Their love and support has always been an overwhelming force in my life.

My ministry assistant Sue and my friend Katharine, who helped edit each page of this Bible study.

My friends Chris, Andrew, and Adam, who spent many hours completing each of these studies and making careful notes and suggestions to improve the content of these lessons.

My friend David, for his diligent work on this book's cover design.

And finally, every member of our church, for allowing me the privilege of learning so much about the process of discipleship through their lives.

CONTENTS

*T*his book has been designed to be used with people at all different levels of spiritual maturity. Whether a new believer or a seasoned saint, everyone can learn from this study. As you move through the study, the lessons build on each other and progressively get into deeper subject matter and require more thought from the student. There are three main ways that this study can be used—self-study, micro group study, or small group study.

While this study has been used successfully as a self-study in which an individual works alone, this method is not recommended. God intends for believers to live in fellowship with others, and we tend to learn more and grow faster and stronger when we join others to study God's Word. Accountability is critical for long-term spiritual success, and without a group, true accountability is difficult. If you are considering doing this study alone, I strongly urge you to consider one of the other two methods, choosing self-study only if you have no other option. If you decide to use this workbook as a resource for self-study, please take the time to visit **www.pastorpete.org** for additional information on each week's lesson along with answers to many of the questions.

This study can also be completed in a micro group. Micro groups usually consist of 3 to 5 people. They generally are less structured then a traditional small group because they rarely have a "leader" or "teacher." Instead, micro groups are made up of like-minded people who voluntarily and willingly agree to meet together and learn from each other. This kind of group encourages high accountability and makes for a very comfortable and effective learning atmosphere. These groups might meet in homes, or at school, work, or church.

Finally, you can use this study in a small group setting. This might be a Sunday school class or cell group, or as a part of a discipleship program at your church. These groups are generally made up of 5 to 20 people and have a designated leader or facilitator. Small groups are a great way to get to know others in the church and to develop healthy biblical relationships while learning from God's Word.

There are several things that the student must do, no matter which learning method is chosen, if you desire to have success with this workbook. They are:

1. ***Focus on the memory verses.*** Each week has a memory verse that the student should focus on and memorize. These verses should be reviewed on a weekly basis using the method explained in Appendix One. The goal

is not to remember a verse for a week but instead to hide it in your heart for a lifetime. This will take effort, discipline, and focus, but it will also return a great reward for those who do it.

2. ***Answer all the questions.*** Even if you think the question is too basic or too hard, attempt to answer every question in the study. When you see the "⚒" or "🎬" symbol, you can go to **www.pastorpete.org**. There you will find expanded explanations, or the answers to some of the questions that require advanced resources. The "⚒" indicates that there is a written explanation, and the "🎬" identifies questions that have a video response or explanation from the author.

3. ***Do one lesson each day.*** Each week contains four lessons. These should be completed ideally in four consecutive days. Do not attempt to do all four lessons in a single day or in the hour before your group study starts. For example, if your group meets on Monday night, you should try to do your studies on Tuesday through Friday, and then use Saturday and Sunday to review your memory verses.

4. ***Don't quit.*** Whatever you do, don't quit or give up before you finish this twenty-six-week study. Make a commitment to finish this workbook today. This workbook is only twenty-six weeks long. You can do it!

Assurance of Salvation—Day One

Memory Verse

Romans 10:9

*O*ver 2000 years ago there was a man who, believe it or not, loved and cared for you so much that, after living a sinless perfect life, he endured incredible torture, pain, and humiliation, and then laid down, was nailed to a cross, and died for you. Through his death, and ultimately his resurrection, Jesus Christ made eternal salvation possible for you and everyone you know. Eternal salvation is impossible without Christ. There is no way to be saved without Jesus. This is the most basic and fundamental truth of the Christian life, so we begin our study here.

WHY IS IT IMPOSSIBLE?

²²This righteousness from God comes through faith in Jesus Christ to all who believe. There is no difference, ²³for all have sinned and fall short of the glory of God, ²⁴and are justified by his grace through the redemption that came by Christ Jesus.

Romans 3:22-24

Verse 23 says that *all* of us have sinned and as a result have fallen short of the glory of God. The Greek word for sin in verse 23 simply means anything at all that is contrary to the will or law of God. Every person to ever walk the face of this planet since the fall in the garden, with the exception of Jesus, can be described by Romans 3:23. We have all sinned and fallen short. Romans 6:23 tells us what those sins have earned us.

⳰ What does Romans 6:23 say the wages of sin are?

_____

_____

ও What does this verse mean to you?

_____

_____

HOW DOES SALVATION HAPPEN?

Look up and read Ephesians 2:4-9.

ও According to this passage, how are you saved?

_____

_____

_____

ও According to this passage, does salvation have anything to do with how hard or how much you work?

_____

_____

_____

ও What do you think it means to be saved "through faith"? ⚒

_____

_____

_____

Salvation comes when individuals place their faith and trust in Jesus Christ. This can happen at church, on the side of the road, in a home, at work, or any other place. You can't earn your salvation and, as we will soon learn, you can never lose it. In the space below, write out our memory verse for the week.

📖 Romans 10:9:

_____

_____

_____

⅋ What are the <u>two</u> things that your memory verse says you must do to be saved?

_____

_____

⅋ Which of these two things require faith? Or do both? Explain. ✖

_____

_____

⅋ According to this verse, how certain can you be of your salvation once you have confessed with your mouth and believed in your heart?

_____

_____

Now look up and read Romans 10:10

⅋ Compare Romans 10:9 and Romans 10:10. Do you notice anything different about the two verses? ✖

_____

_____

_____

⅋ If you were asked how someone could be saved, how would you answer?

_____

_____

⅋ Have you publically confessed Christ as your Lord and Savior? If so, when and where?

_____

_____

⅋ Have you believed in your heart? When? Or, why not?

_____

_____

Write out your memory verse in the space below. Try to do it completely from memory and then double-check yourself.

TAKE TIME TO PRAY

Thank God for sending his Son to die for you. Pray for one person you know who may not be saved.

Assurance of Salvation—Day Two

Memory Verse

Romans 10:9

Start today's study by writing out as much of your memory verse as you can in the space below. Then, look up the verse and make any corrections that are needed. Finally, read it three times from your Bible and pray before completing the following lesson.

_____

_____

_____

_____

*Y*esterday, we learned why salvation is impossible without Jesus Christ and we learned that our salvation comes through faith. Today, we will take our understanding of salvation just a bit further. Others will try to convince you that there are many ways into heaven. The world will tell you that your good works, your money, your status, or some other earthly thing that you generated yourself will get you into heaven. However, the Bible leaves no room at all for us to wonder about where our salvation comes from or how it is received.

The devil always attempts to attack us in this area of our lives. He knows that if he can fool us at the point of salvation, the rest of our faith will fall as well. Your enemy understands that no matter how young or mature you are in your faith, if he can cut you off at the roots you will never grow and produce fruit. So having a clear and well-developed understanding of grace and salvation is essential to your development as a disciple of Christ. Turn in your Bible to Acts chapter 4, then read verses 8-13 and answer the following questions.

- ❧ Where do the disciples say salvation can be found?

  _____

  _____

- ❧ Are there multiple places that humans can receive their salvation according to these verses?

  _____

  _____

Several things strike me as I read this passage. The first is that these "ordinary, unschooled" men are able to so clearly communicate the truth of the gospel. This simple truth is empowering for all Christians. You don't have to be a seminary graduate or a professional theologian to be able to communicate the gospel. In fact, in many respects, the layperson has more in common with the apostles than the professional staff at a church. The second thing that strikes me is the simplicity of the gospel message. Acts 4:12 reads, *Salvation is found in no one else, for there is no other name under heaven given to men by which we must be saved.* Too many times we get side-tracked and try to do too much with the message. When ordinary men and women present the simple message, extraordinary things happen. You are ready today to start telling others the simple message of the gospel.

- ❧ How would you tell someone about the gospel if you had the chance today?

  _____

  _____

  _____

  _____

- ❧ Write out your memory verse for the week and then explain how you could use that to express the simple truth of the gospel.

  _____

  _____

  _____

  _____

❧ Where is the only place salvation can be found?

_____

_____

Now, in your Bible, turn to the gospel of John, chapter 14. Read verses 1-7 before going further.

❧ How does verse 1 relate to having faith like we discussed yesterday? ⚒

_____

_____

_____

❧ Do verses 2 through 4 make you feel safe and secure as a Christian? Why or why not?

_____

_____

_____

❧ Read verse 6 one more time. Where does Jesus say salvation can be found?

_____

_____

❧ According to Jesus, is there any other way to get to the Father? What does that mean? ⚒

_____

_____

_____

The devil will try to tell you that you don't need Jesus to get into heaven. The world will try to convince you that you are good enough, rich enough, famous enough, important enough, or smart enough to get in on your own. God's word, however, tells us the truth! There is only one way into heaven. There is only one way to get to the Father, and that is through Jesus Christ. There is nothing you can do on your own, and there is nothing you can do to earn it. Salvation is a gift that you accept through faith. There is only one way, and his name is JESUS!

Take time to think through what you would say if God gave you an opportunity to share the gospel today. Think about a specific person whom you know, and visualize yourself successfully sharing your faith with that person. Use your memory verse and any other verse you can think of as you play out this scenario in your mind.

Write out your memory verse in the space below. Try to do it completely from memory, then double-check yourself.

TAKE TIME TO PRAY

Thank God for sending his Son and making the way to heaven so simple for you. Ask him to give you opportunities to share your faith in the coming days. Pray specifically for one person you know who does not know Christ.

Assurance of Salvation—Day Three

Memory Verse

Romans 10:9

Start today's study by writing out as much of your memory verse as you can in the space below. Then, look up the verse and make any corrections that are needed. Finally, read it three times from your Bible and pray before completing the following lesson.

_On Day One, we learned that salvation is impossible without placing our faith in Jesus Christ. Yesterday, we took it a step further and discovered that there truly is only one way to get into heaven and that is through Christ. Today, we want to look at the security of our salvation. We know that salvation is impossible without Jesus and we know that there is only one way, but can we lose it? Can it be taken away from us? Can we mess up so badly that God refuses to grant us salvation? These are the questions we will answer today.

In a temporary world, our mind is trained to think in temporary terms. For example, when we think of a lifetime, we think of someone living for seventy to one hundred years. But, in reality, a "lifetime" is eternal and will never end. Everyone will live forever. The question is, where will they live? Everything on this planet is temporary. Even our most treasured relationships with our spouses will come to an end; that's why we say, "'til death do us part." Our money is in the bank today and we spend it tomorrow. Our jobs are secure today and on the rocks tomorrow. Our vehicles are new when we drive them off the lot, but in time they too grow old, break down, and are discarded. Even our bodies are temporary! So, it's easy to see why the devil is so successful in confusing our thinking when it comes to our salvation. He wants you to believe that you can lose your salvation, or that it can be taken from you. He causes you to wonder if it is secure or, like everything else you know, is it only temporary?

Let's look into God's word for the answer to this very important question. Turn to John 10:25-30 and read it carefully, then answer the following questions:

ᑫ Who does Jesus say gives eternal life?

_____

_____

ᑫ In the very next statement, Jesus tells us what the result of eternal life is. What is it? ✗

_____

_____

ᑫ If you are a follower of Christ, who can snatch you out of his hands according to this passage? Why?

_____

_____

ᑫ Does this passage make your salvation sound temporary at all? What words in this passage lead you to your answer?

_____

_____

ᑫ Think about your memory verse for the week. What statement, or words in it, indicates that your salvation is secure and not temporary in any way?

_____

_____

_____

_____

Jesus says we are safe in his arms—not for a day, week, month, year, or generation. He says we are safe there for all eternity. He says that there is no one who can ever steal you or take you away from Him. This is good news for all believers. We don't have to walk on eggshells around God. We can, as the book of Hebrews (4:16) says, *approach the throne of grace with confidence.* This, however, does not mean that we can simply do whatever we want and live life the way we choose. Paul makes it clear in the book of Romans that those who are saved want to please Christ and do everything they can to become like him. Just because our salvation is secure does not give us license to go out and live like pagans. Look up and read Romans 5:20—6:7.

📖 Explain what Paul meant in Romans 6:1-2. ✗

_____

_____

_____

❧ Why is that important? Why should we not take our salvation for granted?

_____

_____

_____

Now look up Romans 8:35-39 and answer the following questions:

❧ What or who can separate you from the love of Christ?

_____

_____

❧ Can you think of anything else that might be able to separate you from Christ? If so, what?

_____

_____

❧ How does it make you feel to know that your salvation is secure?

_____

_____

_____

ঽ€ How would you explain the concept of your salvation being secure to someone else? What would you tell them if they doubted their salvation?

_____

_____

There is nothing in all of creation that can separate you from Christ! You are
safe in his arms and your salvation is secure in his care. Even the devil can't overcome the power of the cross and what Christ Jesus did for you that day. So, never
be fooled into thinking that your salvation is temporary.

Write out your memory verse in the space below. Try to do it completely from
memory then double-check yourself.

_____

_____

_____

_____

TAKE TIME TO PRAY

*Tell God how it makes you feel to know that your salvation is secure. Ask him
to show you others who need to hear this message and to give you the words to
share it with them.*

Assurance of Salvation—Day Four

Memory Verse

Romans 10:9

Start today's study by writing out as much of your memory verse as you can in the space below. Then, look up the verse and make any corrections that are needed. Finally, read it three times from your Bible and pray before completing the following lesson.

_____

_____

_____

_____

Today, we are going to start with another common question about salvation. How do I know if I am saved or not? It is easy to understand why everyone wants to know the answer to this question in light of what's at stake. The Bible teaches us that our eternal destiny must be settled on this side of eternity. In other words, you can't wait until you die, take a tour of heaven and hell, then pick your eternal home. It's not like shopping for a car or a new house; there are not multiple options and many dealers to choose from. There are only two choices, and you must make your choice on this side of eternity. So, if accepting Christ's free gift of grace is the only way to be saved, and if that choice must be made here and now, it is understandable why people want to be sure of their salvation.

One of the saddest thoughts I have about eternity is the great number of people who go through life believing that they are saved, but will ultimately end up spending their eternal lives in a very real place called hell. These people are good people, church people, people who tithe, people who work in the church, people who read their Bibles, and people who have convinced themselves that they are saved because of who they are or what they do. God's word, however, tells us time and time again that salvation comes only by confessing and believing in Christ. Look up Ephesians 2:8-10 and answer the following questions:

- What is the relationship between faith and good works according to these verses?

_____

_____

- Can your works get you into heaven? (circle)

  Yes   No   Don't know

  Explain.

_____

_____

_____

- Do these verses say that works have any place in a believer's life?

  Yes   No   Don't know

  Explain.

_____

_____

_____

Now look up and read Matthew 7:21-27 and answer the following questions:

- Why do you think it is so easy for so many to be fooled and tricked by the devil in this way?

_____

_____

- What do these verses say about good works?

_____

_____

≈ According to these verses, is it possible to be a great person and do good things, but still not get into heaven? How does that make you feel?

_____

_____

_____

I don't bring this subject up to scare you, or to cause you to doubt or become anxious about your salvation. As we have previously learned, our salvation is secure and we are safe in Jesus' care and can never be lost once we are saved. However, if we are fooled into thinking we are saved, it is even worse than not knowing Christ at all. In my years as a Christian, I have found that the person who is lost and does not know Christ is much easier to reach then those who have convinced themselves that they are good people; and therefore believe they will one day, in some miraculous way, end up in Heaven. We must avoid being fooled and allowing our enemy to fool those we love.

So, how can we know for certain? Start with a practical exercise. Take a minute to fill in some points on the timeline below. You might want to get a blank sheet of paper to do this on so that you have more room. Be sure you keep your timeline in your workbook because we will be referring back to it in the coming weeks as well. On the far left, place the year you were born. On the other end, place today's date. None of us are promised tomorrow, so let's not be presumptuous; instead, think of your life in terms of what you have done thus far. On this timeline, you should place a few other major events in your life, such as your wedding day, graduations, the birth of your first child, or other important events that you remember. Now, where on this line did you accept Christ as your Lord and Savior? Put a big 'S' there on the line and the date and year it happened.

There should be a day in your life that you confessed with your mouth and believed in your heart that Jesus is Lord. If there is not, I strongly encourage you to talk to your pastor or Bible study leader immediately to discuss this further.

There is a second thing that can confirm your salvation experience. Like our previous exercise, this too can be seen and experienced in your life. This is particularly helpful since salvation itself is not audible or visible. In other words, people's fingers don't turn green when they are saved, and you don't hear any audible evidence, either. In this way, salvation is like the summer breeze: even though you can't see it, you can see the effects of it. You see the grass moving, or hear the trees as the wind blows through them. In the same way, we can see the effects of salvation in our lives also. Here are a few questions for you: Are you different today than you were before you were saved? Have things significantly changed in your life, heart, spirit, and soul? Are others able to see these changes as well? When God enters a person's life, the effects are immediate and easy to see. The Bible talks about this in many ways and in many places, but for our study we will conclude by examining one passage. Look up Galatians 5:22-26 and in the margin, write out the fruits of the Spirit.

> What are some other fruits of the Spirit that you might be able to see? ⚒

_____

_____

_____

> Do you see these kinds of things in your life? What was the first thing that changed in you that others could see after you gave your life to Christ?

_____

_____

_____

_____

TAKE TIME TO PRAY

If you know for certain that you are saved, thank God for your salvation and pray for someone who does not know Christ. If you are unsure of your salvation, pray the following prayer and then make an appointment to speak with your pastor or Bible study leader as soon as possible. Do it today if you can! Finally, write your memory verse at the bottom of this page.

PRAYER OF SALVATION

Jesus, I know that I have sinned. I invite you into my heart to be my Lord and Savior. Forgive me for my sins and give me the gift of eternal life. Thank you for your grace and goodness. Amen.

To review, use the space below to write all the memory verses you have learned so far, including this week's. You can also use this space for personal notes about this lesson.

_____

_____

_____

_____

_____

_____

_____

_____

_____

_____

_____

_____

_____

_____

_____

_____

_____

_____

Baptism—Day One

Memory Verse

Matthew 28:19-20

Start today's study by writing out your memory verse in the space below. Then, read it three times from your Bible and take just a moment to pray before completing the following lesson.

Baptism in the modern age has been demoted to nothing more than a symbol of one's faith and is seen as something that an individual does only when, and if, they feel like it. Personally, I have found that nearly 50% of those who claim to have given their lives to Christ never follow through with baptism. The goal of this week's study is not to guilt you into being baptized. Instead, the aim is to give you a clear and biblical picture of what baptism is, and who it is for.

Let's start with the question, Who should be baptized? Many think that baptism is only for those who wish to become members of a church or denomination. But the Apostle Peter gives us a clear definition of who should be baptized in Acts 2:37-38.

❧ Who does Peter say should be baptized?

_____

_____

_____

❧ Do you see anything that is a prerequisite for baptism in this passage? What is it? Why? ▰

_____

_____

_____

❧ How many does it say were baptized that very day? (verse 41) What does this tell you?

_____

_____

_____

Baptism is for every believer! He says *repent and be baptized every one of you.* The apostle clearly teaches that this command is for all believers and should be practiced by all Christians after they have confessed Jesus as Lord and repented of their sins. We will learn tomorrow that baptism is a direct command from Christ for all believers to practice. So, Peter was right to advise people in the audience that day to submit themselves to public baptism. Baptism is for all believers and it should be done as soon as possible after repentance.

❧ Last week on day four I asked you to fill in a basic timeline of your life. Did you include your baptism on that timeline? If you did not, go back and place a capital "B" on your timeline to represent when your baptism took place. Did your baptism take place before or after you confessed Christ as your Lord and Savior?

_____

❧ Have you been baptized? If not, what is keeping you from being baptized?

_____

_____

_____

⚘ How important do you think baptism is? Based on what you know now, how would you explain the importance of baptism to a friend or family member?

_____

_____

_____

_____

Write out your memory verse in the space below. Try to do it completely from memory, then double-check yourself.

_____

_____

_____

_____

TAKE TIME TO PRAY

Ask God to continue to help you learn more about him each day. Pray specifically for one person you know who does not know Christ or who has not been baptized.

Baptism—Day Two

Memory Verse

Matthew 28:19-20

Start today's study by writing out as much of your memory verse as you can in the space below. Then, look up the verse and make any corrections that are needed. Finally, read it three times from your Bible and pray before completing the following lesson.

_____

_____

_____

_____

Yesterday, we looked at Acts 2:37-38, where the Apostle Peter challenged over three thousand new converts to be baptized. Baptism is much more than a challenge; it is nothing less than a direct command from Jesus Christ himself. Before you go any further, take a few minutes to seriously think about the question below. Write down as many answers as you can.

ع What are some commands that are found in the Bible? For example, do not murder. ✗

_____

_____

There are thousands of commands in God's word. At the very least, you probably thought about the Ten Commandments and the Golden Rule. But there are many more commands that God gave his people throughout history and each of them is extremely important. In Matthew 28:19-20, we find what is known as the Great Commission for Christians. In this passage Jesus gives some of his final instructions to his disciples before he ascends back into heaven. Read Matthew 28:19-20 and answer the questions below.

    ❧ What commands do you see in this text? ✗

_____

_____

    ❧ Do you think baptism is a command? Why or why not?

_____

_____

Baptism must have been important to Jesus. If it was not important and if he did not intend for all believers to follow him in baptism, why then would he include it as a command in his final words to his disciples? This is why Peter was so quick to say *repent and be baptized every one of you!* Christ had commanded him to go, make disciples, baptize them, and teach them. This is still the work of the church to this very day and this command is still relevant to all believers.

We also know that baptism was important to Jesus Christ himself. In Matthew 3:13-17, we find that Jesus himself was baptized. Sometimes people say, well I don't need to be baptized, or baptism is not for me. If there was ever a person in the history of the world that did not need to be baptized, it was Jesus Christ. Yet Christ made a journey and sought to be baptized himself. This shows us just how important baptism was to Christ. Read that passage, then answer the questions below.

    ❧ Who baptized Jesus?

_____

_____

    📖 What does Matthew 3:13-17 tell you about the importance of baptism for the modern day disciple of Jesus Christ?

_____

_____

_____

So far, we have answered two common questions about baptism: Who should be baptized, and why? Tomorrow we will look at how obedience plays into the importance of baptism.

Write out your memory verse in the space below. Try to do it completely from memory, then double-check yourself.

TAKE TIME TO PRAY

Pray about whatever the Lord lays on your heart today!

Baptism—Day Three

Memory Verse

Matthew 28:19-20

Start today's study by writing out as much of your memory verse as you can in the space below. Then, look up the verse and make any corrections that are needed. Finally, read it three times from your Bible and pray before completing the following lesson.

_____

_____

_____

_____

*H*as anyone ever been totally disobedient to you? Maybe it was a child who, despite your warnings, disobeyed anyway. Perhaps it was an employee, or maybe a friend or family member who willingly chose to disobey what you perceived to be a very reasonable and simple command. The fact is that we have all disobeyed someone at some time in life. So in turn, we all have experiences with the feelings that come with disobedience. As modern day disciples, we understand deeply that disobedience is sin and it will always lead us down the road of destruction.

    How does it make you feel when someone disobeys you?

_____

_____

❤ How do you think our disobedience to Christ makes him feel?

_____

_____

We know that baptism is a command that came directly from Jesus Christ. We know that it was important enough to Christ for him to go and personally be baptized by John. And yet, many still continue to be disobedient to Christ when it comes to this simple command. Baptism has been referred to as the first step of obedience for a believer. Why? Because we are not baptized to get into heaven or to wash our sins away; nothing but the blood of Christ can do such a thing. Instead, we are baptized to show the world that Christ is our Lord, our Master, and our Savior! Being faithful in baptism is a sign of obedience to Christ. Read John 14:21 and then answer the following questions.

❤ Do you think obedience is a sign of love? Explain your answer.

_____

_____

_____

❤ Do you think it is possible to be a disciple of Christ without being obedient to Christ?

_____

_____

_____

❤ Biblically, do you think baptism is a command or an option for believers?

_____

_____

_____

Obedience is also important to success when it comes to anything in life. If you want to find success in the sports world, you must be obedient to the coach. In business, you must learn to obey the commands of the boss. Successful bands obey the lead singer's cues and commands. Successful writers must learn to be obedient to the rules of grammar. Students will find little success until they first learn to obey their instructors. Obedience is key to our spiritual success as well. Until we learn to obey the commands of Christ, we will experience little spiritual success. That obedient heart is clearly seen through baptism as we publically submit our lives to Him.

- ❦ In what areas of your life are you currently being disobedient to Christ? Be specific.

_____

_____

_____

- ❦ Do you have intentions to change these things? If so how? What is your plan of action? ⚒

_____

_____

_____

Write out your memory verse in the space below. Try to do it completely from memory, then double-check yourself.

_____

_____

_____

_____

TAKE TIME TO PRAY

Ask God to show you the areas of your life where you are being disobedient to his will. Pray for forgiveness and make a plan of action to correct these things.

Baptism—Day Four

Memory Verse

Matthew 28:19-20

Start today's study by writing out as much of your memory verse as you can in the space below. Then, look up the verse and make any corrections that are needed. Finally, read it three times from your Bible and pray before completing the following lesson.

So far this week we have looked at who should be baptized and why we should be baptized. Today we will try to answer the question how should we be baptized? There are many different methods of baptism in use around the world. Some sprinkle, others pour, some dunk (immerse), and others claim to use the Holy Spirit himself in baptism. If there are so many different methods of baptism, which one is the right one?

Let's start today by looking at the original Greek word for baptism, which is βαπτίζω (bap-tid´-zo). Strong's Greek dictionary gives the following definition of the word: "to immerse, submerge; to make whelmed (i.e., fully wet); used only (in the New Testament) of ceremonial ablution, especially (technically) of the ordinance of Christian baptism." Thayer's Greek—English Lexicon provides the following commentary.

In the N.T. it is used particularly of the rite of sacred ablution, first instituted by John the Baptist, afterward by Christ's command received by Christians and adjusted to the contents and nature of their religion (see *baptisma,* 3), viz., an immersion in water, performed as a sign of the removal of sin, and administered to those who, impelled by a desire for salvation, sought admission to the benefits of the Messiah's kingdom.[1]

The word used to describe what we know as baptism is defined by immersion, or being submerged into water. So, by pure definition, we can eliminate all but one of the most common methods used today for baptism.

Full immersion is also the only form of baptism that totally depicts what baptism is meant to symbolize as well. Look up Romans 6:3-4 and answer the following questions.

ᐧ From this passage, what would you say baptism pictures or symbolizes?

_____

_____

ᐧ What are some other things that baptism pictures or symbolizes?

_____

_____

ᐧ Why can those things only fully be expressed through baptism by immersion? ✘

_____

_____

_____

If baptism symbolizes our death, immersion is the only form of baptism that will work. When we are buried we are submerged in the earth. We don't just sprinkle a little bit of dirt over the top of those who go on to be with Christ; instead, we completely submerge them when they are buried.

The right method is important when it comes to baptism, but it is not the only thing that should be considered. Baptism also involves the right person, the right reasons, and the right authority. Without looking ahead, try to explain what each of those three things might mean.

---

1   Joseph Thayer, *Thayer's Greek-English Lexicon of the New Testament Coded with Strong's Concordance Numbers* (New York: Hendrickson, 1996).

❧ The right person

_____

_____

_____

_____

❧ The right reasons

_____

_____

_____

_____

❧ The right authority

_____

_____

_____

_____

The right person refers to a believer. Peter said we must repent and then be baptized. Baptism without repentance is worthless. If you come forward for baptism without repenting of your sins, you will not be saved; you will only be wet! Baptism does not save you. Instead, it is an outward symbol of what God has already done in your life. Next, we must be certain that we are being baptized for the right reasons. We don't get baptized out of guilt or because our friends are doing it. Our reason for coming to be baptized should be based on our love and devotion to Christ and a desire to be obedient to His commands. Finally, the right authority should also be a consideration. The right authority is God's church. In the modern day, that normally means that a pastor, deacon, or elder will perform the baptism as a representative of the church.

Baptism is a special event in the life of an individual and in the life of a church. If you have never been baptized, or if you were baptized prior to confessing Christ as your Lord and Savior, you should consider contacting your pastor today to follow Christ in baptism and allow your church to rejoice with you over what God has done in your life.

Write out your memory verse in the space below. Try to do it completely from memory then double-check yourself.

TAKE TIME TO PRAY

Thank God for sending his Son and making the way to heaven so simple for you. Ask him to give you opportunities to share your faith in the coming days. Pray specifically for one person you know who does not know Christ.

To review, use the space below to write all the memory verses you have learned so far, including this week's. You can also use this space for personal notes about this lesson.

_____

_____

_____

_____

_____

_____

_____

_____

_____

_____

_____

_____

_____

_____

_____

_____

_____

_____

Church—Day One

Memory Verse

1Corinthians 12:27

Start today's study by writing out your memory verse in the space below. Then, read it three times from your Bible and take just a moment to pray before completing the following lesson.

This week we will look at the importance of church in a disciple's life. Like salvation and baptism, church must be an essential part of a believer's life. Modern day believers have bought into the lie that says, "I can be a Christian without going to church." This comes from the theology that correctly says, "To be saved, all I need is Jesus." However, what follower of Christ would shun, despise, demean, or refuse to be a part of the church that their savior created? In the New Testament, you will find no examples of Christians who regularly existed outside of the context of God's church. This idea and theology would have been foreign and totally unacceptable to Peter, Paul, Timothy, and Jesus. A Christian without a church home is like a boat without water or a pilot without a plane; it just does not make sense. The healthy disciple engages wholeheartedly in meaningful, God-focused worship experiences on a weekly basis with the family of God.[2]

---

2   Stephen A. Macchia, *Becoming a Healthy Disciple* (Grand Rapids: Baker Books, 2004), 43.

So what is the church? There are several Greek words used to describe what we call the church. In Acts 15:30 we find the word πληθος (plethos) used to describe the church. This word is only used once in the New Testament to describe the church as a whole. Typically, it is used to describe a large crowd or gathering of people. It can also be used to describe a large number of anything else. It is where we get our word plethora from.

The most common word used for church in the New Testament is ε'κκλησι'α (ekkleœsia). Many feel that this word can best be translated "the called-out ones" and that it indicates that we have been called out of the world and into a new life with Christ. However, Louw and Nida argue against this and push for a stronger definition of the word. They say it means "a congregation of Christians, implying interacting membership." They go on to say, "the term ε'κκλησι'α was in common usage for several hundred years before the Christian era and was used to refer to an assembly of persons constituted by well-defined membership. In general Greek usage, it was normally a socio-political entity based upon citizenship in a city-state."[3] This word was not used even once to describe a building or a place of worship. It was only used to describe a group of people who gathered to worship Christ. The word itself implies interacting membership in the group by individuals. It describes a well-defined group of people who are devoted to Christ and to each other. Being a member of a church has nothing to do with your name being written down on a roll sheet. Instead it has everything to do with your activity and overall participation in worshiping with other believers. Every Christian, both past and present, is expected to be actively involved in the life of the church.

So, why should you go to church? Let's start with a few practical reasons. Many studies have shown that being active in a church and attending regularly can increase your level of happiness and literally increase your life span. Other studies have shown time and again that children who are raised in church are less likely to commit suicide, binge drink, have premarital sex, become depressed, go to jail, or do drugs. Children who are active in church, and who have parents who take an active role in church, are also more likely to attend church after they leave home. For these reasons alone it is easy to see why church is worth our time and effort.[4]

Now, let's look at what the Bible says about why we should go to church. Look up the following verses and, in your own words, describe what reasons they give us for going to church.

---

3   Johannes P Louw and Eugene A. Nida, *Greek-English Lexicon of the New Testament based on Semantic Domains.* 2nd ed. (New York: United Bible Societies, 1989).

4   Many of these facts have been picked up over my years of watching research; others are hard facts that will be directly quoted in day four from Neil MacQueen, "The Life Benefits of Regular Church Attendance," an article by Neil MacQueen," Christian software—The Sunday School Software Home Page, http://www.sundaysoftware.com/stats.htm (accessed December 29, 2009).

📖 Service—Romans 12:6-8

_____

_____

_____

📖 Worship—Colossians 3:15-17

_____

_____

_____

📖 Accountability—Hebrews 13:17

_____

_____

_____

📖 Fellowship—Hebrews 10:24-25

_____

_____

_____

📖 Celebration—Acts 15:3

_____

_____

_____

📖 Instruction—Ephesians 4:11-14

_____

_____

_____

There are countless other reasons that Christians should be active and involved in church. Christians who sit on the sidelines quickly become out of shape and spiritually stagnant in their faith. They soon begin to wonder why they are growing bored and why they no longer feel the passion they once enjoyed. To be a Christ follower (Christian) implies that you participate and take an active role in the body of Christ.

    ❧ Are you an active member of your church? If not, why? If so, where and how do you serve?

_____

_____

_____

_____

Write out your memory verse in the space below. Try to do it completely from memory, then double-check yourself.

_____

_____

_____

_____

TAKE TIME TO PRAY

Take time to thank God for making you apart of his church. Ask God where he might call you to get involved and participate in the life of your church.

Church—Day Two

Memory Verse

1Corinthians 12:27

Start today's study by writing out as much of your memory verse as you can in the space below. Then, look up the verse and make any corrections that are needed. Finally, read it three times from your Bible and pray before completing the following lesson.

_____

_____

_____

_____

I once read a quote that said, *The Church is God's creation and design; it is His method of providing spiritual nurture for the believer and a community of faith through which the gospel is proclaimed and His will advanced in every generation.* I could not agree more and the church, when properly understood and experienced, is a powerful and wonderful thing! Yesterday we started our study by examining what the church was. Today you will answer five basic questions about the church. They are Who, What, When, Where, and Why?

✎ Based on what you learned yesterday, who is the church?

_____

_____

📖 Look up Galatians 1:13. What was Paul persecuting? ⚒

    a. A building

    b. An institution

    c. People

    d. Animals

The answer, of course, is people. Paul was doing everything he could to destroy the church and the only way he could accomplish his purpose was to go after individuals. The church is made up of people just like you. The Bible never refers to the church as a building or location for worship. Church is about people and it is made up of people. Who is the church? You are the church!

What is the church? It has to be more than just a group of people, right? If all you needed was a group of people to make a church, then many things in life could meet that definition and claim to be a church. The church is more than just a group of people; it's a group of believers who gather to serve and worship the living God. The Bible calls this group the Body of Christ. Look up Colossians 1:18 and answer the following questions.

❧ Who is the head of the Body?

_____

_____

❧ How would you describe this concept of the church being the body of Christ to a friend?

_____

_____

📖 What does 1 Corinthians 12:27 tell you about your role in the Body of Christ?

_____

_____

When does church take place? Many in today's society think that church only happens on the weekends at the building with the white steeple on top of it, but is that biblical?

📖 When does church take place according to Matthew 18:20?

_____

_____

Church can happen anywhere! It can be held at school, in your home, at work, on the street, in the café, in a hospital room, in your car, at the game, or anywhere else for that matter. Church can happen in the morning, afternoon, evening, or even the middle of the night. Church is not limited to a certain time, at a certain place, or in a specific building. We limit the meaning of church when we think of it in these terms. Of course, every believer should participate in the regular church service that is held each weekend, but they should also find times throughout the week to gather with other believers and worship God as well.

If church can happen anywhere, it can also happen at any time. People are the church and that means wherever God's people are, so is his church! It is a mistake to think that church is a certain geographical place on a map or a building of any kind. The church is the Body of Christ and it is made up of God's people. Therefore, church can and should happen all the time, wherever his people go.

Why church? Why should anyone devote time, effort, energy, and money to a church? After all, churches are not perfect places, and over time Christians find that no matter how great their church is, at some time or another being a part of a church will lead to frustration and even disappointment. This should not catch us by surprise, should it? After all, we know that the church is made up of people. Do you know of any perfect people? Of course not! So, if the church is made up of imperfect people, it should come as no surprise that the church itself will not be perfect. Only upon the return of Christ will the church be perfect. Until then, the church will continue to lack the perfection so many desire from it.

If you go to church because you think it is a perfect place or because you think that church will solve all your problems, you will be disappointed and not stay long. These are not the reasons we go to church. So, why church? Because it is God's best hope for the entire world and for each of us. It has always been the plan and primary vehicle by which God chooses to shape and transform lives. It is one of the only things we can invest in and be a part of on this side of heaven that is eternal. "The church of Jesus Christ, with all its blemishes, its divisions and its failures, remains our best hope of spiritual vitality. However poor it is, life without it is worse."[5]

    📖 Read Matthew 16:18. What does this say about the eternal nature of God's church? ✖

_____

_____

    🕊 Who does the church belong to?

_____

_____

---

5   Elton Trueblood, *Best of Elton Trueblood: An Anthology* (Nashville, TN: Impact Books, 1979), 26.

The church is not perfect, but neither are you! We should view the church as a safe place for imperfect people to gather, worship, serve, and learn about the loving and perfect creator of the universe. The church is the hope of the world and it is an honor to be a part of it. All Christians should place church attendance—and more specifically, church involvement—at the very top of their value system and do whatever it takes to join with others and God each week as the church.

Write out your memory verse in the space below. Try to do it completely from memory, then double-check yourself.

TAKE TIME TO PRAY

Pray for the leaders of your church today and ask God to show you where he would have you help those leaders in the coming weeks.

Church—Day Three

Memory Verse

1Corinthians 12:27

Start today's study by writing out as much of your memory verse as you can in the space below. Then, look up the verse and make any corrections that are needed. Finally, read it three times from your Bible and pray before completing the following lesson.

---

*N*ow that you know a little bit about the church and we have answered the basic questions (who, what, when, where, and why) about the church, let's look at the purposes of the church. Look up Matthew 28:19-20 and answer the questions below:

> ❧ According to this passage, what would you say the overall mission of the church should be? 🎬

❧ Is Jesus speaking to a church in this passage? Explain. ⚒

_____

_____

_____

Jesus clearly gives the church its overall mission in Matthew 28, which is known today as the Great Commission, and his plan to complete this worldwide mission is the church. There is no plan B and there is no other option; we are the plan and the church is his method. In order to succeed in this great endeavor, we must mobilize an army of believers who make up the church. This requires us to understand the five main purposes of the church, which are membership, missions, ministry, magnification, and maturity. Before going further, read the verses below and see if you can find all five of the purposes. Write them above the part of the passage you believe is speaking to each purpose.

> Acts 2:42-47 _42They devoted themselves to the apostles' teaching and to the fellowship, to the breaking of bread and to prayer. 43Everyone was filled with awe, and many wonders and miraculous signs were done by the apostles. 44All the believers were together and had everything in common. 45Selling their possessions and goods, they gave to anyone as he had need. 46Every day they continued to meet together in the temple courts. They broke bread in their homes and ate together with glad and sincere hearts, 47praising God and enjoying the favor of all the people. And the Lord added to their number daily those who were being saved._

Let's take some time to go through each of these five purposes and explain them in more detail. First there is membership. Membership is more than being a member of the church. It is much more than being on the roll at a church or being a person who can vote at the church. Membership means that we are like family to one another. There has never in the history of the world been a perfect family. Even Jesus' family had trials, troubles, and tribulations. Jesus' own brothers and sisters (Mark 6:3-4) did not always agree with what Jesus was doing. Families are not perfect; they never have been and they never will be, but families are important. In the same way, our churches are not perfect but they are very important.

❧ Would you say you are a part of the membership at your church? Why or why not?

_____

_____

_____

☐ According to Hebrews 10:24, why is it important to be *involved* in the life of your church? If you are not involved and active in the life of your church, do you think what this verse speaks of could happen?

_____

_____

_____

Next is maturity. Every Christian should be actively growing in his or her faith. Studies like this one assist you in the process of maturity. Sunday morning worship, times of prayer, and even church fellowship help us grow and mature as believers. Spiritual maturity takes time and effort. It will only happen when you put forth the effort and are willing to discipline yourself and make spiritual growth a priority in your life.

☐ Read Hebrews 5:12-14. Why was the writer frustrated with the readers of the letter?

_____

_____

✾ Do you think you should be further along in your faith by now? Why aren't you?

_____

_____

Ministry is also something all Christians should engage in. There are many definitions of ministry, but simply defined, ministry is something that happens inside the walls or on the campus of the church and is aimed at helping others. When you serve on a team that works primarily on the church property, you are participating in ministry. This may be cutting the grass, greeting people at the door, working with children, or parking cars. All of these and many other things that happen at church are equally important and meet the definition for ministry.

✾ What ministry are you currently serving in?

_____

_____

The fourth area is missions. Missions and ministry differ somewhat from each other. Mission work primarily happens outside of the church, while most ministries happen on the church campus. In general, missions are events that happen away from the church—for example, a mission trip to Africa or Mexico, building a wheelchair ramp at someone's house, or repairing a roof for a widow. Outreach events that focus on evangelism and winning the lost are mission events. Every Christian should take part in missions as well.

> ❧ Do you consider yourself to be a missionary? Why or why not?

_____

_____

_____

> ❧ What have you done in the last month that could be defined as mission activity?

_____

_____

_____

Finally, there is magnification. You should magnify God each and every day! Everything we do as a church and everything you do as an individual should bring honor and glory and magnification to God. We are not called to magnify ourselves or even the church we attend. It is our goal and purpose as believers to magnify Christ alone. We do this in many ways through small groups and as we live our daily lives, but this is most clearly seen each weekend as we gather as a church to worship God. All believers should make it a point to be at church each week to participate in a corporate magnification of our Lord and Savior.

> ❧ List some ways God can be magnified.

_____

_____

_____

You are the church and the church is the hope of the world! God has given us the most important and significant mission of all time. We are called to go and make disciples and ensure that every individual on this planet has an opportunity to respond to the grace of God. This will only happen when the church is willing to unite and engage in membership, maturity, ministry, missions, and magnification.

Write out your memory verse in the space below. Try to do it completely from memory, then double-check yourself.

TAKE TIME TO PRAY

Ask God to help you fulfill these five purposes in the coming days. Thank him for calling you to be a part of his church!

Church—Day Four

Memory Verse

1Corinthians 12:27

Start today's study by writing out as much of your memory verse as you can in the space below. Then, look up the verse and make any corrections that are needed. Finally, read it three times from your Bible and pray before completing the following lesson.

_____

_____

_____

_____

Today we will look at some practical reasons that you and your family should attend and be active in your local church. Being active in church is good for you and your kids; it really is that simple. There has been a great deal of research on the benefits of being involved and active in your local church. Here are just a few things that researchers see time and again from their studies. Here are some possible benefits for children:

- Increase the average life expectancy of your children by 8 years;
- Significantly reduce your child's use and risk from alcohol, tobacco, and drugs;
- Dramatically lower their risk of suicide;

- Help them rebound from depression 70% faster;

- Dramatically reduce their risk for committing a crime;

- Improve their attitude at school and increase their school participation;

- Reduce their risk for rebelliousness;

- Reduce the likelihood that they would binge drink in college;

- Improve their odds for a "very happy" life;

- Provide them with a life-long moral compass;

- Provide children with a caring extended family;

- Get them to wear their seatbelts more often;

- ***And it will also statistically improve the odds that they will lead an active church life in their adult years.***[6]

There are also benefits for adults. A study by a University of Pittsburgh researcher found that people who attend weekly religious services have a longer life expectancy.[7] Other studies have shown that people who are active in church tend to be more positive and more likely to feel fulfilled and satisfied with life. These things alone should give us some motivation about going to church, but the scriptures also outline why we should go to church.

When we are involved in church, we are encouraged and motivated by other believers. Life in the context of community allows us to lean on others when we face the storms and struggles of life. Read Hebrews 10:23-25 and answer the following questions.

> What are we to spur each other on toward?

_____

_____

> What might happen if we give up meeting together?

_____

_____

When we are actively involved in the life of a local church, we also receive the accountability that we all need to stay on the narrow road Christ has called us to walk down. Bible studies, ministry teams, and mission trips allow us to get to

---

6   Neil MacQueen, "The Life Benefits of Regular Church Attendance, an article by Neil Mac-Queen," Christian Software—The Sunday School Software Home Page, http://www.sunday-software.com/stats.htm (accessed December 29, 2009).

7   Joe Fahy, "Going To Church May Help You Live Longer," Post-Gazette.com. http://www.post-gazette.com/pg/06094/679237-51.stm (accessed December 29, 2009).

know others on a personal level. When this happens, we become invested in the spiritual success of others and as a result, we hold each other accountable to the commitments we make to God and to ourselves. We think of accountability as a bad thing, but it is actually one of the most powerful reasons to be involved in a church. When you start to stray, others are there to lovingly pull you back.

We can also accomplish more as a group then we can on our own. When we combine our time, talents, and treasures, we can do far more than any of us could do alone. There is power in numbers, and a group of united believers working for the LORD OF LORDS, and KING OF KINGS is unstoppable. Read 1 Corinthians 12:12-27.

❧ What does the writer describe the church as being?

____

____

____

❧ Can the church reach its full potential without you? Explain.

____

____

____

____

The facts are simple: you need the church and the church needs you! The church is a place where you receive instruction, fellowship, membership, protection, accountability, and where you will find the soil you need to grow and mature as a believer. Just as the church helps you, so also you help to provide each of those things, and much more, to other believers who are involved in the life of God's church. We should take these words to heart for they speak a great truth into our lives. *Let us not give up meeting together, as some are in the habit of doing, but let us encourage one another—and all the more as you see the Day approaching.* (Heb 10:25)

Look up the following verses and try to determine the final reason that all Christians should be actively involved in their local church each week.

📖 Psalms 96:2-6

____

____

📖 Psalms 145:1-5

_____

_____

📖 Revelation 4:8-11

_____

_____

📖 Revelation 5:6-12

_____

_____

We should be involved in our local church because it is worth it, and because God is worthy! God is worthy of our worship, he is worthy of our praise, and he is worthy of whatever effort we have to put forth to be in his house each week to worship with other believers. Make it a point each week to join others in your local church to praise and magnify the KING OF KINGS, and LORD OF LORDS! He is worthy of it!

TAKE TIME TO PRAY

Take some time to thank God for your local church. Ask him to bless your leaders and your church as a whole. Let God know that you are ready and willing to be a part of that process, then listen and see what he says.

MEMORY VERSE REVIEW

To review, use the space below to write all the memory verses you have learned so far, including this week's. You can also use this space for personal notes about this lesson.

Discipleship—Day One

Memory Verse

1 John 2:6

Start today's study by writing out your memory verse in the space below. Then, read it three times from your Bible and take just a moment to pray before completing the following lesson.

```
_____

_____

_____

_____
```

*L*ast week we discovered the importance of church in a believer's life. This week we turn our attention to a much deeper matter that encompasses all of what it means to be a Christian. We will take a close look at what it means to be a disciple of Jesus Christ. To begin our study, we need to first define what it means to be a disciple. Read the following definitions that others have offered before answering the questions below.

1. "A disciple, *mathetes,* is a learner or follower-usually someone committed to a significant master." [8]

---

8   Michael J. Wilkins, *Following the Master: Discipleship in the Steps of Jesus* (Grand Rapids, MI: Zondervan, 1992), 38.

2. The word *disciple* means "a learner," but Jesus infused into that simple word a wealth of profound meaning. As used by Him and by Paul, it means "a learner or pupil who accepts the teaching of Christ, not only in belief but also in lifestyle." This involves acceptance of the views and practice of the Teacher. In other words, it means learning with the purpose to obey what is learned. It involves a deliberate choice, a definite denial, and a determined obedience.[9]

3. A disciple is a follower and student of a mentor, teacher, or other wise figure.[10]

4. ...becoming a complete and competent follower of Jesus Christ. It is about the intentional training of people who submit to the lordship of Christ and who want to become imitators of Him in every thought, word, and deed. On the basis of teaching, training, experiences, relationships and accountability, a disciple becomes transformed into the likeness of Jesus Christ.[11]

❧ Which of the definitions do you most agree with: 1, 2, 3 or 4? Which do you least agree with: 1, 2, 3, or 4? Why?

_____

_____

_____

❧ From the definitions above and what you know about discipleship, write out your own definition of what it means to be a disciple in the space below.

_____

_____

_____

In Week Two you were asked to memorize Matthew 28:19-20 as we studied the subject of baptism. This passage also has a great deal to say about discipleship. In his book, *Growing True Disciples,* Barna says "The Great Commission is not primarily about evangelism,[12] it is about discipleship." To be sure, discipleship was indeed on the mind of Christ as he gave his most trusted followers their final

---

9   J. Oswald Sanders, *Spiritual Discipleship: Principles of Following Christ for Every Believer* (New York: Moody, 2007), 8.

10   "Disciple." *http://en.wikipedia.org/wiki/Disciple* (accessed January 07, 2010).

11   George Barna, *Growing True Disciples: New Strategies for Producing Genuine Followers of Christ* (New York: WaterBrook Press, 2001), 17-18.

12   Ibid., 25.

orders before he departed. Discipleship was at the heart of Jesus' ministry from start to finish, and it is still important to him today.

📖 From memory, write out Matthew 28:19-20.

_____

_____

❦ What do these verses teach us about discipleship?

_____

_____

While most churches in America and around the world have some form of discipleship program in place, few churches are full of disciples. One of the primary reasons this has happened is because we have become so fascinated with and focused on "programs." Discipleship is much more than a program or a ministry; it is a lifestyle. When we make it a program, we lose the ability to transform people into disciples. This kind of transformation can never be achieved through clever programs. It is only possible if individuals are encouraged to live a lifestyle of total obedience and dedication to Christ. Christ did not have a program for his disciples. There were no textbooks or studies that they followed. Why? Because the heart of discipleship is not learning, memorizing, or gaining knowledge that allows us to answer questions or explain scripture. Discipleship is about life transformation, and that will only happen if we make discipleship a lifestyle rather than a program. Christ asked his disciples to do two basic things: follow Him and learn from him. Just like the disciples of the first century, the modern day disciple must make a lifelong commitment to follow and learn from Christ. Read the following verses that relate to the way Jesus made disciples, then decide if they lean more toward a program or a lifestyle of discipleship. ⚒

1. Matthew 4:18-20   a) Program   b) Lifestyle
2. Mark 10:20-22   a) Program   b) Lifestyle
3. Luke 9:59-62   a) Program   b) Lifestyle
4. 1 Peter 2:21   a) Program   b) Lifestyle
5. 1 John 2:5-6 (your memory verse)   a) Program   b) Lifestyle

❦ Up to this point in your spiritual life, have you considered discipleship to be a program or lifestyle? What led you to believe this?

_____

_____

Discipleship is about learning from and following Christ in total obedience. Discipleship is not something we do; it is who we are. It is not a part of our life, it *is* our life. We can no longer accept the lie from Satan that says we can be Christians and not be disciples. The truth is if we are one, then by default we are the other as well.

Write out your memory verse in the space below. Try to do it completely from memory, then double-check yourself.

_____

_____

_____

_____

TAKE TIME TO PRAY

Discipleship—Day Two

Memory Verse

1 John 2:6

Start today's study by writing out as much of your memory verse as you can in the space below. Then, look up the verse and make any corrections that are needed. Finally, read it three times from your Bible and pray before completing the following lesson.

Growing up with a dad who made a living as a farmer and rancher taught me many things. One of the things I learned was that everything needs the right environment to grow and flourish. For example, plants need basic things like soil, sun, rain, fertilizer, and time in order to grow. With these basic things in place, a harvest is produced. Many who do not grow up in farming and ranching families think the meat, milk, and vegetables they consume somehow magically appear on the shelf at the grocery store because they never see or experience firsthand the hardships that come when you try to produce a crop.

After over a decade in the ministry, I have found the same to be true of discipleship. Many people look at a pastor, missionary, or layperson who has found the full and abundant life and who has been transformed into a true disciple of Christ and think it happened magically through a prayer or retreat, or overnight as the individual slept. The truth is that disciples grow the same way everything else does. They must be in the right environment, under the right conditions, and given time to grow. Today I want to look at just a few of the basic things a disciple needs in order to grow and flourish.

The first basic ingredient is trust. Those who refuse or are unwilling to trust Christ, the Bible, and other Christians rarely survive the process of discipleship. The journey of transformation a disciple takes requires trust. You must learn to trust God even when it does not make sense. You must learn to trust your mentor or accountability partner even when you don't like what they have to say. You must trust the Word of God no matter how challenging its commands may be. Trust is key, and without it a disciple's growth will be stunted or will stall out completely.

📖 Read John 14:1. What did Jesus have to say about trust?

_____

_____

❧ What area or part of your life have you been unwilling to trust God with?

_____

_____

_____

❧ What area or part of your life are you unwilling to trust other people with?

_____

_____

_____

❧ Why is total trust so difficult?

_____

_____

_____

The next essential for discipleship is encouragement. Affirmation and encouragement can be the boost we need to get through a difficult task or overcome an impossible problem. Those who attempt to climb to the highest point in the world climb in pairs. Everest is a formidable challenge for even the most seasoned climber. Pairs are used for the assent to the summit for obvious safety reasons, but they are also used to encourage each other along the way. One person in the pair is more than just an experienced climber; he or she has been on the top of the world before and made that journey at least once. Along the way, they encourage their partner and remind them that they can do it! Discipleship, in and of itself, is a difficult and egregious journey. You need someone to help you and encourage you along the way! When we work in pairs or small teams, we stand a much better chance of reaching the summit of discipleship. Read 1 Timothy 4:11-14.

❧ How did Paul encourage Timothy?

_____

_____

❧ Who is your Paul? Does that person know it?

_____

_____

❧ Who is your Timothy? Does that person know it?

_____

_____

Discipleship without accountability at its core lacks a basic ingredient for success. Accountability has become somewhat of a dirty word in recent history. It seems that business leaders, teachers, government officials, and Christians alike despise and retreat from accountability whenever possible. Accountability, however, is essential to becoming a disciple. Those who hold me accountable are there not to pressure me or persecute me; they are there to protect me. In many cases, they protect me from myself! They help me keep the commitments I make to God, as well as to others. God is shaping me, and others join the process to help sharpen me. Disciples don't fear accountability, they embrace it.

📖 Look at Proverbs 27:17, and Hebrews 10:24. What are some of the benefits these verses point out about accountability?

_____

_____

_____

Discipleship also requires every individual to develop a humble and submissive heart. No one can experience transformation without humility and submission. If we are going to become more like Christ, we must become less like ourselves. We must be willing to humbly accept whatever his plans are for our lives. We must submit our lives to his program and abandon our own. A disciple must seek the kingdom of God first, and that requires humility and submission.

   📖 Look up Luke 1:52 and James 4:6-10. What do these verses say about submission and humility?

_____

_____

_____

The final thing a disciple must possess is discipline. There are certain spiritual disciplines that one will always find at the core of a disciple's life. These disciplines include scripture reading and memorization, prayer, fasting, solitude, and meditation. This journey of discipleship is long and the road is narrow. Without discipline and dedication to the process, success is highly unlikely.

Let me close by reminding you once again that discipleship is not a program; it is a lifelong process. Those people you look at and view as true disciples did not arrive where they are overnight, or by some special prayer. Furthermore, they will not be in the same place when tomorrow arrives because they will have continued to progress in their faith and they continue to grow. This is only possible because they have found the basic ingredients needed to grow as a disciple of Christ. While our list is not exhaustive, if you will trust, encourage, be accountable to others, and be willing to be submissive and humble, along with practicing the disciplines that will make you stronger, you will have the most basic ingredients needed for spiritual growth and be on your way to becoming a disciple.

Write out your memory verse in the space below. Try to do it completely from memory, then double-check yourself.

TAKE TIME TO PRAY

Discipleship—Day Three

Memory Verse

1 John 2:6

Start today's study by writing out as much of your memory verse as you can in the space below. Then, look up the verse and make any corrections that are needed. Finally, read it three times from your Bible and pray before completing the following lesson.

_____

_____

_____

_____

Yesterday we looked at the basic environment that will facilitate growth in a believer's life. Today we will turn our attention to the stages or phases in which this growth occurs, and tomorrow we will look at the different kinds of transformation that happen during the process of discipleship. As you go through today's study, please understand that these phases are not intended to be viewed as theological truths. They should instead be viewed as guideposts, or somewhat of a general model that can be used to determine our progress as disciples.

While each stage is clearly biblical, and we see evidence of each in the lives of the first-century disciples, no biblical writer ever defined discipleship in stages. Discipleship should be viewed primarily as a lifelong process for a believer, but having some signposts along the way to mark that progress can be helpful, as well.

Perhaps A. B. Bruce, in his 1871 book *The Training of the Twelve*, most clearly defined the stages of the process of discipleship. He wrote: "They arrived at their final intimate relation to Jesus only by degrees, three stages in the history of their fellowship with Him being distinguishable." [13] The three stages he described are "come and see," "come and follow me," and "come and be with me." Bill Hull adds a fourth stage, which he labels "remain in me." [14] Let's look at each of these four stages briefly.

The "come and see" stage is the first and shortest of the four stages. Some might describe this as the "seeker" stage, or a testing stage, when people start to examine the life and teachings of Christ and begin to make a determination whether or not they wish to follow and learn from him. This is a time when a person comes to look, listen, and observe the life of Christ. The disciples did this firsthand by spending time with Christ. Today, people do this by watching, listening, and observing the lives of modern day disciples, just like you. This first stage can be seen clearly in the first four chapters of the book of John, as Jesus interacts with people he encounters. But for the sake of our study today, go to the gospel of John, read verses 35-45 of chapter 1, and answer the questions below.

    ⁊ What level of commitment is Jesus asking from these people at this stage?

_____

_____

    ⁊ When were you at this stage? What was it like then? If you are still in this stage, describe what it is like now.

_____

_____

_____

The next stage is outlined as the "come and follow me" stage. This is where the rubber meets the road, as they say. The commitment level at this stage increases dramatically and steadily over time. We see an example of this in Mark 1:16-18. Read those verses before continuing on.

    ⁊ Do you think this was the first encounter Christ had with these men?

_____

_____

---

13   B. Bruce, *The Training of the Twelve: Exhibiting the Twelve Disciples of Jesus under Discipline for the Apostleship* (New Canaan, CT: Keats Publishing, 1979; first published 1871), 11.

14   Bill Hull, *The Complete Book of Discipleship* (Colorado Springs, CO: Navpress, 2006), 169.

  List some of the things these men would have left behind to follow Jesus?

_____

_____

  Do you think you would have left everything to follow Him?

_____

_____

When we read this text at the beginning of Mark, we tend to think this was the first time that Jesus met these men. It sounds so dramatic and romantic when you think about Christ walking up to these complete strangers and challenging them to leave everything and follow him. The fact is that this was not their first encounter with Christ. Matthew places this event in Chapter 4 (verse 19). John's gospel also makes it clear that Christ had encountered these men before. They had already had a chance to come and see. There was a brief time of separation when the men returned to their normal way of life; however, the invitation to follow Jesus was soon delivered. What these men left behind to set out and follow Christ is still, to this day, a huge demonstration of incredible faith. From this moment on, they would increasingly be challenged, stretched, and given responsibility in the work Christ was doing. These men were not following Christ in order to write books about him. They were following him to learn from him.

It is in this stage that they learned how to pray, serve, share their faith, help the hurting, minister to the sick, and discern, obey, and articulate the will of God. They learned all of this and much more by following Christ and obeying his commands. Look up and read Luke 9:57-62 before you answer the questions below.

  What is different between the people in Luke 9 and those in Mark 1:16-18?

_____

_____

_____

  Do you think Jesus was too hard on those in Luke 9? Explain.

_____

_____

_____

The next stage is described as the "come and be with me" stage. Many came to see Jesus. While there were fewer people who entered into the "come and follow me" stage, it seems at a minimum there were 70-120 people, if not more, who were actively involved on that level. However, the "come and be with me" invitation during the ministry of Christ was only extended to the twelve disciples. After following him for some time, Christ prayed, and then called the twelve to enter this third stage of discipleship. Read Mark 3:7-19.

✳ Look at the people in the text closely as you read. Who do you see? ✗

- Come and see

_____

_____

- Come and follow

_____

_____

- Come and be with me

_____

_____

✳ Why do you think Jesus limited the number of people who entered the "come and be with me" stage to twelve?

_____

_____

_____

In the "come and be with me" stage, Jesus was selecting the men who would carry on his mission once he departed Earth. He did not select the brightest, wealthiest, or most respected men. He chose those who were loyal, obedient, teachable, and reliable. Christ limited this number to twelve because he needed to be sure he could give them the time and attention that was needed so that they would be prepared to carry on once his physical presence was no longer with them. This would not have been possible to do with hundreds or thousands of people. This is also a stage that none of us today can enter into because we no longer have Christ here with us as a physical presence. It is impossible for us to "be with him" in the way that the disciples were in this third stage. Today, we are left with the Holy Spirit as our guide. We will discuss the role of the Spirit in volume two of the Absolute Basics of Christianity.

Bill Hull correctly adds the fourth stage for the modern day disciple. The "remain in me stage" describes where we are today as believers. Discipleship is not a program, it is a process. The only way the process works is if we remain in Christ. The disciples had Jesus; today we have the Holy Spirit to guide us, and the number of those who enter stage three is no longer limited by those whom Christ can physically be with. However, total obedience, loyalty, willingness to learn, and reliability are still necessary for this stage. Active ministry and mission, under the care and direction of Jesus, defined this stage in the day of Christ. Today, active ministry and mission, under the care and direction of the Holy Spirit, define it. Those who enter this stage have believed what they have seen, learned as they followed, and are now being what Christ calls them to be as they remain in him. This is an endless, lifelong stage for a modern day disciple. We are to remain in him for the rest of our days on this planet! Look up and read John 15:1-17, then answer the questions below.

❧ Why is it so hard to follow Christ or remain in him each day? What are some of the things that distract us or drag us away from him?

_____

_____

_____

❧ Can we avoid these things or are we forced to face them?

_____

_____

_____

❧ As modern day disciples, how can we overcome them?

_____

_____

_____

❧ What stage do you think you are in today?

_____

_____

_____

❧ How would you explain the four stages to someone else?

- Come and see me

_____

_____

- Come and follow me

_____

_____

- Come and be with me

_____

_____

- Remain in me

_____

_____

You won't find these four stages in any New Testament study or any theology book. They are not intended to be theological beachheads or biblical cornerstones. Instead, they are a simple way for us to examine our progress in the journey of discipleship. Where you are in the process is not as important as the fact that you are involved in the process. Don't give up, don't give in, and don't stop now! There is so much you have yet to learn and discover as you walk with Christ.

Write out your memory verse in the space below. Try to do it completely from memory, then double-check yourself.

_____

_____

_____

_____

TAKE TIME TO PRAY

Discipleship—Day Four

Memory Verse

1 John 2:6

Start today's study by writing out as much of your memory verse as you can in the space below. Then, look up the verse and make any corrections that are needed. Finally, read it three times from your Bible and pray before completing the following lesson.

---

*T*he God we serve is all about transformation. In the book of Genesis, we see him transform the world we live in out of nothing. Throughout the ages, God has transformed the lives of people like Moses, Abraham, Jacob, Peter, Paul, James, and John. He has, according to the scriptures, brought us from death to life (John 5:24) by providing for our salvation through Jesus Christ. He is truly a God of transformation. And he is not done with you yet! While being a disciple involves following and learning from Christ, those things should lead to transformation in your life.

Today we will look at a few of the things that mark our progress as disciples along this journey of transformation. This list is not meant to be a complete description of the things that get transformed in our lives, but rather a place to begin the confirmation that God's transforming power is at work in our lives. God is not finished with you yet, no matter where you are in your spiritual journey. Read Philippians 1:6 and answer the questions below.

ᵉ❦ Who is doing a good work in you?

_____

_____

ᵉ❦ What are some of the things you have seen him transform?

_____

_____

So, what is transformed as you walk with Christ and learn from him through the process of discipleship? First, your ability to see clearly is transformed. This does not refer to the blind man's regaining his sight, but speaks of our ability to see the needs of others. A true disciple of Christ is able to perceive the needs of others. These may be physical or emotional needs. A man once called me at my office on a Tuesday and told me that he had just finished praying with a friend he worked with. He'd felt that this friend had a personal, emotional need that needed to be met and he decided to let God use him to intercede on his friend's behalf. Toward the latter part of our conversation, I realized that I had seen this man's name on one of our salvation cards from Sunday and he was on my list of people to call. This man had only been a believer for 72 hours, but he had new spiritual eyes that allowed him to see things he would have missed before. Others have offered up clothing, food, or financial assistance because their sight was transformed and they began to see people around them with God's eyes.

The longer you walk with Christ, the keener your spiritual vision will become. This transformation is seen most clearly when we start to see and respond to the spiritual needs of other people. It is then that we begin to care about the eternal condition of our friends' and families' souls. George Barna reports that less than half of adult believers think it is their responsibility to tell others about Christ.[15] Notice this study was done with *believers*—people who go to church and who have confessed Christ as their Lord and Savior. Why is this? Because many "believers" have stopped at the eternal transformation of their souls and neglected the good work Christ desires to do in them this very day. As a result, their sight has never been transformed.

Early in their walk with Christ, the disciples missed many of the spiritual, emotional, and physical needs of those they encountered. However, after three years with Jesus we see these same men respond very differently throughout the

---

15   George Barna, *Growing True Disciples: New Strategies for Producing Genuine Followers of Christ* (New York: WaterBrook Press, 2001), 66.

book of Acts as they see and meet the needs of those with whom they come in contact. Discipleship leads to our sight being transformed.

⁂ Have you noticed a difference in the way you see people and their needs? Explain.

_____

_____

_____

Your mind will also be transformed. It's one thing to believe in Jesus; it's quite another to believe what Jesus believed.[16] Many claim to believe in Christ, but do they really believe in the things Christ taught and believed: forgiveness, love for their enemies, service, and sacrifice? When we walk with Christ, over a period of time we should begin to think like Christ as well. Our decision-making will reflect his values and standards rather than the world's. Being a disciple of Christ is more than believing in him. It's believing what he believed! Look up Romans 12:1-2 and answer the questions below.

⁂ What are the results of the transformation of our minds?

_____

_____

_____

⁂ What examples have you seen in your life so far that point to the transformation of your mind?

_____

_____

_____

As you walk with Christ, your values will also be transformed. We value many things in our society. We value things like money, fame, power, houses, land, pleasure, vehicles, and success, just to name a few. Sadly, Christians are almost undistinguishable from the rest of our culture when it comes to the values we hold. Christians regularly choose a football game, shopping spree, or hunting blind over church on Sunday. They regularly place climbing the ladder at work or making more money over what God has called them to do in his kingdom. True disciples,

---

16   Bill Hull, *The Complete Book of Discipleship* (Colorado Springs, CO: Navpress, 2006), 130.

however, will find that their value system is transformed into Christ's as they walk with him. So what does God value? Look up Matthew 22:35-39 and see if you can identify the things God values.

1. _____

_____

2. _____

_____

Christ lays out perfectly the values that all believers should have, and will have, if they spend any time at all following him and learning from him. The values to which we aspire are the ones that Jesus himself held while he was among us on this planet. He valued a strong solid relationship with God and with other people. In the same way that we are called to love God with all we have, we are to love other people, too. Jesus does not value money, fame, or a work title, yet we continue to focus on the things that don't matter at all in the scope of eternity. When you walk with Christ as his disciple, it is impossible to not have your values transformed. What do you value? Examine your life as it is right now. Ask yourself the following question and you will clearly be able to see what your priorities and values are. What do I spend my time and money on? That is what you value!

📖 What do you think Paul was saying about values in 1 Timothy 4:8?

_____

_____

❧ How have your values changed since you have been following Christ?

_____

_____

As you close your study today, don't be discouraged if you have yet to see the full effects of these and other transformations in your life. If you are a young believer, or perhaps you have been lying dormant for a while, you must understand that transformation takes time. There are two great big oak trees in my back yard that provide shade for my family all summer long. While I enjoy their shade, I did not plant those trees. My neighbor, who has lived next door for 35 years, told me they were planted just before he moved in. Today my family enjoys the benefit from something another family did over three decades ago. It will be no different for you. Transformation takes time, but when it is fully realized it will pay dividends and leave a legacy that will last for many generations to come.

Mushrooms transform overnight, but they fade and decay just as quickly. God is not interested in making you into a mushroom, but into a mighty oak for the faith. So, follow him, learn from him, remain in him, and be patient. As you do, you will see many transformations take place over the years as you mature in your faith.

Write out your memory verse in the space below. Try to do it completely from memory, then double-check yourself.

_____

_____

_____

_____

TAKE TIME TO PRAY

To review, use the space below to write all the memory verses you have learned so far, including this week's. You can also use this space for personal notes about this lesson.

_____

_____

_____

_____

_____

_____

_____

_____

_____

_____

_____

_____

_____

_____

_____

_____

_____

_____

_____

_____

Evangelism—Day One

Memory Verse

Mark 16:15

Start today's study by writing out your memory verse in the space below. Then, read it three times from your Bible and take just a moment to pray before completing the following lesson.

So far in our walk through the ABC's of the Christian Faith we have looked at the **A**ssurance of Salvation, **B**aptism, **C**hurch, and **D**iscipleship. This week we will study **E**vangelism. At this point you might be tempted to think you have bitten off more than you can chew. Let me assure you that you have not! That is exactly what the devil wants you to believe, but the scripture speaks the truth when it says in Philippians 4:13, *I can do everything through him who gives me strength.* You are memorizing scripture, studying God's word, growing healthy spiritual relationships with other believers, and looking more and more like Christ each day. This does not make the devil happy, so he will feed you all kinds of lies to sink your ship just as you are picking up steam and getting near the deep water. Don't stop now. If you will keep your heart open and embrace this week's lesson with all you have, I promise you will be blessed beyond measure.

So what is evangelism? In the context of the Christian faith, evangelism is telling others the good news of Jesus Christ. We have already studied Matthew 28:19-20, which tells us we are all to go and make disciples. Jesus clearly taught that his disciples were supposed to be evangelists. But the truth is we are all called to be evangelists. When we hear the word evangelist, we tend to think of Billy Graham, our pastor, or the traveling evangelists who preach countless revivals each year. Evangelism at its best happens in the work place, school, on the sports field, at the bus stop, in the car, around the dinner table, at the store, or on your back porch. You are just as capable as Billy Graham or your pastor when it comes to evangelism. In fact, many people who would not give professional ministers ten seconds will give you all the time you need to tell them the good news. All you have to do is tell them what Christ has done for you.

❧ Before today, did you think of yourself as an evangelist? Do you now?

_____

_____

_____

_____

❧ How would you define evangelism?

_____

_____

_____

_____

❧ What are some of the reasons you have not told others about Christ in the past?

_____

_____

_____

_____

Now that we know that evangelism is telling others about Christ, the next question we must answer is who should we tell and why? Jesus gives us the answer to both questions many times in scripture. Look up your memory verse for the week again (Mark 16:15-16) and answer the questions below.

❧ What did he tell them to do? Is that what we (the church) are doing today? If not, what is the common thing most churches are doing today?

_____

_____

_____

_____

❧ Who are we to tell?

_____

_____

_____

❧ Why do you think it is important to tell others about Christ?

_____

_____

_____

❧ Does this verse make evangelism sound like an option or a command for Christians?

_____

_____

_____

When we leave evangelism to the professionals, we condemn the world because most people will never listen to or come in contact with a professional minister. Many who do come in contact with a minister will never listen because they don't have a relationship with that minister. This is why Jesus did not leave the hope of the world to the professional minister. He left it to all Christians. We are all called to be evangelists for Christ. We are all called to go and tell everyone we can about the good news we have received ourselves. Evangelism was always intended to be a community effort in which all people of the church participate. When this happens, we see evangelism at its best!

Now that we know what it is, and how Christ intended for it to work, we will spend the next few days learning how to do it.

Write out your memory verse in the space below. Try to do it completely from memory, then double-check yourself.

_____

_____

_____

_____

TAKE TIME TO PRAY

Tell God why you have been afraid to tell others about him in the past. Be honest and open, and ask God to help you get over those things. Start to pray for those people you have relationships with who do not know Christ. Ask God to give you opportunities to share the good news with them.

Evangelism—Day Two

Memory Verse

Mark 16:15

Start today's study by writing out as much of your memory verse as you can in the space below. Then, look up the verse and make any corrections that are needed. Finally, read it three times from your Bible and pray before completing the following lesson.

---

*Y*esterday we learned some of the basics about evangelism. Today we are going to learn how to actually do it. Learning to tell others about Christ is like learning to ride a bike or play almost any sport. It is slow and nerve-racking at first, but the more you do it, the better you get and the easier it becomes. Just like riding a bike or playing a sport, you have to learn the basics first, then as you learn more and gain confidence, you can expand your game, so to speak. Like most boys, I started riding a bike with the assistance of training wheels. Within an hour I begged my dad to take them off. In just a few months I was jumping ramps and popping wheelies. When I started playing baseball, I literally got my glove and bat the day before tryouts. I knew nothing at my first practice, but within a few weeks I was able to turn a double-play. At my very first game, and my very first time at bat, I hit the fence and got a stand-up triple. Why do I tell you all this? Simple; it takes time and practice to build competence and confidence. There is no telling how many times I crashed that bike, or how many times I struck out at batting practice, but with persistence, practice, and patience, I was able to succeed. It is no different when it comes to evangelism. If you will give it some time, and work at it, telling others about Christ will get easier, I promise.

One of the best ways to learn is by watching others. If I wanted to learn how to throw a football, I would look at a great quarterback. If I wanted to learn how to sail on the open sea, I would spend time on the bridge observing a captain with many years of experience. When I was learning how to fly, I started by watching my instructor and any other pilot who would let me sit beside him. When I wanted to learn about evangelism, I turned to one of the greatest evangelists of all time; Paul. Read the entire chapter of Acts 26 and then answer the questions below.

> What are some of the things you notice that you like about his evangelistic style?

_____

_____

> Paul breaks his testimony down into three general sections: before, how and after. Can you identify each section? Write the verses that correspond with each of these three areas in the space below.

• Before he met Christ—

_____

_____

• How he met Christ—

_____

_____

• After he met Christ—

_____

_____

What do verses 29-32 tell you about Paul's passion for evangelism?

_____

_____

If you don't feel you are good at telling others about Christ, it's probably because you have not done it enough. There are few things in life that we learn and master quickly. Even the simplest tasks for us today, like eating with a fork or tying our shoes, took practice, persistence, and patience. Paul did not stand and give this soaring testimony his first time. It came after lots of practice and telling many other people about Jesus. Don't make the mistake of thinking evangelism is about being great the first time you try it. If you do, you will make the greatest mistake of all and give up on it all together.

Write out your memory verse in the space below. Try to do it completely from memory, then double-check yourself. Be sure to review your past verses as well.

TAKE TIME TO PRAY

Ask God to give you the courage and boldness to fail so you can experience what it is like to succeed in the area of evangelism. Continue to pray for opportunities to share with your lost friends and family.

Evangelism—Day Three

Memory Verse

Mark 16:15

Start today's study by writing out as much of your memory verse as you can in the space below. Then, look up the verse and make any corrections that are needed. Finally, read it three times from your Bible and pray before completing the following lesson.

---

*Y*esterday we looked at the way Paul presented the gospel through his testimony in Acts 26. Today we are going to work on your testimony so you too can start to use it to present the gospel to those the Lord places in your path. There are many different clever and eye-catching models that can be used to share the gospel. I have even read a small pamphlet called 24 Ways to Explain the Gospel, and there are certainly many more than that. Things like the four spiritual laws, evangelism cube, and FAITH are all useful and effective, to be sure, but God seems most often to work through the personal testimony of people just like you. Just as Paul shared his testimony in Acts 26, by the end of today you will be able to do the same, so let's get started.

ॐ Yesterday we broke Paul's testimony down into three general sections. Can you list them? If not, go back and review the lesson from yesterday. Write them out in the space below.

_____

_____

ॐ What are some of the benefits of using your personal testimony as the primary method of evangelism?

_____

_____

_____

Using your personal testimony is great for many reasons. First, it's personal, which means it matters to you and therefore others are naturally more inclined to listen to you and be interested. Because you are simply reporting what God has done in your life, you don't have to memorize any script, verses, or methods to share your personal testimony. Your personal testimony is also flexible and can be adapted to almost any situation. Instead of a set script, it is fluid and the Spirit is free to move through you as you share the gospel. Finally, I find it useful because it can be shared in a matter of minutes. If you read Acts 26, it is conceivable to think that Paul's entire testimony to the King only took about three or four minutes. I have found that, in general, the shorter and more concise your testimony is, the more powerful it becomes.

Before you work on your testimony, let's look at the three sections together. First, you want to tell the person you are sharing with about what your life was like *before* you met Christ. Who were you before you were a disciple of Christ? What did you do? How did you act? What defined your life then? They don't need all the details, just enough to be able to see how you have changed since that time.

Next, tell them *how* you met Jesus. For Paul, it was on the road to Damascus. How did you meet him? Was it through a friend, at church, or perhaps a Billy Graham crusade? Just tell them about the day you gave your life to Christ. Again, you don't need to give every last detail, just enough so they can clearly see how God worked to bring you to the point of salvation.

Finally, tell them how your life has changed since you met Christ, or what is different *after* you met Christ. You should be able to tie this in with the "before" and show the contrast between the two lives. For example, if you say, "Before I met Christ, I was always worried about what would happen when I died." Then your "after" should include something like, "I don't fear death anymore because I know that my eternal salvation is secure in Christ."

Now it's your turn. Read Acts 26 again to refresh your memory, then write out your personal testimony in the space below, section-by-section. Again, this can change from situation to situation, but it is good practice to write out what I call your basic testimony. After you get it down, you will be able to share it to build your confidence and it won't be long before you will be turning double-plays and popping wheelies.

    ❧ Describe your life _before_ you met Christ:

_____

_____

_____

    ❧ Describe _how_ you met Christ:

_____

_____

_____

    ❧ Describe what your life is like now, _after_ you met Christ:

_____

_____

_____

Write out your memory verse in the space below. Try to do it completely from memory, then double-check yourself.

_____

_____

_____

_____

TAKE TIME TO PRAY

Pray a dangerous prayer today. Ask God to give you an opportunity to share your testimony with someone in the next 48 hours! Then keep your eyes open and be ready to share.

Evangelism—Day Four

Memory Verse

Mark 16:15

Start today's study by writing out as much of your memory verse as you can in the space below. Then, look up the verse and make any corrections that are needed. Finally, read it three times from your Bible and pray before completing the following lesson.

We are going to finish our study on evangelism today by taking your testimony to the final step, which is asking for a response. Sharing your *before, how,* and *after* is great, but we can't stop there. Once you have shared your testimony, you should give those who have been listening the option to respond or reject what you have told them. I generally try to use a statement rather than a question for this. So instead of saying, "Would you like to give your life to Jesus now?" I say something like, "I would be glad to pray with you if you're ready." They understand what this means because in my *how,* I explained that I prayed to receive Christ as my Lord and Savior. Whatever question or statement you choose to use, there are three responses you are likely to get. No thanks, maybe later, or yes. If you get one of the first two responses, don't act surprised or disappointed; instead, make sure they know that you are always ready and willing to talk to them about this subject should they ever change their mind. Then, DON'T GIVE UP on them. Take every opportunity you get to continue to live your life in a manner that is worthy of the Lord and continue to share the good news with them. If your subjects say yes and are ready to pray with you, take a minute to make sure they understand what they are doing by receiving Jesus as their Lord and Savior. You might consider using the following three verses to do this.

📖 Romans 3:23-24. What would you reinforce about this scripture? ⚒

_____

_____

📖 Romans 6:23. What would you reinforce about this scripture? ⚒

_____

_____

📖 Romans 10:9-13. What would you reinforce about this scripture? ⚒

_____

_____

After you have covered these basic things, ask them to follow you in a short and simple prayer. If the situation permits, ask them to pray out loud after you. Many people worry that they are going to mess the prayer up somehow. Let me assure you that this is not possible. There is no special prayer, and prayers don't save us. It is the blood of Christ that transforms us and if this person is truly repenting of their sins, God will know it, no matter what you say in the prayer. Your prayer should, in some way, lead the person to admit their sinful nature, ask for forgiveness, and thank God for his salvation. The following prayer is a basic sample of what this might sound like.

> **Prayer of Salvation:** Jesus I know that I have sinned. I invite you into my heart to be my Lord and Savior. Forgive me of my sins and give me the gift of eternal life. Thank you for your grace and goodness. *Amen*

When you are finished, congratulate them with a hug, handshake, high-five, or whatever seems appropriate to you. Then invite them to church and encourage them to join a Bible study or go through this study with you as they start their journey with Christ. Don't just say goodbye and leave, if you can help it. Follow-up is very important.

The final thing you must understand about evangelism is that it is not your job to save people. In fact, you can't save anyone. Our job is simply to go and tell. God must do the rest. Don't take it personally if people tell you no. Don't get discouraged if someone you care deeply for rejects the gospel on your first attempt. Continue to pray for them and continue to share. God's timing is perfect, and salvation for most is a process that may take months or years before they come to the point of salvation. Even the Apostle Paul did not convert everyone he shared with. As we close our study on evangelism, take some time to examine Romans 10:14-16 and answer the questions below.

⚕ According to these verses and our memory verse for the week, what is our job in evangelism?

_____

_____

_____

_____

⚕ Who did not believe?

_____

_____

_____

_____

⚕ Why is it important that we continue to share the message of the gospel?

_____

_____

_____

_____

Paul writes these words in Philemon 1:6—*I pray that you may be active in sharing your faith, so that you will have a full understanding of every good thing we have in Christ.* You will never have a full understanding of every good thing until you become active in sharing your faith. When you become active in sharing your faith, you grow, mature, change, and honor God. We will never experience the full and abundant life as believers if we refuse to be active in sharing our faith. Make it your goal to share your testimony with as many people as possible in the coming days. Be active in sharing your faith. Not only will you bless the lives of others, but you too will be blessed beyond measure.

Write out your memory verse in the space below. Try to do it completely from memory, then double-check yourself. Don't forget to continue to review your past memory verses as well.

TAKE TIME TO PRAY

Ask God to give you an opportunity to share your testimony at least once a day for the next ten days! Pray specifically for as many people by name as you can who may not have a relationship with Christ. Tell God your testimony (even though he already knows it). Ask him to help you refine it and remember it so when the opportunity comes, you will be prepared to share it boldly.

To review, use the space below to write all the memory verses you have learned so far, including this week's. You can also use this space for personal notes about this lesson.

_____

_____

_____

_____

_____

_____

_____

_____

_____

_____

_____

_____

_____

_____

_____

_____

_____

Forgiveness—Day One

Memory Verse

Matthew 19:26

Start today's study by writing out your memory verse in the space below. Then, read it three times from your Bible and take just a moment to pray before completing the following lesson.

This week we will tackle another basic yet critical aspect of a disciple's life: forgiveness. Throughout the course of our lives, we will be wronged or hurt by others. At times, this happens by accident and is nothing more than an unintentional mistake, or it can be a deliberate attempt on the part of someone else to demean and destroy you. In the same way throughout the course of your life, no matter how wonderful you are as a person, you too will hurt or offend others, even if it is nothing more than an accident.

During my freshman year in college, I met another guy in my dorm whom I will call Bill. We struck up a quick friendship and had many things in common; however, midway through the spring semester Bill cut off all communication with me. He would not answer my phone calls, he ignored me in the hallways, and he refused to even be in the same room with me. Bill and I remained in the same dorm on the same floor our sophomore year as well, and despite my efforts to figure out what the problem was, it was apparent that Bill was done with me. I later learned that Bill was upset with me because one evening I had asked his roommate to go to dinner and did not ask Bill. I tried to explain that if I had done such a thing, it was not on purpose. Bill's roommate informed me that the night this happened Bill was on the top bunk under the covers taking a late nap and he was offended that I did not wake him up. I told Bill that I did not know he was up there. Forgiveness was granted and our friendship continues to this day, but the damage had already been done and many days of our lives and friendship that can never be replaced had passed us by. Because of that small unintended event, we lost almost a year of friendship, simply because I did not know what the problem was and Bill was unwilling to forgive.

     ∾ Have you ever been mad at someone and unwilling to forgive them for something that you later found out was an accident on their part?

_____

_____

_____

     ∾ Have you ever withheld forgiveness from someone? Was it worth it?

_____

_____

When we refuse to forgive, the devil wins. It really is that simple! It does not matter what the reason is or how bad the offence is. If you refuse to forgive, you are allowing your enemy to win. Forgiveness brings freedom; anything less brings frustration, guilt, destruction, and pain. Read 1 Timothy 1:14-17 and then answer the questions below.

     ∾ Would you say that these words could be written of you? Do you see yourself as the worst of sinners?

_____

_____

     ∾ Who would have won the victory if Christ would not have forgiven you and died for your sins?

_____

_____

_____

✱ Why do you think Jesus would forgive you, the Apostle Paul, or anyone else for that matter? ✖

_____

_____

_____

The word of God is clear: each and every one of us is a sinner. Romans 3:23 says we have *all* fallen short. For this reason we are all equal in the eyes of God and we are all the worst of sinners. Why would Jesus forgive us? Why would he go to the cross and die for sinners like you? Because with forgiveness comes freedom! You can't be set free until you have been forgiven. Many today are living their lives in bondage because they refuse to forgive someone else. Forgiveness is not always easy, but it is essential in the life of a believer. We must learn how to give and receive forgiveness if we want to fully experience the freedom that Christ died to bring into our lives. Look up Luke 23:34 and read some of Christ's final words as he hung from the cross.

✱ Do you think Jesus is serious about forgiveness? Why or why not? ✖

_____

_____

_____

✱ Does his example of forgiving others teach you anything about forgiveness in your own life? If so, what?

_____

_____

_____

_____

✱ Have you ever experienced the peace and freedom that comes with true forgiveness? When was it?

_____

_____

_____

_____

Take a few minutes to examine the list of people below. Think about each one for a moment, and if you have something that you have never forgiven them for, simply place a check mark beside their name.

- ☐ Your spouse
- ☐ Your father
- ☐ Your mother
- ☐ Your children
- ☐ Your boss
- ☐ Your co-workers
- ☐ Your friends
- ☐ A cousin
- ☐ An uncle
- ☐ An aunt
- ☐ A teacher
- ☐ An ex-boyfriend or girlfriend
- ☐ An ex-spouse
- ☐ A roommate
- ☐ Another believer
- ☐ A stranger
- ☐ In-laws
- ☐ List any others:

Write out your memory verse in the space below. Try to do it completely from memory, then double-check yourself.

TAKE TIME TO PRAY

Ask God to guide you this week as we examine the issue of forgiveness. As you look at those check marks above, ask God to help you grant forgiveness so you can experience the freedom that comes with it.

Forgiveness—Day Two

Memory Verse

Matthew 19:26

Start today's study by writing out as much of your memory verse as you can in the space below. Then, look up the verse and make any corrections that are needed. Finally, read it three times from your Bible and pray before completing the following lesson.

_____

_____

_____

_____

*Y*esterday, we started our study by taking a very basic look at forgiveness. At the end of the first lesson you were asked to look at different people in your life and determine if forgiveness was needed in those relationships. Today we will take it a step further and examine what happens when we refuse to forgive others.

If you have not granted forgiveness to someone on the list from yesterday, there is probably a reason behind your unwillingness to forgive. Maybe you feel that person doesn't deserve it, or perhaps the pain, anger, and hurt are simply too much and you don't think you can forgive them for what they have done. Sometimes the inability to be able to forget makes it hard to forgive. The bottom line is that forgiveness is something we must choose to do and you certainly have the choice to grant or withhold forgiveness from others. However, I would like to remind you that if you refuse to forgive, you will never experience the freedom that comes with forgiveness. Furthermore, you are left with no other good options. If you don't take the path of forgiveness, you will take one of the following destructive roads.

Those who refuse to forgive easily fall into the destructive cycle of bitterness. When we become bitter towards someone, our willingness to forgive vanishes. That affects all of our relationships. It will eventually penetrate your relationship with God, as well. Bitterness makes us cold and hard, and ultimately it leads to mistrust. Over time, we become skeptical of others' intentions and motives. Individuals who refuse to forgive and choose the path of bitterness become distanced from others and as fellowship decreases, isolation increases. This, in turn, leads only to more bitterness, and the cycle can be difficult to break. It also places us in dangerous territory. Look up 1 Peter 5:8 and answer the questions below.

ੴ Why is bitterness dangerous?

_____

_____

_____

ੴ Who wins when we refuse to forgive and choose bitterness instead? Explain why.

_____

_____

_____

_____

Not everyone who refuses to forgive becomes bitter. Some just become angry. Anger is an emotion that can at times be harnessed for good and the Bible does not teach that it is a sin to be angry. However, when anger takes control of our lives it can have devastating results. Anger causes us to become blind to the things God is trying to teach us and show us. If you have ever been really angry at someone, you have probably experienced the tunnel vision that comes along with it. When I was growing up, like most boys I wrestled and fought with my brothers and others on occasion. Generally this was nothing more than casual horseplay. However, after being hit in the face one day, I became angry with a close friend and a real fight broke out. There were eleven other kids around me during that time, but I saw only one person. The others were screaming and shouting as we went at it with each other; however, all I heard were his voice and my own. Anger is debilitating because it takes such intense focus that we can easily miss other things that are going on around us. When we choose anger over forgiveness, we run the risk of missing God's blessings and his will for our life.

📖 How does Ephesians 4:26-27 say we should handle anger? If we don't deal with our issue, who wins?

_____

_____

_____

📖 Look up James 1:19-20. Why does it say we should avoid the emotion of anger?

_____

_____

_____

When someone hurts us or harms those whom we love, forgiveness is generally not the first thing that enters our mind, although it should be. Bitterness and anger don't always surface first, either. Sometimes revenge is all we can think about. We take the approach of "an eye for an eye" and "a tooth for a tooth." Despite knowing that two wrongs never make a right, we are quick to convince ourselves that this is the best option. There are several problems with choosing revenge. The first problem we are faced with is that it won't help anyone. Getting revenge will not replace your lost belongings or bring back a loved one. Revenge won't even make you feel better in the long run. Instead, it simply compounds the issue and makes matters worse. The second major issue with revenge is that it lowers you to the level of the one who hurt you. As believers, we are called to be different, and by seeking revenge we simply look like everyone else. Paul gives us a better solution when it comes to revenge. Look up and read Romans 12:17-21.

📖 Focus on verse 18 for a minute. What does that mean? �

_____

_____

_____

📖 What does verse 19 require us to do? Can you do it?

_____

_____

_____

  ❧ If we seek revenge, who wins? If we do what Paul says, who wins?

_____

_____

_____

If we choose bitterness, anger, or revenge, the devil wins every time. Our flesh cries out when we are wronged and pushes us toward these emotions, but our Lord and Savior cries even louder and urges us to choose forgiveness instead. It may be impossible to forget, but forgiveness is attainable for any disciple who will seriously consider God's Word and his ways. Forgiveness may still seem impossible, but I believe that with God's help and a willing and teachable heart, you can embrace forgiveness. Then you will find the power and freedom that comes with it.

Write out your memory verse in the space below. Try to do it completely from memory, then double-check yourself.

_____

_____

_____

_____

TAKE TIME TO PRAY

Ask God to guide you this week as we examine the issue of forgiveness. Ask God to help you grant forgiveness so you can experience the freedom that comes with it.

Forgiveness—Day Three

Memory Verse

Matthew 19:26

Start today's study by writing out as much of your memory verse as you can in the space below. Then, look up the verse and make any corrections that are needed. Finally, read it three times from your Bible and pray before completing the following lesson.

Finding the strength and boldness to forgive others is one of the hardest things we are called to do as disciples. As humans, we come to rely on others. We trust others with our hopes, dreams, and desires. Many times it seems that when we finally get to the point where we are willing to become vulnerable and totally trusting, we are disappointed to find that someone has betrayed that trust. They may have talked negatively about us or spread rumors and lies. Perhaps they've just let us down, or maybe they took something we valued, or cheated on us with another person. No matter what it was or who did it to you, it hurts! That pain can cause us to naturally fall back on the things our flesh desires to do, as we discussed yesterday.

⁊ From yesterday's lesson, do you remember the three roads we go down if we choose not to forgive? Take a minute to look back over yesterday's notes and review them.

_____

_____

We should forgive others not only because that is the best option, as we discussed yesterday. There is a second reason that we should be quick to forgive. It's a command! Jesus commands us to forgive others, and when we choose to disobey the commands of Christ, there are consequences for our disobedience. We can see just how serious Jesus was about the issues of forgiveness in Matthew 6:14-15, Mark 11:24-25, and Luke 6:36-37. Read these three passages and then answer the following questions.

⁊ Do you think God's eternal forgiveness is contingent upon your forgiveness of others? Explain why or why not. ✗

_____

_____

_____

_____

⁊ According to these three passages, do you think we should take forgiveness lightly or be slow to grant it to those who sin against us? Explain. ▰

_____

_____

_____

_____

These three passages are difficult truths to accept and understand. Many commentaries offer only a limited explanation of these three sections of scripture. For example, the Life Application Study Bible says this:

> Forgiving others is tough work—so much so that many people would rather do something totally distasteful than offer forgiveness to someone who has wronged them. For a person to pray while bearing a grudge, however, is like a tree sprouting leaves and bearing no fruit (Mark 11:13). True faith changes the heart. Real prayer dismantles

pride and vengeance, filling the holes with love. Real faith seeks peace. Harmony and forgiveness must be evident among the body of believers for our churches to have prayer power. Let go of hurts, abandon grudges, and forgive others.[17]

While that offers some explanation, it does not offer any help on the most obvious question that most people have about these passages. If I don't forgive someone, will I go to hell? After all, if I can't be forgiven then I can't enter heaven, right? So what are we to conclude about this text?

First, we must understand that this is indeed a command from Christ. At the end of today's study you will look up some other scriptures that help reinforce that a command such as this is indeed in line with the character of our Lord and Savior. But is the command to forgive linked with our eternal salvation? For this, we must examine these texts in their proper context.

Jesus did not utter these words while speaking about the eternal salvation of the individual soul. The passages in Matthew and Mark are set in the context of prayer, and the phrase in question in the gospel of Luke is spoken in the context of hypocrisy. As we discussed in Week One, the eternal salvation of one's soul is contingent on one thing alone: faith in Christ! Jesus is not implying that our lack of forgiveness will exclude us from entrance into the kingdom. However, it will always affect our ability to communicate freely with God and it sets a bad example for the unbelieving world around us due to the hypocrisy we spread by claiming the forgiveness of Christ but withholding our own forgiveness of others.

God has granted us eternal, unending, and unconditional forgiveness for all of our sins. Those sins are as numerous as the stars in the night sky or the sand on the seashore. The forgiveness he granted us was indeed free, but it certainly was not cheap. It cost him his one and only begotten Son. Christ lived a perfect life, yet was slaughtered as a sinless lamb for your sins. The forgiveness we freely receive came at an awful price for the KING of KINGS and LORD of LORDS. So, when we refuse to forgive those who have sinned against us, it is easy to see how this will affect our ability to communicate and receive further blessing from the one who paid such a high price for our forgiveness. No matter how deep the wound is or how horrible the offence, the forgiveness you are being called to grant can never compare with what Christ did for you. When we refuse to choose forgiveness, we slap God in the face and say "The price I am paying to forgive is higher than the price you paid."

Next, as a follower of Christ, we are called to be different. We have been transformed. We are supposed to look and act differently from the world around us. When we choose to forgo forgiveness for bitterness, anger, or revenge, we look just like the rest of the world. This causes us to exhibit the exact opposite of Christ-like

---

17   *Life Application Study Bible, Accordance electronic ed.* (Carol Stream: Tyndale House Publishers, 2004), n.p.

behavior, when we show the world how hypocritical we are. The world looks at us and says, "They freely receive forgiveness, but are unwilling to grant it." Our light is dimmed and our witness is diminished by a lack of forgiveness.

I know a couple who was faced with the issue of forgiveness some time ago. A family friend recommended another friend to help them sell one of their vehicles. The agreement was that the salesman would sell this vehicle for free to help this young ministry couple. This person sold their vehicle, but refused to give them $6,000 from the sale. This came as a shock, since the vehicle only sold for $8,000. Many told them to take the man to court, but they instead decided to take this man's name to God in prayer. While praying, they felt God say, "Fully forgive this man of this debt." They granted that forgiveness in full by informing the man in person that he could keep the $6,000 and they would not pursue him anymore. The man seemed shocked at the news and stunned as they walked away. Later that month, they received $6,000 from that man, along with a note that informed them of his newfound faith and upcoming baptism at a local church. Their total forgiveness cut this man to his very soul and caused him to long for the freedom they had. Forgiveness is powerful, but only if we choose to grant it.[18]

This command to forgive others is not out of question when it comes to the character of God. Take some time as you end the study today to look up the following verses. Make notes and be familiar enough with each verse to discuss them in your next class. Pay particular attention to how foreign these things sound in our culture today and how they might positively affect others if we chose to follow these teachings from Christ.

📖 Luke 6:32-38

_____

_____

📖 Colossians 3:12-14

_____

_____

📖 Ephesians 4:29-32

_____

_____

---

18   It should be noted that this family chose to do more then forgive, by releasing him of his debt because God told them to. They sought the Lord's guidance and obeyed his commands to the fullest extent with total faith. While we should always be quick to forgive, God may or may not call us to give even more depending on the situation. The key is seeking his guidance in every situation.

Forgiveness may not seem the logical or natural choice in most situations. Then again, many things Christ calls us to do are not logical or sensible from the outside looking in. Only when we have experienced them from the inside out can we know the blessing that comes with each of the commands of Christ. The command to forgive freely is a blessing, but it can only be experienced once you fully embrace it.

Write out your memory verse in the space below. Try to do it completely from memory, then double-check yourself.

TAKE TIME TO PRAY

Thank God for his eternal forgiveness and for the assurance of salvation that he offers to all who call on his holy name. Ask him to help you come to a place where you can fully embrace forgiveness for those in your life. Look at your list again from day one and pray about each situation and person that you have never fully forgiven.

Forgiveness—Day Four

Memory Verse

Matthew 19:26

Start today's study by writing out as much of your memory verse as you can in the space below. Then, look up the verse and make any corrections that are needed. Finally, read it three times from your Bible and pray before completing the following lesson.

_____

_____

_____

_____

There was once a man who was considered to be an expert fisherman. This person was always up-to-date on the most current technologies and methods being used in the fishing world. He could tell you anything you wanted to know about every kind of boat, rod, reel, bait, or lures. He was a subscriber to all of the greatest fishing magazines and was a frequent columnist in many of them. He was said to be one of the most sought-after speakers at the biggest fishing shows and conferences, and it was at one of those conferences during the question-and-answer time that he stunned the world. The question from a fan in the audience had never been asked of this man before and this simple question turned the fishing world upside down. The man asked, "How many fish has a great fisherman like you caught in your lifetime?" The expert fisherman paused for a long time and then looked at the floor and said, "I have never caught a single fish in my life." The crowd was stunned and shocked at the expert's shocking admission. The audience member who had asked the question said, "What do you mean, you have never caught a fish. Why not? I don't understand." The expert replied, "I am terrified of water. I can't even make myself stand on the dock near the lake, much less get in a boat."

Why do I share this funny and facetious story with you? Because when it comes to forgiveness, this is how most Christians look to the rest of the world. We know a lot about forgiveness. We talk about it, we pray about it, we read about it, and we recommend it to others who come to us for advice. We look like and act like experts, but when it comes right down to it, most of us have never even gotten near the water. C. S. Lewis said it this way: "Everyone says forgiveness is a great idea, until they have something to forgive."

So far this week, we have learned about forgiveness, but if we don't take what we learn and apply it to our faith, we are no better than the fisherman. We must actively apply what we have learned and dare to forgive those who have hurt, harmed, or attempted to destroy us in the past. This will not be easy and it will not come naturally to us at first. However, if we are willing to obey the commands of Christ and forgive those who have hurt us, we will be amazed at the transformation that it will usher into our lives and the lives of others. Look up Matthew 26:26-28 and answer the questions below.

    ❧ Jesus shows us the ultimate and most incredible example of true forgiveness. What does it teach us about the sacrifice involved in forgiveness?

_____

_____

_____

_____

    ❧ Does forgiveness require pride or humility? Explain.

_____

_____

_____

    ❧ With this passage and what you have learned about forgiveness this week in mind, do you think forgiveness will ever be "easy"?

_____

_____

_____

Forgiving others may become "easier" over time but it is doubtful that it will ever be "easy." Just hours before Christ died on the cross for the forgiveness of our sins, we see him in extreme agony in the garden as he wrestled with what was about to happen. No one else in the history of the world will ever have to deal with such a dilemma, but this shows just how difficult forgiveness can be. But, like Christ, we must do what God has called us to do and that involves forgiving those who have mistreated us, no matter how recent or old the wound may be. While our memory verse this week does not deal specifically with the issue of forgiveness, it does speak an incredible truth into our lives: with God all things are possible. Read what the Apostle Paul said in Philippians 4:13.

    ❖ Do you think there is anything that is impossible for God? Seriously consider this question and write out anything you think of in the space below.

_____

_____

_____

_____

    ❖ Do you think that anything is impossible for you if you attempt it through Christ?

_____

_____

_____

You can forgive and you can experience the freedom that comes with forgiveness. This is one of the basic things all disciples of Christ will be faced with as they walk with Jesus in this journey through life. The sooner we submit to Christ and decide to obey his commands fully, the better for us and for the world. As you prepare to close out this week, embrace the following challenge. Go back to Day One and think about those people you identified who you have withheld forgiveness from in the past. Pray and ask God how he would have you grant that forgiveness. The question is not whether we should forgive, but how God wants us to forgive. It may be a verbal conversation that God calls you to have with the other party. It might be confessing your own error and asking forgiveness that must take place before you can grant forgiveness yourself. It may be a letter or email that you feel compelled to write. As you pray and listen, then respond quickly and fully by forgiving those who have hurt you. You can do it!

Write out your memory verse in the space below. Try to do it completely from memory, then double-check yourself.

TAKE TIME TO PRAY

As you pray today, be sure to listen more than you speak. Give God time to respond to your request for guidance in the area of forgiveness. When we pray, we must be very intentional about listening to God, too.

To review, use the space below to write all the memory verses you have learned so far, including this week's. You can also use this space for personal notes about this lesson.

Gifts—Day One[19]

Memory Verse

Romans 12:1

Start today's study by writing out your memory verse in the space below. Then, read it three times from your Bible and take just a moment to pray before completing the following lesson.

M any studies avoid the subject of spiritual gifts all together because there is so much disagreement and controversy surrounding the subject. For example, when it comes to the number of gifts, some say there are seven gifts, others say seventeen, still others say twenty-nine, and some even say there is an infinite

---

19   The majority of my research for this study comes from notes I took in college from a sermon series my pastor preached on the subject of spiritual gifts. Glen Howe based his series on the notes he took from a taped series that he heard Dr. Charles Stanley preach sometime in the 1980's. Dr. Stanley has since produced a workbook entitled *Ministering through Spiritual Gifts*. I was not aware of Dr. Stanley's study or sermons until months after this chapter was completed. This study was originally written directly from my notes and to the best of my knowledge I have not directly quoted either Glen Howe or Dr. Charles Stanley. If you feel that I have, please contact me and I will be glad to add quotation marks and proper citations in the next edition of this work.

number of gifts, with only a small portion of them being listed in scripture. Admittedly, the framework this study will use in teaching about spiritual gifts is open to debate. It is not within the scope of a basic study like this one to outline and explore all of the possibilities and controversies surrounding spiritual gifts. Instead, this study's aim is to give the student a *basic* understanding of spiritual gifts and what they look like when used in real life. It will also provide guidance in how to determine what your primary spiritual gifts are.

So what is a spiritual gift? It can be described as a supernatural gift that is measured and given by God to all believers at the time of their spiritual birth and conversion. God imparts these gifts to believers for the purpose of serving the church and humanity, in order to advance his kingdom and the good news of the gospel of Christ. God grants each of us certain natural talents and abilities at the time of our physical birth. In a similar way at the time of our spiritual transformation God gives us our spiritual gifts so that we will be able to accomplish the spiritual purposes and plans he has for our lives.

📖 In 1 Peter 4:10-11, what reason is given for God granting us spiritual gifts?

_____

_____

_____

The following passages are the primary texts in God's word concerning spiritual gifts. Take some time to open up your Bible and read each passage carefully. Then list the gifts that are mentioned in that passage in the space provided below.

📖 1 Corinthians 12:8-10

1. _____

2. _____

3. _____

4. _____

5. _____

6. _____

7. _____

8. _____

9. _____

📖 1 Corinthians 12:28-30

    1. _____

    2. _____

    3. _____

    4. _____

    5. _____

    6. _____

    7. _____

    8. _____

📖 Romans 12:6-8

    1. _____

    2. _____

    3. _____

    4. _____

    5. _____

    6. _____

    7. _____

❧ Of the gifts mentioned above, list the gifts you have seen at work in your own life.

_____

_____

_____

❧ Are there any gifts you have never seen at work in your life?

_____

_____

❧ Why does God give us these gifts?

_____

_____

❧ Who benefits from these gifts if we use them? 🎬

_____

_____

Next, we need to answer the following two questions: who has spiritual gifts, and what are they for? It is clear as we read scripture that our God is a God of purpose. He does not do things randomly. He does not give or take away without reason or purpose. Before we can discover what the purpose of these incredible gifts might be, we must first have a clear understanding of who possesses them. Look up and read 1 Peter 4:7-10 carefully.

❧ Who has these gifts according to this passage? Does it seem specific or general?

_____

_____

The Greek word translated as "each one" in verse 10 is εκαστος (hekastos). This word simply means each person and could be applied to mean many things. Some have used this to say that "everyone," Christian and non-Christian alike, have received spiritual gifts. However, when we read this text in context, it seems very unlikely that the author was speaking to nonbelievers. This portion of his letter seems to be addressed specifically to believers. The other texts you studied earlier in the lesson also imply that the gifts are given only to believers. 1 Corinthians 12:4 puts the issue to rest by saying, _There are different kinds of gifts, but the same Spirit._ Those who do not know Christ clearly do not possess the same "Spirit" as those who have been transformed by the blood of Jesus. As we will discover in later lessons this week, we can see signs of these gifts in the lives of people in the Old Testament as well. While these men and women were not "Christians" in the sense that they had accepted Christ, they were following God in the days in which they lived. However it is important to remember that for those living under the New Covenant in Christ today, we now only receive our spiritual gifts upon our conversion to Christianity.

The next question that arises is when we receive these gifts. The answer is that when we receive the Holy Spirit, we receive our spiritual gifts as well. It should be noted here that God might impart certain gifts into a believer's life for a specific time and purpose and later decrease those gifts in order to increase others and use that person for another purpose. For example, your primary gift at your spiritual transformation may be hospitality and giving. The Lord may use those gifts in your life to serve as a leader or member of a team at your church for months or years. Then, a staff member may move to another church, or a strong leader within the congregation may pass away, or there may be no apparent reason at all and out of nowhere, when you least expect it, you might start to experience the gift of administration in your life and sense God calling you to serve in a new ministry that you had never considered before. Our spiritual gifts should not be viewed as concrete things that will never change, because the Spirit of God directs them—they are fluid and active. However it is extremely unlikely that they will change often in our lives. Once again, our God is one of purpose and he has planned and prepared to such a degree that it seems unlikely that our gifts, which come from him, will change on a weekly or monthly basis.

    📖 Look up Ephesians 1:13-14. What do these verses tell you about when we receive the Holy Spirit?

_____

_____

_____

    ❧ What do these verses tell you about the security of our salvation in Christ?

_____

_____

_____

Now that we know who gets these gifts and when they are delivered into our lives, the next question is, "what are they there for?" Because most Christians have never considered this question, many gifts go unused each day in the kingdom of God.

    📖 According to 1 Corinthians 12:7, what are our spiritual gifts used for?

_____

_____

    📖 What are the gifts in Ephesians 4:11-12 for, according to the Bible?

_____

_____

The gifts given to each of us by the Spirit are to be used to build up the body of Christ, serve others, and advance God's kingdom. They are for his glory and fame, not our own. Whatever gifts we have been given should be used to serve God to accomplish whatever purpose and plan he has for our lives. Sadly, many use their gifts for their own purposes and many more simply don't use their gifts at all. In Week Three, we studied the church and we focused on the picture of the church as "The Body of Christ." When believers refuse to use their spiritual gifts, the entire body suffers. God has equipped every believer in a special and unique way through his gifts. Only when we are willing to discover our gifts and use them can the body truly be healthy and function at its full potential.

📖 Look up 1 Timothy 4:14, then write out the first five words of that verse in the space below. What does this verse mean to you?

_____

_____

_____

❧ Have you been using your gifts for God's glory, for something else, or not at all? Explain.

_____

_____

_____

❧ Are you satisfied with the way you have been using the gifts that God has given you? If not, what do you plan to change?

_____

_____

_____

❧ If you are not using your gifts for God's glory, what is holding you back?

_____

_____

_____

As we close this study today, be sure you spend some extra time in prayer asking God to guide you as you attempt to understand and discover the gifts he has given you. Over the next two days, we will look at these gifts in the light of scripture and see if we can uncover their true meaning and purpose in our lives.

Write out your memory verse in the space below. Try to do it completely from memory, then double-check yourself.

TAKE TIME TO PRAY

Thank God for sending his Son and making the way to heaven so simple for you. Ask him to give you opportunities to share your faith in the coming days. Pray specifically for one person you know who does not know Christ.

Gifts—Day Two

Memory Verse

Romans 12:1

Start today's study by writing out as much of your memory verse as you can in the space below. Then, look up the verse and make any corrections that are needed. Finally, read it three times from your Bible and pray before completing the following lesson.

---

*Y*esterday in our study, we discovered that God imparts spiritual gifts into the lives of all believers and those gifts are given for a reason and a purpose. Believers are supposed to put their gifts to work for the glory of God and the advancement of his kingdom. Today we will look at some people in the Bible and examine their primary gift and see what that particular gift looks like when it is put into action. It is not within the scope of this study to examine every gift in detail, so we will focus on the gifts listed only in Romans 12:3-8. This will be sufficient to see what the spiritual gifts look like in action.

The gift of prophecy is listed first among these seven gifts in Romans 12. Many in our modern day misunderstand this gift. When we hear the word prophet or prophecy, our mind automatically thinks of someone who can foretell the future. God has used people in this role in the past; however, with the completion of the biblical canon the office of prophet passed away. We now have God's complete revelation through his written word. Today, God primarily uses those with the gift of prophecy to speak about what has already been revealed. We see this gift clearly at work in the life of Peter. Like the Apostle Peter, those with the gift of prophecy have a hard time keeping their mouths shut. I once heard a pastor say that Peter spoke more than any other disciple in the four gospels. Prophets feel compelled to speak especially when they see someone doing something wrong or leading others astray. Peter was generally the first to speak. Read Matthew 16:13-23 and you will see this gift at work in the life of Peter.

    ⤳ How can this gift be a blessing to the church or to other people?

_____

_____

    ⤳ From this passage, can you see the downfall of those with this gift? ✘

_____

_____

In Acts 2:13-14, Peter stands up to preach. He does not foretell the future; rather, he proclaims the gospel boldly. While others are thinking about what to say, the prophet stands and speaks. Those with this gift also have the ability to discern the character and motives of people. It was Peter who called out Ananias and Sapphira in Acts 5:3-10. Those with this gift also have a genuine concern for the things God is doing and will fight to defend those programs at all costs. It was Peter in John 18 who drew his sword when they came to arrest Christ. It was Peter who boldly said *For we cannot help speaking about what we have seen and heard* to the Sanhedrin (Acts 4:20). Those with this gift are extremely loyal to the people they love and care about, and they have a very deep dependence on scripture. Look up and read 1 Peter 4:11, then answer the question below.

    ⤳ From these verses, how serious do you think Peter was about scripture? Explain.

_____

_____

_____

Those who have this gift also have some problems that, if they are not careful, can overtake them and cause them to stumble in terrible ways. Because of their strong desire to speak the truth, people with the gift of prophecy are not always quick to think or pray before speaking. Like Peter, their tongues can get them into trouble. They can also come across as being intolerant, harsh, and uncaring. Prophets, if not careful, can quickly become poor listeners if they are not intentional about slowing down and letting others speak. Prophets are quick to say when accused of these things, "Well, that's just the way I am!" Those who are quick to use that as a defense of their unholy actions are probably misusing the gift that God has blessed them with. All of God's gifts are given to be a blessing to his people and the church, not a curse. In 1 Corinthians 14:3, the Apostle Paul explains what the gift of prophecy looks like when used correctly.

📖 What are the three things that Paul says those with the gift of prophecy will do in 1 Corinthians 14:3?

1. _____

2. _____

3. _____

📖 Those with this gift should also strongly consider what Paul says in 1 Corinthians 13:2. He says that prophecy is useless without what?

_____

If you desire to study this gift more and see it at work in the lives of others in the Bible, you might consider studying the following people.

1. Hananiah, Mishael, and Azariah in the book of Daniel;
2. John, later in his life, as he speaks to the seven churches in Revelation 1-3;
3. The life of Joseph in Genesis 37-50.

The second gift listed in Romans 12 is serving. The word in the Greek text is *diakonia*. My pastor in college gave the following definition for this word: "Someone who executes the commands of others." This is also the same Greek word from which we get our English word *"deacon."* Louw and Nida's Greek—English Lexicon defines it this way: "to render assistance or help by performing certain duties, often of a humble or menial nature." The life of Timothy gives us an accurate picture of what this gift looks like in the real world. Those with the gift of service like Timothy long to be around other people. They want to be around and have relationships with as many people as possible because they are looking for people whom they can serve and help. They love working in groups as well. In the book of Acts, each time Timothy is mentioned (Acts chapters 16-20), he is working with others in a group. Paul often sent Timothy to check on or work with groups of believers and churches that they had started on their missionary journeys. Why? Because

Timothy was good with people and he enjoyed working with them through his gift of service. Those with the gift of service have a strong desire to help others and, more specifically, to meet practical needs. Read Philippians 2:20.

    ❧ Why did Paul say he was sending Timothy?

_____

_____

    People with the gift of service also work best on short-term projects. They want to use their gift and be able to see the results quickly. In 2 Timothy 4:13, Paul says this to Timothy: *When you come, bring the cloak that I left with Carpus at Troas, and my scrolls, especially the parchments.* He knew Timothy needed specific instructions but he was fully confident that Timothy would carry those instructions out completely once he had them. Twice in 2 Timothy 4:9-21, Paul reminds Timothy to stay on task and come as soon as possible. Those with the gift of service do best with short-term projects and can easily get distracted when the finish line is too far down the road. These people also need more verbal praise then others. Prophets, for example, need little if any praise. Those with the gift of service, however, need a great deal of verbal praise and encouragement. Paul encourages and builds Timothy up more than any of his other disciples. First and Second Timothy are both full of praise for this young man. Sometimes people think of servants as being high-maintenance because they need attention and praise. The truth of the matter is that they don't care if their name is in the paper or if they are publically recognized, and they could care less if they have a seat at the head table. But they need to be verbally encouraged. They see their service as an investment in the lives of others and God's ministry. But serving the church and other people will drain such hard workers, and they must be filled back up! They can tell if your verbal praise is sincere or not as well, so don't ever attempt to give them praise if you don't really mean it.

    Those who have this gift tend to feel inadequate and unqualified for spiritual leadership. When asked to lead a home Bible study, the person with the spiritual gift of service will gladly bring the refreshments, clean the house, set up the chairs, or do anything—other than teach. Not because they are bad Bible teachers but they just feel drawn to do the more practical parts of the ministry. No fewer than three times does Paul encourage Timothy to step up and lead (1 Tim 4:14; 2 Tim 1:5, 3:14). These people have a hard time saying no as well. They can easily become overworked and may burn out if others are not sensitive to their needs and help them keep a steady pace in their ministry.

    Individuals with this gift must guard against being judgmental of others who are not as quick to meet the needs of others as they are. They tend to be critical of others who do not volunteer as much as they do. People with this gift have trouble understanding why others are so unwilling to give and sacrifice as much as they

THE ABSOLUTE BASICS OF CHRISTIANITY

do for the kingdom. They can also rush into situations without fully understanding what God is trying to do. When they see a need, they launch into action to meet that need and don't always take time to look at the big picture first. They must also be extremely careful that they don't neglect their own spiritual and physical health, along with their families, in the name of service. The gift of service can also come across as being pushy, because those with this gift are always trying to jump in and help, even if they have not been invited or asked to do so.

If you desire to study the gift of service more and see it at work in the lives of others in the Bible, you might consider studying the following people.

1. Tabitha. We don't have a great deal of information about her life but she was clearly a servant. See Acts 9, specifically verse 36;

2. Epaphroditus is another interesting figure who clearly had the gift of service. To learn more about him you can read the book of Philippians, especially 2:25-27; 4:16-19;

3. Martha was also a servant and from her life you can see the downfall of servant hood if it is not kept in the proper perspective. Read Luke 10:38-42.

The final gift for today's lesson is the gift of teaching. Luke will be our biblical example for this spiritual gift. Individuals with this gift have a strong desire to present truth in a systematic sequence. For example, in the first chapter of his gospel, Luke states that his purpose in writing this book is to lay out an "orderly account" (Luke 1:3). He also notes that others have already written about the life of Jesus; however, he feels compelled to do so as well presumably because he was not completely satisfied with the other accounts. Teachers like Luke are concerned with facts and accuracy. Look up the following verses in different gospels and compare them to see if you notice any differences.

📖 Mark 1:30 and Luke 4:38. ✖

_____

_____

📖 Mark 3:1 and Luke 6:6. ✖

_____

_____

📖 Mark 1:40 and Luke 5:12. ✖

_____

_____

📖 Read Matthew's genealogy of Jesus in Matthew 1:1-16, and then the account given in Luke 3:23-38. Pay close attention to Matthew 1:1 and Luke 3:38. What is the difference? ⚒

_____

_____

The gospel of Luke gives more details when it comes to names, cities, towns, dates, events, and side points than any of the other gospels. Luke's account of the early church in the book of Acts is equally precise. Those with the gift of teaching pay close attention to the details and stick to the facts more than those with any other gift. They also tend to wait for all the information to come in before they speak. Prophets speak first and think later, servants serve first and think later, teachers think first and act later. They are more anticlerical and thoughtful than most. They may not have a lot to say but when they say it, everyone listens because it is well thought-out and worth listening to.

Those with the gift of teaching must be careful not to become prideful in their knowledge. Because they have a solid grasp on spiritual matters, they can easily become proud and arrogant. Individuals with the gift of teaching sometimes look down on others who have not done the research and put in the time they have to learn about a subject. They will at times lord their knowledge over others, and pride will start to creep in. They should keep in mind that this gift, like all the others, is meant to build up the body of Christ and to be a blessing, not a curse. They should also remember that the Apostle Paul said in 1 Corinthians 13 that even if you can fathom all mysteries and knowledge but have not love, you are nothing. Those with the gift of teaching must keep in mind that Christ has called us to be doers of the word, not knowers. They must also be careful not to engage others with petty arguments that serve no purpose. The great knowledge these individuals have can sometimes lead them to spend too much time arguing about issues and topics that in the end don't matter, or perhaps can't even be solved or explained. Finally, because they are generally slow to speak, they must constantly remind themselves that no one benefits from their silence. Speak up and share your gift with the rest of us. If you can't verbalize your thoughts, write them down!

If you desire to study the gift of teaching more and see it at work in the lives of others in the Bible you might consider studying the following people.

1. In Acts 8:26-40, we find the story of Philip. He spent a short amount of time teaching the Ethiopian eunuch about a certain passage of scripture. While little is known about Philip the evangelist, it seems that he indeed possessed the gift of being able to relate to other people and teach them about God's Holy Word.

2. Aquila and his wife Priscilla helped teach Apollos in Acts 18:18-27. Apollos was also gifted as a teacher, according to this passage of scripture. While

Aquila and Priscilla are only mentioned a few other times in the New Testament in general greetings (Rom 16:3; 1 Cor 16:19; 2 Tim 4:19), Apollos seems to have become a major figure in the early church and his ministry is mentioned many times by Paul (Acts 19:1; 1 Cor 1:12; 3:4-6, 22; 4:6; 16:12; Titus 3:13).

3. In tomorrow's lesson we will look at the Apostle Paul as our example for the gift of encouragement. Paul, however, was also gifted greatly in the area of teaching. He is able to communicate and clearly teach the early church on so many difficult theological issues. Read the books of Romans, 1 Corinthians, or Ephesians, or any other book that Paul authored and you will see that God enabled him with a strong teaching gift.

Tomorrow we will look at the last four gifts outlined in Romans 12. Then we will be prepared to discuss how we can identify what gifts the Spirit has blessed us with personally in our final lesson on day four.

Write out your memory verse in the space below. Try to do it completely from memory, then double-check yourself.

TAKE TIME TO PRAY

Gifts—Day Three

Memory Verse

Romans 12:1

Start today's study by writing out as much of your memory verse as you can in the space below. Then, look up the verse and make any corrections that are needed. Finally, read it three times from your Bible and pray before completing the following lesson.

_____

_____

_____

_____

Yesterday we looked at the first three gifts mentioned in Romans 12—the gifts of prophecy, service, and teaching. Today we will examine the next four, which are encouragement, giving, leadership, and mercy. All of these gifts are given to God's people to be a blessing to others and to the church as well. A gift is useless if you don't use it, so as we examine these gifts, think about your own and how God has used or can use the gifts you have.

In Romans 12:8, Paul speaks of our next gift—encouragement. Those with this gift have the desire to motivate other believers to take the action that is necessary to grow and mature their faith in Christ. We will look at two biblical examples of this gift. They are Barnabas and Paul.

The first time we encounter Barnabas in scripture is in Acts 4. The name Barnabas was given to him by the apostles (Acts 4:36) because of the kind of man he was. The name itself means "son of encouragement." Barnabas was the kind of man who was willing to build others up without giving any thought or consideration to his own needs or desires. We see this all through the book of Acts as we follow the life of Barnabas. For example, look up and read Acts 4:32-37.

✂ What was Barnabas's real name?

The early church was in big trouble. They were being persecuted, and because of the great persecution there were many in the church who had lost their jobs or the ability to make money because they had converted to Christianity. So Barnabas sold some land and brought the money to the church to be used to meet the needs of others. He did not have to do this. No one made him sell his property and bring all of the money to the church. However, the working of the Spirit in his life compelled him to do this incredible thing and to practice generosity in a way that few in the history of the world ever have. In doing this he encouraged the church.

Barnabas was a respected leader in the early church. Saul, on the other hand, was a despised enemy of the church. Saul, who would later become known as Paul, was busy persecuting the church and even overseeing the deaths of some Christians (Acts 7:58). In Acts 9, Saul had an encounter with the resurrected Christ on the road and ultimately converted to Christianity himself. After spending three years in the desert (Gal 1), Paul attempted to join the disciples in Jerusalem (Acts 9:26-28). The disciples, however, were afraid and unwilling to accept him, fearing that he might just be trying to infiltrate the group to destroy it. But Barnabas bridged the gap and, through his influence, brought Paul into the group.

Barnabas and Paul would do a great deal of ministry together and through the encouragement of Barnabas, the greatest missionary and church planter the world has ever known was trained. In Acts 13, we see a major shift in the roles of Barnabas and Paul. It is here that Paul becomes the leader and Barnabas becomes Paul's follower. Barnabas does not complain, or desperately try to hold on and control the group. Instead, he continues to encourage Paul.

In Acts 15, Barnabas has a strong desire to encourage John Mark. John had quit on a previous missionary journey (Acts 13:13) and Paul was unwilling to give him another opportunity to join the group. The disagreement between Paul and Barnabas caused them to disband and go in different directions. But Barnabas saw potential in John Mark, and so he and John went to Cyprus, while Paul and Silas set out for Syria and Cilicia.

When Barnabas encouraged the church, he lost his land. When he encouraged Paul and brought him into the group of disciples, he ultimately lost his position, as Paul eventually overshadowed him and became the leader. And when he encouraged young John Mark, he lost his place in scripture and history. We never hear of Barnabas again after he departs for Cyprus, because Luke, who would write the book of Acts, went with Paul.

We do, however, hear about John Mark. He wrote the earliest gospel; we know it simply as the book of Mark. We also know that Mark was a strong leader in the early church and through his ministry many were won to the faith. We also hear about Mark in the very last book that Paul wrote. Just before his death, in writing to Timothy Paul writes, *Get Mark and bring him with you, because he is helpful to me in my ministry* (2 Tim 4:11). Mark was useful to Paul's ministry because of the encouragement of Barnabas. Paul was useful in the kingdom of God because of the encouragement of Barnabas. Without the encouragement of Barnabas, it is doubtful that the church of God would be what it is today.

ᘐ How would you have felt if you would have been Barnabas?

_____

_____

ᘐ What natural emotions might you have expressed through your flesh?

_____

_____

ᘐ Why do you think that Barnabas was able to stay focused on the overall mission rather than himself?

_____

_____Paul was willing to stand for Christ and the church when called upon and he would ultimately give his life in his effort to spread the Good News, which might make him sound more like a prophet. However, when examining the life of Paul closely, we find that he was a great encourager as well. The time that Paul had spent with Barnabas allowed him to see the power of this gift. Because of the example he had witnessed in the life of Barnabas, he was all the more willing to allow this gift the freedom to work in his ministry as well. There are many things we see in his life that show us what the spiritual gift of encouragement looks like in the real world.

First, those with this gift are great at discerning the spiritual maturity of others. Paul does this in 1 Corinthians 3:1-2 when he tells his readers that he gave them milk, not solid food, because they were not mature enough to handle it. These people have the gift that allows them to see the untapped spiritual potential in a person's life and then they can show others the steps to achieve that potential. Yesterday we talked about Timothy's gift of service and how much encouragement he received from Paul. The Apostle Paul was great at giving encouragement and instruction to others. Just take a few minutes to read 2 Timothy 2:22-26 and you will see how Paul carefully encouraged and guided Timothy's spiritual development. Individuals with this unique gift are also very optimistic even in the face of tragedy, sorrow, pain, or suffering. They are not concerned with why things happen; instead they are always trying to figure out how to use what has happened to build others up. Look up 2 Corinthians 1:5; 2 Corinthians. 4:17; 2 Corinthians 12:9-10, and then answer the questions below.

> ⚘ What does Paul emphasize more in these passages: problems, or God's ability to pull these people through?

_____

_____

> ⚘ List the words of encouragement he uses in these verses.

_____

_____

People with this gift want to see others reach their full potential in Christ more than anything else. They don't care about getting the credit for it, they just want to be able to see the fruits of their labor in the lives of others. People with this gift prefer to work in small groups or one-on-one with people, if possible. They naturally seek small groups and one-on-one relationships because it is the most effective way to find out where others are spiritually and then guide them toward spiritual maturity. We can see this in the life of Paul in many places (1 Thess 2:17; 1 Thess 3:10; 2 Tim 1:4). He cared deeply for people and loved spending time with others on an individual basis.

Those with this gift must guard against the weaknesses of encouragement as well. For example, because they are quick to discern what it is that people need to grow, they can easily become bad listeners and jump to conclusions when it comes to the needs of others. It is also tempting for those with this gift to only encourage people who are making great progress in their faith. Encouragers are not always the most patient people. They prefer to put their encouragement efforts into the lives of those who are moving forward, rather than those who are standing still. In doing this they can forget that their encouragement might be what God desires to use to nudge others along. Finally, people with the gift of encouragement must be careful not to treat people like projects. When our encouragement becomes more about the project than the relationship, there will always be trouble.

If you desire to study the gift of encouragement more and see it at work in the lives of others in the Bible you might consider studying the following people and books.

1. Little is known about the life of Tychicus. However, he was considered to be a faithful follower and co-laborer with Paul. You can read about his

encouragement in Ephesians 6:21-22, and about who he was from these references: Acts 20:4; Colossians 4:7; 2 Timothy 4:12; Titus 3:12

2. You might also consider reading the book of James. This book was probably written by the half-brother of Jesus. It contains many forms of encouragement for the early believers. This letter seems to have been "prepared for public reading as a sermon to the congregations addressed. The tone is clearly authoritative but not autocratic. James included 54 imperatives in his 108 verses—an average of one call for action in every other verse!" [20] James seems to have been a man of encouragement among other things.

The next spiritual gift is generosity, or giving. We will look at Matthew the tax collector as our example of someone with the spiritual gift of giving. Matthew may seem at first to be a strange choice. However, as we examine his life I believe you will see that he did indeed have this gift in abundance. To start with, Matthew included more counsel about the use of money than any of the other three gospels. For example, look up Matthew 6:19-21 and answer the question below. Matthew is the only gospel that records this truth taught by Christ.

❧ Where should we store our treasure? Why?

_____

_____

People with the gift of generosity and giving, like Matthew, are financially wise individuals in general. They are the people who make budgets and plan their expenses down to the penny. Their primary motivation for doing this is so that they will be able to give more to God and those in need. The heartbeat of a person with this spiritual gift is found in Luke 6:38. They understand and believe that no matter how much they give, their investment in God's kingdom will always return eternal rewards. They also desire to give privately in most cases. They are not motivated by the applause or recognition of other people. They are blessed the most when they see God working through their gift. Being pressured to give turns them off! Matthew is the only gospel to discuss the importance of giving in private (Matt 6:1-4).

It may seem strange, but people with this gift also have a unique ability to be satisfied with the basic necessities of life. In Luke 5:27-28, we are told that Levi (Matthew) was willing to leave everything to follow Jesus. Such people tend to be thrifty and very frugal. They believe that God's money flows *through* them, not *to* them, so they make every effort to be stewards that God is pleased with.

---

20 John F. Walvoord and Roy B. Zuck, eds., *The Bible Knowledge Commentary: New Testament.* Accordance Electronic Edition (Wheaton: Victor Books, 1983), n.p.

They also want to make sure their gift is of the highest quality. Matthew describes the gifts of the magi as being "treasure," and Mary's ointment as being "very costly," and the tomb that the body of Christ lay in prior to his resurrection as being a "new tomb." Those with the gift of generosity desire that their gifts be of the highest quality and they also expect that their gifts will be used to produce something of quality as well. Let me share a quick story about the way a gift like this can be used.

Years ago, a man asked if he could make an appointment to meet with me in my office at our church. We set a time and day that worked for both of us for the following week. When he arrived at our office (a 3-bedroom trailer house), he wanted some information about the building project that we had started to raise funds for just five weeks earlier. Our church at the time had outgrown the barn that we were meeting in and desperately needed a bigger facility with air-conditioning, heat, and children's space. We had estimated that this project would cost 1.2 million dollars and we believed that God would provide the money. This individual asked if we could drive out to the land that had been donated to our church and look at it. As I climbed into his sixteen-year-old pickup truck and looked at this tall lanky farmer with holes in his tan cotton shirt and stained Wrangler jeans, I thought to myself, This is probably going to be a huge waste of time. After spending five minutes out at the property, we drove back to the office. There in our driveway he handed me a folded check and said "This will be a good start for your building fund." I thanked him and walked inside, tucking the check into my shirt pocket. As I sat down, I pulled the check out and discovered that this man had written a check to our church for $900,000. When added to the money that had already been collected, we had reached our goal almost to the penny. This man's only request was, "I don't want anyone to known who gave this money." This was not a wealthy athlete, Hollywood movie star, or talented musician. He was a normal person with the gift of generosity!

Individuals with this gift, however, must be careful not to fall into the devil's traps as well. They can be tempted to use their gift to control the ministry of God. Sometimes, those with this gift feel that because they give more, they should have more say or control in the church. They can at times withhold their gifts from the church to punish the board or the pastor. They can also become too frugal and stingy, to the point of causing suffering and pain for their own families. Their thriftiness at times can become more of an obsession then a part of their ministry. People with this gift may also move too fast without praying and consulting others about the gifts they desire to make or the needs they want to meet. Instead of praying about whether or not they should meet a need, they just do it, and they can steal blessings from others whom God is trying to grow in the area of generosity.

If you desire to study the gift of generosity more and see it at work in the lives of others in the Bible, you might consider studying the following.

1. The Macedonian churches, at 2 Corinthians 8:1-5.
2. The nameless widow in Mark 12:41-44 shows us what the gift of generosity looks like as well.
3. Mary in the book of Luke 7:37-46.

The next gift is leadership. Not everyone is a leader. To be a leader you must have followers. So God clearly intends for some to lead and others to follow. One is not better than the other, and both are needed in God's economy. The important thing is that we are true to what God has called us to be. God may use you in both roles as well. Our example for this gift is Nehemiah. God used this man as a follower *and* a leader. He was cupbearer to the King and the man God used to organize the effort to rebuild the wall around Jerusalem. As we look at his life we can see the characteristics that those with the gift of leadership possess.

Leaders have the ability to take dreams and put them into action. We might call them visionaries. There are many people in the world who have dreams, but leaders have a unique ability to connect the dots and make a plan work. They know what the end goal is and they have the ability to outline the steps to reach that goal. They can see the big picture and at the same time they understand how all the parts work to make that big picture come together. This is easy to see in the life of Nehemiah. You can see an example of this in Nehemiah 2:6-8.

⤳ What did Nehemiah say he needed?

_____

_____

Nehemiah was able to think the project through and discern what he would need for both the project and the journey. In Nehemiah 2:11-16, Nehemiah himself sets out to survey the damaged wall and make his plans for its restoration. He was also able to motivate both the king and the people to participate in the project. It would not have been common or acceptable for a cupbearer to make a request like this one to a king. Nehemiah however was bold and put it all on the line and persuaded the king to allow him to embark on this journey. When he arrived on the scene in Jerusalem, the wall was in ruins and the people had no intention to rebuild it. He rallied the common people and assigned them tasks, and the construction began. He was not only able to motivate them to build a wall of brick and mortar, but in Nehemiah 4:10-15, he motivates them to take up arms to defend the city! Leaders are able to motivate others.

They also delegate tasks to others. Good leaders understand that they can't reach their full potential without others. So they focus on building others up, and then delegating tasks and responsibilities to those people and entrusting them to complete the work. Look up and read Nehemiah 3:1-13 to see how masterfully he delegated responsibility to others.

๛ What was Nehemiah's part in building the wall?

_____

_____

๛ Without delegation, do you think it would have been possible to complete this project?

_____

_____

_____

Individuals with the gift of leadership are very loyal to those they lead. They feel a responsibility and personal connection with those who are entrusted to their care. In return they expect those they lead to be loyal as well. Good leaders will do everything possible to bless and govern diligently. They never use their power or authority in selfish ways. Instead, they are humble and thankful for the gift they have been given and desire to use that gift to build others up.

People with this gift should be careful not to put projects ahead of people. Sometimes leaders get so focused on the task and project at hand they can lose perspective and sight of the priority that God places on people. Leaders must also be careful to communicate clearly with those they lead. Because leaders see the big picture easily, they can start to assume that everyone else sees it as well. Leaders must always communicate what the end goal is. Leaders should also be willing to follow. No one will lead all of the time. It can become difficult for a leader to be a co-pilot instead of the person in charge. However, leaders can improve their leadership skills by following others and learning from them. God also places leaders in the position to follow so that we never forget what it is like on the other side of the table. Finally, leaders must be careful not to move on to the next task or project before ensuring that the current project is finished and that solid leadership is left behind to continue the work. Too many times, leaders jump from project to project, and they leave their organizations and ministries in disarray because they failed to train and equip others before they left.

If you desire to study the gift of leadership more and see it at work in the lives of others in the Bible, you might consider studying the following people.

1. Moses as he leads Gods people in the books of Exodus, Leviticus, Numbers, and Deuteronomy.

2. King Solomon as he leads the people to build the temple for God in 1 Kings 5—9:1

3. The life of King Josiah is an incredible testament to the power of leadership as well. He inherited a broken kingdom at the age of eight. This

kingdom, which had become corrupted and separated from God because of poor leadership in the past, was assured certain destruction by God's own words. Yet Josiah, knowing that God would not turn his wrath away, still chose to lead the people toward God. You can read his story in 2 Kings 22-23. In 2 Kings 23:25, you will find one of the most powerful statements that can be made about a man.

The final gift mentioned in Romans 12 is seen clearly in the life of John. It is the gift of mercy. Those with this gift are able to sense who is hurting emotionally, physically, or spiritually. They are drawn to these people and feel compelled to help them in some way. Those who are hurting will run to people of mercy in times of crises because they know without a doubt that they will find help there. John is described as the disciple that Jesus loved. He is the disciple that Christ turned to so many times throughout the most difficult times in his ministry. As Jesus hung from the cross, he directed John to take care of his mother as well (John 19:25-27). John was a person of compassion and mercy.

People with the gift of mercy are dependent on deep friendships and commitment from others. In return, they are some of the most dependable and committed people you will find. All of the other disciples fled the side of Jesus as he was arrested, beaten, and finally nailed to a tree. Peter followed at a distance, but then even the mighty prophet Peter fled the scene after denying Christ three times (Luke 22:54-62). John, however, was near the cross, along with the mother of Jesus and some other women. Those with the gift of mercy really want to help others no matter what the cost may be. They will even place themselves in harm's way if they think it will help those who are in need. Their hearts are broken when they see others hurting. Those with the gift of mercy try to avoid confrontation at all costs. The only time they will get involved in a confrontation is when there is no other option and if they feel it will somehow help. Look up and read Acts 3:1-16 and Acts 4:1-20.

ᚱᚴ Who does most of the talking in these verses?

_____

_____

ᚱᚴ In which verse does John first speak up? Why do you think he stepped in there? ✕

_____

_____

Like all of the other gifts, the gift of mercy has some downfalls that you must be careful to guard against. For example, if you have this gift, you must be careful not to take up someone else's offense and make it your own. When we think with our hearts, we can be lead astray. It is also important to understand why someone is suffering before you set out to meet her or his need. Those with the gift of mercy can make the situation worse if they don't fully understand what the root of the problem is. When we fix the symptoms but don't address the illness, it will only return and continue to cause pain. You must also not become bitter because others don't share your sense of compassion and rush to aid those in need. Finally, be careful to show people God's truth as you show them his mercy. It is God's truth that ultimately sets people free and that truth is expressed through your mercy.

If you desire to study the gift of mercy more and see it at work in the lives of others in the Bible, you might consider studying the following people and churches.

1. Read about the life of Esther. We see the gift of mercy most clearly in chapters 5-8, as she risks everything by standing up at the right moment for her people.

2. In 1 Samuel 25, we read about the life of another woman who was merciful, in the sense that she sought mercy for her family and people. Her name was Abigail and she went against her husband and king to stop the impending attack and certain destruction by David's army. Read about her in 1 Samuel 25:14-35.

3. The name Onesiphorus is only found twice in the Bible (2 Tim 1:16, 4:19). Paul writes that this person refreshed him and was not ashamed of Paul's chains. From these two verses, it seems that this person had a caring and merciful heart. The church in Philippi sent aid to Paul at least twice (Phil 4:16) and Paul counted those faithful as being partners in the gospel from the first day (Phil 1:5). This church cared deeply for Paul and his ministry and they provided for his needs and proved to be people of great mercy.

Write out your memory verse in the space below. Try to do it completely from memory then double-check yourself.

TAKE TIME TO PRAY

Gifts—Day Four

Memory Verse

Romans 12:1

Start today's study by writing out as much of your memory verse as you can in the space below. Then, look up the verse and make any corrections that are needed. Finally, read it three times from your Bible and pray before completing the following lesson.

_____

_____

_____

_____

Today we will conclude our survey of spiritual gifts by asking the question: How can I discover what my gifts are? God has blessed you with these gifts so that you will use them for his glory and for the benefit of his church. Sadly, many never use their gifts. Instead, they lay dormant for years or even a lifetime and the power and potential of those gifts go untapped. As a result, the entire church suffers. Modern day disciples must view spiritual gifts in a serious way and desire to discover and use the gifts they have been given.

This week we looked at the lives of Peter, Luke, Timothy, Paul, Barnabas, Nehemiah, Matthew, and John. They did not have spiritual-gift inventories and tests. There were not clever personality-profiling systems during their day and time. But they discovered and used their gifts to their fullest potential. I don't think there is anything wrong with tests and profiles, unless we make them the sole authority when it comes to our gifts. At the conclusion of today's study, you should take the spiritual gifts test located in the appendix at the back of the book and be prepared to discuss your gifts next week in our class. As you take this test and evaluate your results, remember that this is only *one* indicator, and probably the least effective when it comes to determining what your gifts are. Before we talk about the other three indicators, take some time to answer the questions below.

    ❧ Identify which gift belongs to each person listed below. Then write a few of the main characteristics of that gift and a few of the weaknesses as well. If you have trouble, you can look at the notes from Days Two and Three again.

- Peter _____

_____

_____

- Luke _____

_____

_____

- Timothy _____

_____

_____

- Paul _____

_____

_____

- Nehemiah _____

_____

_____

- Matthew _____

_____

_____

- John _____

_____

_____

We can learn from these people a very sure and quick method to discover our gifts. The first thing we must do is to think about what the desire of our heart is. What is it that breaks your heart? What do you want to do? Where do you want to serve? What makes your heart beat fast and causes your blood to rush through your veins? Is it helping a homeless person or feeding the hungry? Is it preaching and defending God's Word? Is it building people up and making them feel good? Do you love to give your time, talents, and money to others? When you discover what your passion is, you will be on the right road to discovering where you are gifted.

    ❧ Write down some things that have recently broken your heart in the space below.

_____

_____

_____

    ❧ If you could do anything in the world what would you do?

_____

_____

    ❧ Thinking about the two questions above, as well as the seven gifts we discussed, what gifts do you think might be yours?

_____

_____

_____

The next thing you should look at honestly is the opportunities that God has given you. God will never give us more then we can bear, so naturally we can look at the things that God has called us to do and be reasonably certain that we possess the gifts that would be needed to fulfill that call. Do people always come to you for help? Do people ask your opinion when they have questions about the Bible? Have you been asked to teach in children's church or an adult class? When you are in a group, do people turn and look at you when there is no leader and ask you to make a decision?

     ❧ What are some things you feel God has given you the opportunity to do over the last few weeks or months?

_____

_____

_____

     ❧ Which gifts would those things tend to point to?

_____

_____

_____

     ❧ Is there any pattern between your heartfelt desires and the opportunities that God has given you as it relates to spiritual gifts?

_____

_____

_____

After you have examined your desires and the opportunities that God has placed in your life, you should then look at the evidence. Is there any evidence that you might be gifted in a certain area? Have others made positive comments about a certain gift you think you might have? Do you see consistent positive results when you use that gift? Is there any evidence at all that you are gifted in that area? Everyone will make mistakes and we all fall short from time to time, even in the areas in which we are gifted. But if you have tried to teach and no one came back to your class the next week, teaching may not be your spiritual gift. What we want our gifts to be and what God wants our gifts to be can be two different things. We must make sure that we are not trying to be something God has not called or equipped us to be. If we do that, we will frustrate others and ourselves.

     ❧ List some evidence you have seen in the past that might help you in determining what your gifts are.

_____

_____

❧ List the gifts that might be associated with this evidence.

_____

_____

❧ Is there any pattern between your desires, opportunities, and evidence when it comes to a specific gift?

_____

_____

By now you should see a pattern emerging when it comes to your gifts. If you still can't see a pattern between your desires, opportunities, and the evidence, then chances are you are not being honest with yourself or have not seriously considered each category. If you have seen a pattern, then you are well on your way to confirming the gifts God desires to use in your life right now. As I stated at the start of this week, these may change as you take your journey with Christ through this life. If you walk with the Lord long enough, he will use you in many different ways, and there will be seasons when he gives you the desire, opportunity, and evidence that will point to a different gift. Don't fear this change; accept and embrace it! God has given us each a set of unique gifts that empower and enable us to run our race. May we use them to their highest potential.

Write out your memory verse in the space below. Try to do it completely from memory, then double-check yourself.

_____

_____

_____

_____

TAKE TIME TO PRAY

Thank God for sending his Son and making the way to heaven so simple for you. Ask him to give you opportunities to share your faith in the coming days. Pray specifically for one person you know who does not know Christ.

To review, use the space below to write all the memory verses you have learned so far, including this week's. You can also use this space for personal notes about this lesson.

_____

_____

_____

_____

_____

_____

_____

_____

_____

_____

_____

_____

_____

_____

_____

_____

_____

Heaven & Hell—Day One

Memory Verse

John 14:6

Start today's study by writing out your memory verse in the space below. Then, read it three times from your Bible and take just a moment to pray before completing the following lesson.

This week we are going to look at some of the basics about heaven and hell. In the past, these two places have been thought of by many to be imaginary places that are too good or too bad to actually exist. The truth is that both places are very real and every person that has ever lived will spend their eternal lives in one of these two real places. So let's start with heaven and look at a few myths about this very real place.

Myth #1: Heaven will be boring! Many people cite this as one of their major reasons for not accepting the gift of salvation that Jesus offers. They feel that heaven will simply be too boring for them. They view heaven as a place where we all sit on clouds, play harps, and watch eternity creep by. This could not be further from the truth. Heaven will be the most exciting, alive, joyful, peaceful, magnificent place you have ever known. Matthew 22:2 says this about heaven; *The kingdom of heaven is like a king who prepared a wedding banquet for his son.*

This tells me that heaven is going to be amazing! Real estate tycoons, sports stars, and celebrities spend tens of millions of dollars on their weddings. But even these people have limits when it comes to their pocket books. There are no limits at all, no boundaries, and nothing that is off limits for the KING of KINGS and LORD of LORDS. The streets are made of gold and the gates of large pearls (Rev 21:21). Heaven is going to be anything but boring!

Myth #2: I can get into heaven on my own terms. I don't need Jesus! The devil loves it when we think we can do anything on our own, but this myth is one he sells all the time to those we care for and love. And it could not be further from the truth.

📖 Write this week's memory verse out again. What does it say in reference to myth number two? ✗

_____

_____

_____

_____

📖 Look up and read Matthew 22:11-14. What does this tell you about who will be and who will not be in heaven?

_____

_____

_____

To understand this passage, you must understand one of the customs of Jesus' day and time. Kings generally provided wedding clothes for their guests to wear to the wedding. This was done primarily to ensure that no one would out-dress the bride and groom. It ensured that the wedding party would stand out and be the best dressed at the party. One of the guests, however, decided he would go to the party on his own terms and dress in his own clothes instead of the dress that was provided. This got him a one-way ticket out of the party. We cannot enter heaven on our own terms. Eternal life in heaven is impossible without Christ!

Myth #3: I have plenty of time to get ready. What's the hurry? Many have convinced themselves that they have lots of time to prepare for eternity so they will just live their lives the way they please and try to fit God in sometime down the road when the end is a bit closer. This is a dangerous and foolish strategy.

📖 Look up and read James 4:13-15 and explain why believing myth number three is dangerous.

_____

_____

Myth #4: All good people go to heaven. Jesus revealed the truth in Matthew 7:21-23. Jesus clearly and unmistakably stated that not everyone who is good or does good deeds on earth will enter heaven. In fact, he says he will not know them at all. Why? Because while the Bible calls Christians to do good works, our good works do not define our faith or secure our eternal salvation. They are simply by-products of who we are in Christ. We don't do good things because we have to; we do good things because of who we are. No matter how good you are, that alone will never get you into heaven.

📖 Read your memory verse again, and then read Ephesians 2:8-10. What do these verses tell you about salvation and good works?

_____

_____

Myth #5: If I believe in something (a higher being), I will get into heaven. This myth has become accepted in recent years especially among teens and college-age singles. Our society, and their culture in particular, has come to accept that what you believe is not as important as simply believing in something. If you believe in God, Buddha, Muhammad, Karma, Scientology, or just a higher power in general, you will end up on the right side of eternity. This is a myth! James 2:19 says even the demons believe in God. The devil himself believes in God! Believing alone is not enough. Salvation can only be found in believing and confessing that Jesus Christ is Lord.

📖 Read Acts 4:12, and then explain how it counters myth #5.

_____

_____

Myth #6: Religious people who go to church and read the Bible are all going to heaven! Salvation is not found in religion; it's found in a relationship with Christ. Just because you go to church, read the Bible, and know the right answers to all the questions does not mean you are going to heaven. In Matthew 23:25-28, Jesus made this truth abundantly clear. Religious people may look nice on the outside but they are dirty and rotten on the inside, and it's the inside that counts. Religion does not matter unless you have been transformed by a relationship with Christ!

> ❧ Which of these six myths have you believed at one time or another?

_____

_____

_____

> ❧ What other myths about heaven have you heard people say?

_____

_____

_____

Write out your memory verse in the space below. Try to do it completely from memory, then double-check yourself.

_____

_____

_____

_____

TAKE TIME TO PRAY

Pray for those you know who currently believe in one or more of these myths. Ask God to give you opportunities to share the truth with them about heaven in the coming days. Take time to thank God for creating this special, exciting, and amazing place called heaven for you.

Heaven & Hell—Day Two

Memory Verse

John 14:6

Start today's study by writing out as much of your memory verse as you can in the space below. Then, look up the verse and make any corrections that are needed. Finally, read it three times from your Bible and pray before completing the following lesson.

Yesterday we looked at six myths and misconceptions about heaven. They are:

1. Heaven will be boring;
2. I can get into heaven on my own terms;
3. I have plenty of time to get ready;
4. All good people go to heaven;
5. If I believe in something (a higher being), I will get into heaven;
6. Religious people who go to church and read the Bible are all going to heaven!

❧ Take a moment to think about each of these again and write down how you might counter each of these myths.

_____

_____

_____

_____

_____

_____

_____

_____

Today we are going to attempt to discover what heaven will actually be like. In this basic introductory course, it is impossible to fully outline all of the details of heaven. However, if we use scripture as our guide, we can obtain a clear and solid foundational view of what heaven will be like. The three passages of scripture you are going to look up today all come from the book of Revelation. Many people are intimidated by this book of the Bible because it can at times seem confusing, scary, and strange. Today your goal is not to understand the entire meaning of these passages. DO NOT get wrapped up in the parts you do not understand. Instead, read the passages and focus on what heaven will be like.

📖 According to Revelation 4, what will heaven be like?

_____

_____

_____

_____

📖 According to Revelation 21:1-7, what will heaven be like?

_____

_____

_____

_____

📖 According to Revelation 21:15-27, what will heaven be like?

_____

_____

_____

_____

❧ Based on what you learned yesterday and today about heaven, is there any reason you can think of that would cause you to not want to live for eternity in this place?

_____

_____

_____

_____

❧ Do you know for certain that you will live in heaven for eternity? List some scriptures that back that up. (You might review Week One)

_____

_____

_____

_____

❧ God calls us to do more than just know about heaven. We are called to tell others how to get there. Do you remember the three main parts to sharing your testimony? What are they? Who have you told about Jesus in the last two weeks? (Review Week Five if you need help here)

_____

_____

_____

_____

_____

Write out your memory verse in the space below. Try to do it completely from memory, then double-check yourself.

TAKE TIME TO PRAY

Sit in stillness for a few minutes and dwell on what heaven will one day be like. Ask God to guide your imagination and help you picture it. Clear your heart and mind and simply focus on God and the eternal home he has created for you. Then pray as you feel led.

Heaven & Hell—Day Three

Memory Verse

John 14:6

Start today's study by writing out as much of your memory verse as you can in the space below. Then, look up the verse and make any corrections that are needed. Finally, read it three times from your Bible and pray before completing the following lesson.

Over the past two days, we have focused on heaven. We talked about the myths that have been associated with heaven as well as what heaven will be like. For the next two days, we will focus on a place that is much different and far less desirable. It is known as Hades, or Hell.

Hell is a frequently overlooked topic in our churches today. As a result, many people are surprised when they learn the truth about hell. We should not be ashamed or embarrassed to approach this subject. After all, Jesus talked at length about both places. Just as we started with the myths about heaven, we will start today with the surprises about hell. Before going any further, look up Luke 16:19-31 and read the story about the rich man and Lazarus. All of the surprises in our lesson today can be found in this story that Jesus told as well. As you go through the study, try to find them in this passage of scripture.

The first thing people are surprised to hear about hell is that there is not a single second or moment of rest in this place. This place, like heaven, is an eternal home with no eight-hour work day or twenty-four-hour day. It is a never-ending eternal home without morning or evening. As a result, there are no holidays, birthdays, New Year celebrations, no naps, no goodnights or see you tomorrow's. Hell is forever, and the pain and torment is as well. There will not be a single moment of rest for any who spend their eternity in this place.

📖 What does Revelation 14:11 say about rest for those who will spend eternity in this place? ⚒

_____

_____

🕮 When will this end for them?

_____

_____

Many are also surprised to learn that there is no hope in hell, either. There is no hope of rescue, no hope of relief, no hope of escape; there is simply no hope at all in this eternal home that is void of God's holiness. Without God there is never any hope. The Bible says that before we knew Christ, we were without hope and without God (Eph 2:12). As a result of God's absence in this place, there is subsequently no hope at all here, either. Proverbs 11:7 says, _When a wicked man dies, his hope perishes; all he expected from his power comes to nothing._ There is not an ounce of hope in this eternal place.

There is no peace in hell, either. Without God there can be no hope and there can be no peace. People are always looking for peace at home, work, school, church, in marriage, and every other area of life. In hell there will be no reason to search for peace because it does not exist in this place. Many live under the illusion that hell is going to be a place they can kick back with their buddies, watch the game, drink, and eat some BBQ ribs. That sounds very appealing and peaceful, doesn't it? If it were true, it would be, but this is nothing more than a lie from the devil. Individuals who arrive in this place will soon find there is no peace at all. They will be all alone. There will not be friends, family, TV, beer, or ribs in hell. All you will find there is never-ending torment, pain, torture, and agony.

📖 Look up Isaiah 57:20-21. Which two surprises about hell do you see in these verses? ⚒

_____

_____

❧ For whom is there no peace?

_____

_____

_____

It is our natural human nature to assume that nothing could be as painful and horrible as hell is described to be in the Bible. As a result we are quick to think that we will somehow be numb to the pain in this horrible place. The truth, however, is very surprising. You will be conscious in hell and you will not be exempt from anything in this place. Look at the passage in Luke 16:19-31 closely again. Was the rich man aware of the agony of this place? Does he seem unaware or unconscious when it comes to the effects of hell? If he was not aware of the pain, why ask for pity or water? Those who spend eternity in hell will be conscious and they will experience this place and all of its wrath for all eternity.

People are surprised to learn that hell does not care who you are, either. This is one of the only things that heaven and hell have in common: they are no respecters of persons. It does not matter if you are a pauper or a prince, a king or a slave, or if you live in a mansion or a cardboard box. You will be just another pitiful soul in hell. Money won't matter; earthly fame, status, or deeds will not matter. Everyone will be in the same boat in this river of misery. This place will not be better for some and worse for others; it will be hell for all!

❧ Did hell care at all about the rich man's wealth? Did it make his experience in this very real place any better?

_____

_____

_____

📖 Look up 2 Peter 2:4. What does this teach us about eternity not being prejudiced? ⚒

_____

_____

_____

Finally, hell will make a believer out of you! The Bible teaches that every knee will bow and every tongue will confess that Jesus is Lord (Rom 14:11; Phil 2:10). The rich man in Luke 16 begged for Lazarus to be able to go to his house and tell his brothers so they would not suffer the same fate as he did. Hell made a believer out of this man and it will make a believer out of even the hardest, meanest, and most defiant individuals the world has ever known. Those who refuse to believe in Christ on this side of eternity certainly will on the other. Every knee will bow and every tongue will confess that Jesus is Lord.

Hell will hold far more surprises than we have time to discuss in the course of this lesson. However, the larger point is that we should not spend any time there at all. Christ came and died on the cross for the sins of the world. God's will is that all persons would be saved and come to a saving knowledge of the truth that Christ brought us through the cross (1 Tim 2:3-4). However, many will reject his love, mercy, grace, and ultimately, the eternal home that he created for them in heaven. As a result they will spend their eternity in a place that will have many horrible surprises waiting for them.

ૐ Why is it important that we share our faith with others?

_____

_____

ૐ How would you share your faith with someone? What are the four steps in sharing your personal testimony?

_____

_____

ૐ Which memory verses that you have learned so far might come in handy as you share your faith? ✖

_____

_____

ૐ Can you think of anyone you need to share with? Write down their names and make plans to go share with them as soon as you can.

_____

_____

ૐ What other surprises do you think hell might hold for those who choose this place as their eternal home?

_____

_____

_____

Write out your memory verse in the space below. Try to do it completely from memory, then double-check yourself.

TAKE TIME TO PRAY

Heaven & Hell—Day Four

Memory Verse

John 14:6

Start today's study by writing out as much of your memory verse as you can in the space below. Then, look up the verse and make any corrections that are needed. Finally, read it three times from your Bible and pray before completing the following lesson.

---

*A*s with Day Two, your goal today is simple. Look up the following verses to gain a better picture of what hell will be like and what this place is in general. You may not understand all of the text you read today. That's OK; just focus on what this place will be like so that you will have a better understanding of what those in this place will experience. Once you truly understand the devastating eternal consequences of this place, your passion to share the gospel with others will be stronger than ever.

📖 Matthew 13:40-43

📖 Luke 13:26-30

_____

_____

📖 Revelation 9:1-11

_____

_____

📖 Revelation 20:10

_____

_____

📖 Revelation 21:6-8

_____

_____

❧ Do you see anything good about spending eternity in hell?

_____

_____

_____

❧ What would you tell someone who said they wanted to go to hell?

_____

_____

_____

❧ What are some of the surprises about hell and how would you counter them if they were brought up by a friend or family member in conversation?

_____

_____

_____

_____

Write out your memory verse in the space below. Try to do it completely from memory then double-check yourself.

TAKE TIME TO PRAY

Thank God for sending his Son and making the way to heaven so simple for you. Ask him to give you opportunities to share your faith in the coming days. Pray specifically for one person you know who does not know Christ.

To review, use the space below to write all the memory verses you have learned so far, including this week's. You can also use this space for personal notes about this lesson.

_____

_____

_____

_____

_____

_____

_____

_____

_____

_____

_____

_____

_____

_____

_____

_____

_____

I AM—Day One

Memory Verse

1 Peter 1:15-16

Start today's study by writing out your memory verse in the space below. Then, read it three times from your Bible and take just a moment to pray before completing the following lesson.

```
_____

_____

_____

_____
```

This week we are going to take a basic look at who God and Jesus say they are. In a later week, we will also examine the Holy Spirit, but this week we will focus on some of the scriptures that give us a good idea about the nature and character of God and Christ. For the first two lessons this week, we will focus on God, and in the last two lessons we will turn our focus to the person of Christ and who he is according to the Bible.

In Exodus 3, Moses is concerned that the people will not believe him when he returns to Egypt to be used by God to set them free. So he asks God, What do I tell them if they want to know your name? Look up and read Exodus 3:10-14.

❧ What did God say Moses was to tell them if they asked for the name of God?

_____

_____

❧ What do you think this means?

_____

_____

There are several very important things to consider in this passage as we attempt to understand who God is. The first is that we must remember that God never calls us to do something that he has not equipped us to do. Furthermore, he will never make us go and do it alone. God gives Moses two assurances. He says, *I will be with you,* and he assures Moses that they will come back and *worship on this mountain* (verse 12). God wants Moses to understand that he is not alone on this journey, and that the outcome is already in place and the people will be released and they will find their way back to this mountain to worship. The second thing that we must remember as we start this study is that our God is one of purpose. He does not do anything without a purpose and a plan. Your life has a purpose; everything that he calls you to do serves a purpose. The spiritual gifts you have received are there for a purpose, and God reveals his purpose in these verses as well. God's purpose in delivering the Israelites out of Egypt was so that they would come and "worship Him." We see this repeated many times throughout the book of Exodus (4:23; 7:16; 8:1, 20; 9:1, 13; 10:3, 7-8, 11, 24, 26; 12:31). The Hebrew word for worship interestingly is the same word that is used for slave. The picture for the Israelites would have been very clear. They have been serving pharaoh as slaves, but with their freedom they would now serve God as worshipers. So as you study the following qualities of God, keep in mind that he is always present, and everything he does is on purpose.

God reminds us many times that he never changes. He is always the same. God is consistent, reliable, steady, and solid. Look up the following verses and as you read them, look for the things they have in common.

📖 Genesis 26:24

_____

_____

📖 Genesis 28:13

_____

_____

📖 Genesis 46:3

_____

_____

📖 Exodus 3:6

_____

_____

✳ What does God say over and over in these verses? What do you think is the purpose behind these statements? ✘

_____

_____

_____

_____

God clearly wants his people, both from the past and in the present day, to know that he does not change. He is a God of consistency upon whom we can trust and rely. He says, I never change. I am the same today as I was then!

Isaiah 48:17 says, *This is what the LORD says—your Redeemer, the Holy One of Israel: "I am the LORD your God, who teaches you what is best for you, who directs you in the way you should go."* God is our teacher, our guide, and the director of our lives as modern disciples. Like any good teacher, God does not force his perfect ways on us, but when we are willing to submit our lives to his plans and purposes, he is sure to guide us, teach us, and lead us in the way we should go.

In Genesis 28:15 we also hear God say, *I am with you.* Hebrews 13:5 says; *Keep your lives free from the love of money and be content with what you have, because God has said, "Never will I leave you; never will I forsake you."*

📖 What other promises does God make in Genesis 28:15? ✘

_____

_____

_____

_____

📖 Look up Haggai 1:13 and 2:4. According to these verses, God says:

I am _____

📖 Look up Genesis 35:11. According to this verse, God says:

I am _____

❧ How do these things make you feel?

_____

_____

As you can see, God is many things. He is the same, he is with us, he is mighty, and he is our guide. God is the great I AM! He is all that we need, and more then we deserve. Tomorrow, we will look at some more scripture and learn about some more of the many things that God truly is.

Write out your memory verse in the space below. Try to do it completely from memory, then double-check yourself.

TAKE TIME TO PRAY

I AM—Day Two

Memory Verse

1 Peter 1:15-16

Start today's study by writing out as much of your memory verse as you can in the space below. Then, look up the verse and make any corrections that are needed. Finally, read it three times from your Bible and pray before completing the following lesson.

_____

_____

_____

_____

Yesterday, we started this week's study by looking at some of the verses in scripture where God reveals to us who he is. Today, we will continue that study and examine some more of the wonderful things that God is. Before we do, try to recall the five things we learned yesterday.

    ❧ I am _____

    ❧ I am _____

    ❧ I am _____

    ❧ I am _____

❧ I am _____

For today's study we will start by looking at something that humans rarely give God credit for. In the Bible, we learn that God is generous! Many times we think that God takes more than he gives. Too many people feel that God only places requirements on their lives and commands them to do things that they are uncomfortable with and unwilling to do. While God does require much from his disciples, and there is no denying that his word is full of commands for the modern day believer, we must never forget that we serve a very generous God.

📖 What does God give in Genesis 15:7, Exodus 20:12, Numbers 15:2, and Leviticus 25:2?

_____

_____

These verses illustrate just how generous God is. There isn't enough space in this text to elaborate and explore this point to its fullest potential, but scripture declares that all we have is actually God's, from the clothes on our backs to the vehicles in our driveways. Our homes, our children, our spouses, and the money we have in the bank all belong to God and have been given to us by him. Even the air we breathe and water we drink is a gift from God. Every beat of your heart brings another precious gift from our heavenly Father. No matter how much or little you think you have, you can't deny that God Almighty has been generous and blessed you. If you remain unconvinced about God's generosity, consider the following questions.

📖 According to John 3:16-18, what did God give each of us?

_____

_____

❧ In your mind, who has given more: you or God? Explain.

_____

_____

_____

God also frequently introduces himself as *The LORD your God* (Exod 6:7, 16:12, 20:2, 29:46; Lev 11:44, 18:2, 25:38). While most of us want a Savior, few long for a LORD. Throughout the history of humankind, lordship has gained a reputation for being undesirable. Ruthless kings *and* queens, dictators, slave owners, and in some cases the modern day boss, politician, pastor, or priest, have used their position to do only what is in their personal interests. As a result, people have become skeptical of allowing anyone to control their lives and act as lord, even the LORD himself. We have wrongfully assumed that we can have a loving savior and reject our loving LORD, for they are one in the same! He is lord and savior. We don't get to choose one and deny the other.

    ❧ Have you ever resisted God's lordship? When, how, be specific.

_____

_____

    ❧ How would things be different if we submitted to God's lordship?

_____

_____

    ❧ Is there really any reason to resist his lordship?

_____

_____

People have said that God is too removed and unconcerned. They feel that the creator of the universe simply does not care about them on a personal level. The truth is, however, that God is deeply concerned and involved in every area of our lives. He desires to walk with us through both the good times and the bad. God himself tells us that he is concerned.

    📖 Look up and read Exodus 3:7. How concerned was God?

_____

_____

    ❧ Who was he concerned for?

_____

_____

God is kind. Jeremiah 9:24 says, *but let him who boasts boast about this: that he understands and knows me, that I am the LORD, who exercises kindness, justice and righteousness on earth, for in these I delight, declares the LORD.* God is not only kind; he delights in being kind, and he longs to be kind and generous to each of us. He is a good, loving, caring Father who prefers kindness over things like anger, and wrath. When we examine our lives and all that God has done for us, who can deny his patience and kindness? The New Testament makes a great point about God's kindness in Romans 2:4.

    ❒ Toward what does God's kindness leads us?

    ❒ List some of the ways you have seen or experienced the kindness of God.

📖 Jeremiah 3:12 shows us a similar trait. It says:

    I am _____

We will close with this final thing that God says he is. He is holy. There is nothing else like him in all creation. He is unique, set apart from all else. He is pure in a way we can't even comprehend. His holiness makes him unlike any other person place or thing. He is holy! Look up Leviticus 11:44-45 and 1 Peter 1:16.

    📖 Both of the verses above speak of God's holiness, but what is the message in these two passages for us? ❂

    ❒ Do you think this is possible? How?

We could certainly mention many more things that God himself is, such as love, righteous, victorious, just, faithful, true, or available, just to name a few. However, this subject alone would require its own volume to thoroughly examine all that God is and claims to be. With a basic foundation laid for who God says that he is, tomorrow we will turn our attention to Christ for the remainder of the week.

Write out your memory verse in the space below. Try to do it completely from memory, then double-check yourself.

TAKE TIME TO PRAY

I Am—Day Three

Memory Verse

1 Peter 1:15-16

Start today's study by writing out as much of your memory verse as you can in the space below. Then, look up the verse and make any corrections that are needed. Finally, read it three times from your Bible and pray before completing the following lesson.

People have tried to make Jesus out to be many things. Some have tried to make him out to be a liar; others have claimed he was a lunatic, some say he was a magician or the devil himself, and still others say he never even existed, or was only a human whose life was nothing like what we see in the New Testament. But who does Jesus say he is? It is not in the scope of this study to defend Christ or try to answer all of the critics who say the above-mentioned things. Instead, our goal is simple: analyze the scriptures and allow Jesus to tell us who he is.

   📖 Look up and read John 8:12. What is the promise that Christ gives us in this verse?

Jesus says, *I am the light of the world.* This is quite a statement and one you'd better be able to back up. Even a small light can transform a dark room. Jesus was no small light; he was the light of the world! He came to bring the good news and he came to shine his holy light on this sinful world. He came to offer each of us something better then we deserved. The world we live in today is still a cold, dark, unforgiving place. If you are tired of stumbling through this life in the darkness, Jesus alone can bring an eternal light into your life that will illuminate your path as you continue on your journey.

Jesus also says that he is always with us. Have you ever been stranded some place? I mean really lost, or stuck without any hope of immediate rescue? This is rare in our day and time, with cell phones, laptop computers, and GPS devices, but it is a scary, lonely, uneasy feeling when we find ourselves in these rare situations. Jesus, however, speaks truth into our lives and reminds us that no matter how alone we may feel, he is always with us.

📖 Several weeks ago you memorized Matthew 28:19-20. Write it out in the space below and underline the part of the verse that speaks to Christ's never-ending presence in our lives.

_____

_____

_____

_____

In John 10:11, Jesus tells us that he is also the "good shepherd." A good shepherd loves his sheep. He feeds and waters the flock. Shepherds also protect the sheep from wild animals or other things that might cause them harm. They tend to them when they are sick. They rush out to find them when they get lost or separated from the others. Shepherds are even willing to lay down their lives for their sheep (John 10:15). And Jesus says that he is our good shepherd.

📖 Read John 10:7-15. What else does Jesus claim to be in this passage? What does that mean? ⚒

_____

_____

🌾 Who is the thief in verse 10?

_____

_____

- List the differences between the thief and the good shepherd.

- Do you think Jesus was just a hired hand, sent to do something for God? Why, or why not? What are the differences between a hired hand and the good shepherd?

Write out your memory verse in the space below. Try to do it completely from memory, then double-check yourself.

TAKE TIME TO PRAY

I Am—Day Four

Memory Verse

1 Peter 1:15-16

Start today's study by writing out as much of your memory verse as you can in the space below. Then, look up the verse and make any corrections that are needed. Finally, read it three times from your Bible and pray before completing the following lesson.

$\mathcal{S}$tart today's study by reviewing what we learned yesterday. See if you can fill in the blanks below. If you are unable to fill in the blanks, go back and review yesterday's lesson.

    ❧ I am _____

    ❧ I am _____

    ❧ I am _____

Jesus had a very close and personal relationship with his disciple John. When all the other disciples fled as Jesus was hanging from the cross, it was John who, according to the Bible, was near the cross. Jesus turned to John and asked him to take care of his mother (John 19:25-27). Because of his close relationship with Jesus, John is described as the beloved disciple my many. So it should come as no surprise that it is from John's gospel we learn so many personal details about who Jesus was.

In John 11:25, Jesus reveals another truth about who he is. He says, *I am the resurrection and the life.* That is a bold statement, to say the least. Jesus claims to be the key to eternal life. He is saying "I control death and life," as he tries to console Martha who is grieving over the loss of her brother.

    📖 What question does Jesus ask Martha in John 11:26? How would you answer that question?

_____

_____

_____

    📖 What does Jesus do in John 11:43-44? What does this tell us about Jesus as being the resurrection and the life?

_____

_____

_____

In John 15, Jesus outlines not only who he is, but he also gives us a picture of who we are as well. Look up and read John 15:1-5 and answer the questions below.

    ❧ According to these verses, what is Jesus?

_____

_____

    ❧ According to these verses, what are we?

_____

_____

    ❧ What does that mean to you?

_____

_____

_____

❧ What happens if we switch the order? ✖

_____

_____

❧ As of right now, do you think that spiritually you have both Christ and yourself in their proper places in reference to this passage of scripture? If not, what do you need to do to make things right?

_____

_____

_____

❧ What can we do apart from Jesus?

_____

_____

In John 14:1-5 we find another truth about who Jesus is. He says, *"Do not let your hearts be troubled. Trust in God; trust also in me. ²In my Father's house are many rooms; if it were not so, I would have told you. I am going there to prepare a place for you. ³And if I go and prepare a place for you, I will come back and take you to be with me that you also may be where I am. ⁴You know the way to the place where I am going." ⁵Thomas said to him, "Lord, we don't know where you are going, so how can we know the way?"* Jesus said that he was going to prepare a place for each of us. And he also promised to come back and take us to be with him one day. He follows this up with another truth about who He is.

Six times in the book of Revelation Jesus is described as the first and the last (Rev 1:4, 8, 17; 2:8; 21:6; 22:13). He is said to be the *Alpha* and the *Omega*. The Greek alphabet consists of twenty-four letters. The first is alpha and the last is omega. So when the Bible states that Jesus is the Alpha and the Omega, it is referring to Christ being both the first and the last. Just like even small children today know that A is the first letter in our alphabet and Z is the last, those in the day of Christ would have clearly understood this comparison. Look up the following verses and decide if they refer to Christ being the first, last, or both. ✖

📖 John 8:58

_____

📖 Colossians 1:17

_____

📖 Hebrews 7:3

_____

📖 Look up and read Revelation 22:12-13. What is the other "I am" in those verses?

_____

It is easy to get wrapped up in our fast-paced busy world and lose sight of the fact that Jesus will one day return. Because so much time has passed since we last saw Christ on the cross and then being lifted up to heaven (Acts 1:9), it seems that we struggle to remain focused on the return of Christ. But he said that he is coming and he is coming soon! Therefore, we must prepare ourselves and as many others in the world as possible for the imminent return of Christ.

📖 What does 1 Thessalonians 5:2 say the day of the Lord will be like?

_____

_____

This week, you have learned many things about who God and Jesus say they are through the Bible. As you read your Bible daily, look for the two words "I am." Pay close attention each time you see them and you will continue to increase your knowledge and awareness of who both the Father and the Son are.

Write out your memory verse in the space below. Try to do it completely from memory, then double-check yourself.

_____
_____
_____
_____

TAKE TIME TO PRAY

To review, use the space below to write all the memory verses you have learned so far, including this week's. You can also use this space for personal notes about this lesson.

_____

_____

_____

_____

_____

_____

_____

_____

_____

_____

_____

_____

_____

_____

_____

_____

_____

Joy—Day One

Memory Verse

Philippians 4:4

Start today's study by writing out your memory verse in the space below. Then, read it three times from your Bible and take just a moment to pray before completing the following lesson.

---

*J*essica seemed to have it all! Her parents loved her, she was on the Dean's list, all the young men wanted to date her, and she lived in the nicest dorm on campus and drove a brand new car. Despite all of this, Jessica walked into my office one day and said she was considering suicide because her life lacked any joy. Ben's story is not all that different. When he failed to show up for a basketball game, I picked up the phone and gave him a call. He sounded extremely depressed and I asked if we could meet for dinner. He agreed. Shortly after sitting down at our table, Ben started to sob uncontrollably, and made a statement I will never forget, "I want it all to end. This life is not worth living!" "But Ben," I replied, "what about your wife and 2 year old son? What about your great job? You are a great Sunday school teacher. What about all those youth you have ministered to? What about all your friends?" As I continued, Ben seemed unconvinced and said, "But why am I so unhappy? Why is there no joy in my life?"

Years later, I met a lady whom I will call Rebecca. Sadly I did not get to meet her until her husband called and asked me to drive to a rehab center and speak to his wife. Rebecca had a husband who loved her and two grown boys with families of their own. She lived in one of the nicest neighborhoods, and after a lifetime of hard work, they had accumulated over 20 million dollars of wealth. She had it all, but her addiction to pain medication and sleeping pills almost took her life. Over several months, with the help of doctors in the rehab clinic, we got to the root of Rebecca's problem. Like Jessica and Ben, she had no joy. I have seen these kinds of things throughout my ministry.

Sometimes people fall into depression or addictions due to psychological issues. However, it has been my experience that the most common cause is not psychological, but spiritual. Many simply don't understand what joy is. The goal of this week's study is to give you a biblical perspective on joy.

> ❧ Before you go any further, think about the things that bring you joy and write them out in the space below. These things might be people, material possessions, hobbies, etc.

> ❧ Now list the things that drain you and steal your joy.

> ❧ Are there more things in your life today that bring you joy or steal your joy?

To better understand what biblical joy is, spend the rest of today's lesson looking up the verses below which are all related to instances of joy as portrayed in the Bible. There are many more than are included in this selected list, but these passages will set the stage for tomorrow's lesson. As you read these verses, make notes and get familiar with the text so that you can discuss it in your next small group meeting. You should also take the time to relate each of the following instances of joy to something that might be similar in the modern day.

   📖 **Example:** 1 Samuel 18:6-7. David has just killed Goliath and he and his comrades are returning from the battlefield, celebrating their victory. Today this might be parallel to the victorious celebration of a job promotion, beating cancer, finishing school, or reaching a goal.

📖 Exodus 15:1-22

_____

_____

📖 Esther 8:11-17

_____

_____

📖 Nehemiah 12:27-43

_____

_____

📖 Matthew 2:9-12

_____

_____

📖 Luke 15:3-10

_____

_____

📖 Acts 12:11-17

_____

_____

📖 Philippians 1:3-11

_____

_____

Write out your memory verse in the space below. Try to do it completely from memory, then double-check yourself.

TAKE TIME TO PRAY

Joy—Day Two

Memory Verse

Philippians 4:4

Start today's study by writing out as much of your memory verse as you can in the space below. Then, look up the verse and make any corrections that are needed. Finally, read it three times from your Bible and pray before completing the following lesson.

Yesterday we concluded by looking at some instances of joy in the Bible. Today we will attempt to define what joy is and what it is not. Yesterday I told you about three people that had every reason in the world to be happy and to experience the joy of life. Yet for some strange reason, joy eluded them. Why? Because they bought into the lies our enemy is selling when it comes to joy. This caused them to become defeated, and in their despair, they contemplated taking their own lives, all because they did not understand what joy was and, perhaps more importantly, what joy is not.

The first lie that many have accepted is that joy is an emotion. The three people mentioned yesterday all believed that joy was an emotion that came and went, depending on the circumstances of life. This leads to what can only be called a "roller coaster" lifestyle. When we view joy as an emotion, we are up, then down, then up again. One minute we are right side up, and the next we are upside down. The fact is that life is unpredictable and is full of success and failure, encouragement and discouragement, happiness and disappointment. If joy is an emotion, we have it one minute and lose it the next. Over time we lose perspective and, despite the blessings of life, we become frustrated with the "roller coaster" and we just want off the ride!

If joy is not an emotion, then what is it? Biblical joy is a state of being that exists in the lives of those who have a relationship with Christ. It is not contingent upon the external forces of this life. It has nothing to do with money, power, fame, or status. It has everything to do with Jesus Christ! Joy is not an emotion; it is a state of being that exists for Christians in both the good times and the bad. Look up the following verses and notice how they emphasize that joy is independent of circumstances and emotions.

📖 Colossians 1:24-27

_____

_____

📖 1 Peter 1:3-9

_____

_____

📖 1 Peter 4:12-16

_____

_____

The next lie that many believe about joy is that we can somehow create it. The kind of joy we long for and desire is so pure and so special that it can't be created. Think back to yesterday's study and consider the things you wrote down that brought joy to your life. At first glance, you may be tempted to think that you created them, but look closer. Did you really? Some of the things that might have made your list yesterday are your children, your spouse, your friends, your job, your pet, or a hobby you have. Did God not create all of these things? When you look at your children, it is impossible to miss seeing God's fingerprints. When you consider the success of your marriage and the way God brought you and your spouse together, can you really claim to have done it yourself? That great passion you have for your hobby or job was planted inside of you by God. God alone can create joy. We can only experience it. When we start trying to create joy by earning more money, buying more things, going on fancy vacations, or altering our lives with drugs, sex, or medication, true joy will always elude us. We must understand that God alone creates the things that bring us joy. We should praise him for the things in our lives that bring us joy and then experience them for all they are worth.

📖 According to 1 Thessalonians 1:6, who gives us our joy? ⚒

_____

_____

Tomorrow we will look at a few more misunderstood facts about true joy. Finish today's lesson by reading the whole book of Philippians. As you read, count up the total number of times Paul uses the words joy and rejoice.

✺ Joy _____

✺ Rejoice _____

Write out your memory verse in the space below. Try to do it completely from memory, then double-check yourself.

_____

_____

_____

_____

TAKE TIME TO PRAY

Joy—Day Three

Memory Verse

Philippians 4:4

Start today's study by writing out as much of your memory verse as you can in the space below. Then, look up the verse and make any corrections that are needed. Finally, read it three times from your Bible and pray before completing the following lesson.

_____

_____

_____

_____

The Apostle Paul suffered greatly as he planted churches and traveled throughout most of the known world spreading the gospel. While we don't know the exact time, place, or manner of Paul's death, Christian tradition says it was in the mid-60s A.D. during the reign of Nero, in or near Rome. The letter to the Philippians was written close to the end of Paul's life, perhaps from Caesarea, Rome, or Ephesus. "The traditional view places the writing of Philippians during Paul's first imprisonment in Rome during A.D. 59-61 (Acts 28:30). This is the most natural understanding of "palace guard" (Phil 1:13) and "Caesar's household" (Phil 4:22). Paul's trial was evidently going on during the writing, and its outcome could bring either life or death. Apparently there could be no appeal from its verdict (Phil 1:19-24)." [21]

By this time, Paul was a well-seasoned believer who had seen the best and worst of the church and the people who make up the church. He had been imprisoned (Phil 1:7, 13, 16-17), beaten (2 Cor 11:24), left for dead (Acts 14:19), and run out of town (Acts 9:25, 2 Cor 11:32-33), and he had been shipwrecked on more than one occasion (2 Cor 11:25). He had suffered great pain and hardships for the sake for the gospel. And despite all this, his passion and his joy were stronger than ever and he encouraged those in Philippi to REJOICE! He did not whine or complain; in fact, he told them that there is no place for such things in the life of a believer (Phil 2:14-17). Despite all that Paul had been through, he still had joy, because he understood better than most that joy is not an emotion or something you create. It is a state of being for those who live in a right relationship with Christ.

    📖 Read 2 Corinthians 11:23-28 and list the different trials that Paul himself recounts in this passage.

_____

_____

_____

    ❧ If you had faced the same things Paul faced, do you think you would still be able to lead others to rejoice?

_____

_____

_____

Happiness comes from family, friends, jobs, success, children, and many other things. However, as Jessica, Ben, and Rebecca proved, there is a huge difference between happiness and true joy. So where does joy come from? Look up Galatians 5:22-25 and answer the questions below.

    ❧ According to these verses, where does joy come from?

_____

_____

21   Kenneth L. Barker and John R. Kohlenberger III, *Zondervan NIV Bible Commentary* (Grand Rapids: Zondervan, 1994), 788.

ᝍ What else comes from this source?

_____

_____

_____

_____

ᝍ Do you think any of these things are emotions or states of being for those who are in a right relationship with Christ? Explain. ✗

_____

_____

_____

_____

ᝍ Do you think you can create any of these things? Or do they all come from God? ✗

_____

_____

_____

_____

ᝍ Would you say that you are happy today or joyful?

_____

_____

_____

_____

ᝍ What is the difference between happiness and joy?

_____

_____

_____

_____

Ș Do you think there can be joy without happiness? Explain, and give an example.

_____

_____

_____

_____

Write out your memory verse in the space below. Try to do it completely from memory, then double-check yourself.

_____

_____

_____

_____

TAKE TIME TO PRAY

Joy—Day Four

Memory Verse

Philippians 4:4

Start today's study by writing out as much of your memory verse as you can in the space below. Then, look up the verse and make any corrections that are needed. Finally, read it three times from your Bible and pray before completing the following lesson.

---

*O*ver the last three days, we have talked about what joy is and isn't, and where it comes from. Today we will discover how we can keep our joy. As we have already learned, joy is not something we can create, but it is something we can keep once we have it. Knowing how to keep our joy is important because, as John Ritenbaugh writes:

> A Christian's joy can be just as short-lived as anyone's in the world if we are seeking it for itself as the world does. Biblical joy is a fruit, a byproduct, an additional blessing, not the end in itself. It flows into and grows within the person whose life and energies are not focused merely on being "joyful." The lives of those in this world who are so zealously chasing after it prove this point. If they are still chasing it,

they must not yet have it. God's Word also substantiates this... We can seek joy, but we cannot find true joy merely by seeking pleasurable excitement. The best and longest sustained joys result from self-forgetful activity. True joy can be sought, but it must be sought God's way. It must arise as a product of yielding wholeheartedly to the creative purpose God, the Master Creator, is working out in our lives. Joy that is a fruit of God's Spirit has its roots in the realization of God's purpose and its outworking that transforms us into His image. Biblical joy begins when God calls and we hear the gospel, understand, and believe it.[22]

If you want to regain your joy or keep it, you must commit to living a focused life. First, you must focus your faith. Because we cannot create joy and it is only truly obtained from a divine source, we must focus our faith. When we become active in our churches and when we participate in other things that God is doing, true joy will always be nearby. When you help lead someone to Christ or take part in some work that God is doing, the joy you experience is unexplainable! Focus your faith and make sure that you are doing things that make an eternal impact. Transform your thinking from the temporal to the eternal and you will keep your joy all the days of your life. In the book of Philemon, we once again find the Apostle Paul in prison (Phlm 1). However, he continues to speak about joy and guide others to find and keep their joy as well. Look up Philemon 6 and answer the questions below.

⊱ What does Paul pray that Philemon would do?

_____

_____

⊱ What does he say the result will be?

_____

_____

⊱ Are you currently sharing your faith with others? If not, what do you think you are missing?

_____

_____

_____

---

22 John W. Ritenbaugh, "The Fruit of the Spirit: Joy," Bible Tools, http://bibletools.org/index. cfm/fuseaction/Library.sr/CT/PERSONAL/k/280/Fruit-of-Spirit-Joy.htm (accessed March 15, 2010).

Next, you must focus on others! You will lose your joy if you focus on yourself and try to create your own joy. If you want to keep your joy, selflessly deny yourself and focus on others. When we examine the lives of Peter, Paul, Timothy, and others in the Bible who overcame incredible odds and circumstances and maintained their joy, we see the common thread of sacrifice and selflessness. They focused on others, and ensured that they maintained healthy relationships with people, not possessions. If you want to keep your joy, make eternal investments in other people. When you do this, your investment will be returned immeasurably in the currency of joy.

📖 Look up verse 7 in the book of Philemon. What does Paul say has given him great joy? Why was Paul proud of Philemon?

_____

_____

_____

If you want to keep your joy, you must also focus on Jesus Christ. When you live your life in a right relationship with Christ, joy will never be far away. As a modern day disciple, living your life under the lordship of Christ should be your highest priority. This point seems obvious, but many believers make this mistake each and every day, and as a result, they live their lives in the context of occasional happiness, but with the absence of true joy. When we selfishly attempt to tackle life on our own, we are certain to lose our joy. Look up and read Hebrews 12:1-3 and answer the following questions.

✺ What do you need to throw off? Be specific—what is hindering you and keeping you from true joy?

_____

_____

✺ Who should we fix our eyes on? Why?

_____

_____

Staying focused is the secret of keeping your joy. Without focus, you will likely fall prey to your enemy the devil, *who prowls around like a roaring lion looking for someone to devour* (1 Pet 5:8). His chief aim is to kill, steal, and destroy (John 10:10), and that can be accomplished very easily simply by killing, stealing, and destroying your joy. When he takes your joy, he paralyzes your faith, your influence, and your impact on the world for Christ. Furthermore, you are thrown into what seems to be a never-ending cycle of ups, downs, and frustrating in-betweens where, despite having every reason in the world to be happy, you still lack the only thing that can fill the void of your soul: joy.

📖 Read John 10:9-11. Why did Jesus say he came to earth?

____

____

❧ Do you think you can ever find joy outside of living in a right relationship with Christ? Explain.

____

____

____

Write out your memory verse in the space below. Try to do it completely from memory, then double-check yourself.

____

____

____

____

TAKE TIME TO PRAY

To review, use the space below to write all the memory verses you have learned so far, including this week's. You can also use this space for personal notes about this lesson.

_____

_____

_____

_____

_____

_____

_____

_____

_____

_____

_____

_____

_____

_____

_____

_____

Kingdom—Day One

Memory Verse

Matthew 6:33-34

Start today's study by writing out your memory verse in the space below. Then, read it three times from your Bible and take just a moment to pray before completing the following lesson.

This week we are going to examine the kingdom of God, or what is sometimes referred to as the kingdom of heaven. In the NIV Bible, this phrase "kingdom of God" appears in sixty-five verses in the New Testament alone, and 31 of those occurrences can be found in the book of Matthew. It is a frequent theme in the parables and teachings of Jesus, yet most never take time to unpack the significance of these words. It's been said, "The key to the history of the world is the kingdom of God," [23] and understanding God's kingdom is indeed at the heart of understanding both humanity and eternity. Therefore, it is our task this week to lay a foundation to build upon in the future as it relates to the kingdom of God.

---

23   John Blanchard, *The Complete Gathered Gold: A Treasury of Quotations for Christians* (Darlington, England: Evangelical Press, 2006), 366. Quote by D. Martyn Lloyd-Jones.

To begin our study this week you should look up the following passages of scripture related to the kingdom of God. Read each passage carefully and fill in the form below. Your goal today is not to understand each of the passages or to gain a full and comprehensive understanding of this theological concept. Instead, the aim is to become familiar with the texts that we will be working with for the remainder of the week. It is imperative that you spend time today doing this assignment so that these verses can be quickly referenced in your class discussion next week, and to lay a foundation for the remaining three days of study. I have purposefully not listed all of the scripture references that deal with this topic. Furthermore, I have laid the verses out in the same order you will find them in the New Testament, to make looking them up as quick as possible. Many of them are in the same chapter, as well.

📖 Matthew 13:24-30. The kingdom of heaven is like:

_____

_____

• What does this mean to you? (see Matt 13:36-39 for Jesus' explanation)

_____

_____

_____

📖 Matthew 13:31-32 (see also Mark 4:30-32, Luke 13:18-19). The kingdom of heaven is like:

_____

_____

• What does this mean to you?

_____

_____

_____

📖 Matthew 13:33 and Luke 13:21. The kingdom of heaven is like:

_____

_____

- What does this mean to you?

_____

_____

_____

📖 Matthew 13:44. The kingdom of heaven is like:

_____

_____

_____

- What does this mean to you?

_____

_____

_____

📖 Matthew 13:45-46. The kingdom of heaven is like:

_____

_____

_____

- What does this mean to you?

_____

_____

_____

📖 Matthew 13:47-51. The kingdom of heaven is like:

_____

_____

_____

- What does this mean to you?

_____

_____

_____

📖 Matthew 18:21-35. The kingdom of heaven is like:

_____

_____

_____

- What does this mean to you?

_____

_____

_____

📖 Matthew 20:1-16. The kingdom of heaven is like:

_____

_____

_____

- What does this mean to you?

_____

_____

_____

📖 Matthew 25:1-13. The kingdom of heaven is like:

_____

_____

_____

- What does this mean to you?

_____

_____

_____

📖 Matthew 25:14-30. The kingdom of heaven is like:

_____

_____

_____

- What does this mean to you?

_____

_____

_____

📖 Luke 6:20-23. The kingdom of God is like:

_____

_____

_____

- What does this mean to you?

_____

_____

_____

📖 Luke 9:59-62, The kingdom of God is like:

_____

_____

_____

- What does this mean to you?

_____

_____

_____

📖 Colossians 1:13-20. How is this verse different than the others you have read?

_____

_____

_____

- What does this mean to you?

_____

_____

_____

❧ What surprised you about these passages?

_____

_____

_____

_____

❧ Write down any questions you have about these verses in the space below. I would also encourage you to contact your group facilitator either by phone or e-mail prior to class with your questions about these verses. This will allow your leader to spend the necessary time to think about your specific questions and prepare good answers for you and the rest of the class.

_____

_____

_____

_____

_____

_____

_____

_____

_____

_____

Write out your memory verse in the space below. Try to do it completely from memory, then double-check yourself.

_____

_____

_____

_____

TAKE TIME TO PRAY

Kingdom—Day Two

Memory Verse

Matthew 6:33-34

Start today's study by writing out as much of your memory verse as you can in the space below. Then, look up the verse and make any corrections that are needed. Finally, read it three times from your Bible and pray before completing the following lesson.

*Y*esterday you looked up thirteen passages of scripture that deal with the theological concept of "the kingdom." Now that we have some familiarity with the subject, we are going to go a bit deeper and examine the three primary ways that Jesus and the New Testament use this concept. The word we most often translated as kingdom comes from the Greek *basileia* (βασιλεῖα). The New Testament concept of "the kingdom" that we translate from the word *basileia* is almost always used in one of the following three ways.

The first is to describe the people who are under the rule of the kingdom. It refers to actual individuals or groups of people who are living under the reign of the king. For example, Revelation 1:6 says, *and has made us to be a kingdom and priests to serve his God and Father — to him be glory and power for ever and ever! Amen.* God has made his people to be a kingdom. This is one specific use of the term and much different than the other two primary uses.

The next way we see the term "kingdom" used is in reference to an actual place or a realm over which God rules. This use of the concept of heaven refers to an actual physical place. For example, Matthew 25:34 says, *Then the King will say to those on his right, "Come, you who are blessed by my Father; take your inheritance, the kingdom prepared for you since the creation of the world."* In this verse, the kingdom is a place that has been prepared for those who will inhabit it. In other words, it refers to a real place that can be experienced.

Finally, the New Testament also uses this same word to refer to the actual lordship, or rule, of God in the life of a believer. For example, Matthew 6:33 says, *But seek first his kingdom and his righteousness, and all these things will be given to you as well.* In this verse, it is easy to see that the follower of Christ is not being encouraged to seek out a group of people, or an actual physical place or area that God rules. Instead, they are being encouraged to seek the will of God. The only way we can truly *seek first his kingdom and his righteousness* is to submit our lives to him completely.

Now, test your knowledge of these three uses by looking up the following scriptures and attempting to determine the primary context of the use of the word "kingdom." This is a difficult assignment so don't feel overwhelmed if you struggle to determine the exact use for each passage. To check your answers visit www. pastorpete.org. ✗

   📖 Matthew 21:31-32 (start where it says "Jesus said to them")

       ☐ People
       ☐ Place
       ☐ Lordship

   📖 Revelation 5:9-10

       ☐ People
       ☐ Place
       ☐ Lordship

   📖 Matthew 19:23-30

       ☐ People
       ☐ Place
       ☐ Lordship

   📖 Mark 10:13-16

       ☐ People
       ☐ Place
       ☐ Lordship

📖 Matthew 13:43

    ☐ People
    ☐ Place
    ☐ Lordship

✺ Why do you think understanding these three primary meanings of the "kingdom" concept is important?

_____

_____

_____

Write out your memory verse in the space below. Try to do it completely from memory, then double-check yourself.

_____

_____

_____

_____

TAKE TIME TO PRAY

Kingdom—Day Three

Memory Verse

Matthew 6:33-34

Start today's study by writing out as much of your memory verse as you can in the space below. Then, look up the verse and make any corrections that are needed. Finally, read it three times from your Bible and pray before completing the following lesson.

Now that we have a basic idea of the overall concept behind the "kingdom" and have laid the foundation for the three main ways the Bible speaks about that kingdom, we can now spend some time examining the specific details of the kingdom of God. Today we will start by looking at the kingdom as it refers to an actual physical place. Tomorrow we will explore the other two aspects of the kingdom: its people and its Lord.

So what is the kingdom actually like? What are some of its characteristics? The first thing we must understand is that the kingdom of God is eternal. Unlike the world we presently live in that will one day be destroyed, God's kingdom will last forever. It will never end, and can never be destroyed or defeated. It is eternal in all three of the meanings we learned about yesterday. God's people will live forever in his kingdom, the place itself is eternal, and God will reign as the leader of both the people and the place forever. The kingdom is about eternal people, an eternal place, and the eternal God.

📖 2 Peter 1:10-11 says: *"Therefore, my brothers, be all the more eager to make your calling and election sure. For if you do these things, you will never fall, ¹¹and you will receive a rich welcome into the eternal kingdom of* _____

_____."

📖 What does Hebrews 1:8 say will last forever?

_____

_____

📖 Read Luke 1:32-33. Over what house does it say Jesus will reign? For how long?

_____

_____

The kingdom of God is not of this world (John 18:36). We did not make it, we do not control it, and we cannot rule it. The kingdom of God belongs only to him. Jesus told Pilate that if his kingdom was of this world, his disciples would surely be physically fighting for it. But Christ did not come to organize an army. He already had an army (Rev 19:14) He came to redeem the world, not rule it! But Jesus does not shy away from claiming to be a king. Read John 18:36-37 and answer the questions below.

📖 What did Jesus say he came to testify to? What do you think that means?

_____

_____

_____

📖 Write out John 14:6. What does it have to do with John 18:36-37? ✗

_____

_____

_____

_____

God's kingdom is also growing. Because of the gospel and the work of God through people just like you, many are coming into the family of God. In our first study this week, you looked at two parables of Jesus that speak to the growth of the kingdom. In the space below, write out the imagery that Jesus used to describe the growth of the kingdom.

📖 Matthew 13:31-33 and Luke 13:18-21

_____

_____

_____

The final point we will make about the kingdom is that it is available for all who believe. We see this first through the life of the messianic king. Jesus frequently ate, ministered, and spent time with the dirtiest, lowest, most pitiful people of his day. How incredible is it to think that Jesus, the King of Kings, would make time for those whom others simply passed by? So we know that the kingdom is not an exclusive place only for the rich and well-to-do, based on who the king spent the majority of his time with.

In Matthew 21:31-32, Jesus also explains the all-inclusive aspect of the kingdom. *Jesus said to them, "I tell you the truth, the tax collectors and the prostitutes are entering the kingdom of God ahead of you. ³²For John came to you to show you the way of righteousness, and you did not believe him, but the tax collectors and the prostitutes did. And even after you saw this, you did not repent and believe him."*

📖 In our first lesson this week, you looked up Matthew 20:1-16. How does it express this same concept about the kingdom?

_____

_____

_____

📖 Write out your memory verse, Romans 10:9, in the space below and explain how it backs up this point about the kingdom.

_____

_____

_____

_____

Write out your memory verse in the space below. Try to do it completely from memory, then double-check yourself.

TAKE TIME TO PRAY

Kingdom—Day Four

Memory Verse

Matthew 6:33-34

Start today's study by writing out as much of your memory verse as you can in the space below. Then, look up the verse and make any corrections that are needed. Finally, read it three times from your Bible and pray before completing the following lesson.

So far this week, we have looked up many different scriptures that speak about the kingdom of God. We have looked at the three main ways the kingdom is spoken of in the Bible. Then yesterday, we examined some of the characteristics of the kingdom as it relates to it actually being a physical place. Today we will finish our study by looking at the other two aspects of the kingdom of God: its people and its Lord.

Who will be in the kingdom of God? What are the prerequisites for entry into the kingdom? Is it luck, chance, or the mood of God on the day we arrive that determines our eternal fate? The Bible is very clear about who the people of God's kingdom are. According to God's Holy Word, it is the "righteous" who will inherit the kingdom (Matt 13:40-43). It will be a place that is without evil, sin, and the other shortcomings of our present world. To put it simply, it is a perfect place. This poses a problem for those who desire to enjoy the kingdom of God, because we have all fallen short and sinned (Rom 3:23). Our only hope is the purification that can only be attained through the grace and blood of Christ (Rom 3:24). This is why Christ said in John 14:6, *"I am the way and the truth and the life. No one comes to the Father except through me."* Jesus is the only way that anyone will enter into the kingdom because it is only through his incredible grace that we can be redeemed and cleansed to the sinless standards God demands for those who will inherit the kingdom. Entrance into this kingdom is synonymous with entering into eternal life through Christ. Perhaps Henry Drummond said it best: "The entrance fee into the kingdom of God is nothing; the annual subscription is all we possess." [24] Look up the following verses and be prepared to explain how they relate to the people who will be in the eternal kingdom of God.

📖 John 3:1-9

_____

📖 John 10:27-30

_____

📖 Romans 6:19-23

_____

📖 Colossians 3:1-4

_____

📖 1 John 5:11-13

_____

✄ Are you confident that you will be in the kingdom? Why, or why not? You might consider reviewing Week One, "Assurance," if you are unsure about your entrance into the kingdom.

_____

_____

_____

---

24 John Blanchard, *The Complete Gathered Gold: A Treasury of Quotations for Christians* (Darlington, England: Evangelical Press, 2006), 366. Quote by Henry Drummond.

When it comes to the ruler of heaven, great detail and extensive elaboration are not needed. The answer is simple and final: the Godhead will rule this eternal home for the people of the kingdom. There will be no political campaigns, or committees gathered to nominate who will rule, for while this place was created for God's people, the creator himself created it, and he will rule it. The most difficult thing to understand about the ruler of the kingdom is the Trinity itself. How God the Father, Son, and Spirit rule in unity and at the same time express their individual traits and characteristics is and will continue to be a mystery for those who are awaiting our physical entrance into this eternal kingdom. We will study the issues surrounding the Trinity in week 20 (Volume 2) of *The Absolute Basics of Christianity*. While we may not be able to comprehend all of the details around the rule of the kingdom, we are able to confidently say that the Godhead will rule our eternal home. Look up and examine the following scriptures relating to the rule of the kingdom. Be prepared to discuss them in your next group study.

📖 Ephesians 1:9-10

_____

📖 Colossians 1:15-23

_____

📖 Revelation 19:11-16

_____

📖 Revelation 22:1-5

_____

📖 Revelation 21:22-27

_____

This week's study has helped us to learn of the simplicity, complexity, and great wonder that surrounds the simple phrase "kingdom of God." While we did not explore every scripture or examine every possible angle, we did lay a solid foundation for understanding what this place is, who will be there, and who rules the kingdom. As you continue your walk with the Lord, God will reveal more details about the kingdom as you spend time in prayer and with God's Word.

Write out your memory verse in the space below. Try to do it completely from memory, then double-check yourself.

TAKE TIME TO PRAY

To review, use the space below to write all the memory verses you have learned so far, including this week's. You can also use this space for personal notes about this lesson.

_____

_____

_____

_____

_____

_____

_____

_____

_____

_____

_____

_____

_____

_____

_____

_____

_____

Love—Day One

Memory Verse

John 3:16-17

Start today's study by writing out your memory verse in the space below. Then, read it three times from your Bible and take just a moment to pray before completing the following lesson.

---

*L*ove is a powerful word that carries with it a variety of ideas, emotions, and definitions. While the English language only has one primary word to describe the almost limitless levels of love, other languages use many different words to describe what love is. Both the Hebrew and Greek languages express love using a variety of words. For today's study we will look at the different ways the New Testament expresses the idea of love.

In the Hebrew language, three primary words are used in the Old Testament to express the idea of love. Four Greek words are used to describe love in the New Testament. For this study we will not take the time to unpack the meanings of the Hebrew words relating to love. Instead, we will focus on the New Testament and the way the Greek language expresses love.

While there are four Greek words that are used for love, we only find two of them used in the noun or verb form in the New Testament. They are the words *agape* and *phileo*. Phileo is used to describe what we might call "brotherly love." This is also where we get the name for the city of Philadelphia, which is known as the city of brotherly love. Phileo is the kind of love that is not physical, but instead is focused on a deep, growing, personal relationship. This is not a surface relationship, or some kind of casual, shallow love, but is indeed a very intimate and deep love for another person or thing.

The second word that is used in the New Testament is agape. This is the highest and purest expression of love in the Greek language. It conveys the idea of a person who places others above themselves, and is willing to generously give everything they have out of their love for others. This kind of love is so strong that others do not have to earn it. Instead, it is given freely and fully to others. It is used to describe the way God loves each of us fully, without expectations, and before we ever made any kind of response to Him.

There is another word that is used for love in the New Testament. However, it is never used as a verb or noun. Instead, it is only used twice (Rom 1:31, and 2 Tim 3:3) in its negative form. The word is *stergo* and this normally would refer to the familial love that exists between parents and their children. When used in its negative form *astorgos,* it means "lacking love" or to be "heartless," without normal affection for others.

The final word that the Greeks used to describe love is *eros*. This word is never used in the Bible, but it refers to a sensual love that exists between a man and a woman. This word is not just used to describe sexual encounters; it also implies a deep caring relationship that is shared between a man and a woman, but is based on physical attraction.

Having a basic understanding of these concepts in the Greek language is important as we study and learn about biblical love. Take John 21:15-19, for example. The passage in English loses some of its impact without a proper understanding of the different levels or expressions of love. Read this passage from your Bible and answer the questions below before going on.

> Which Greek words for love do you think are used in this passage?

_____

_____

_____

> From the English translation, can you identify the true meaning of this passage?

_____

_____

_____

❧ Now let me identify the words for you:

John 21:15-18. *When they had finished eating, Jesus said to Simon Peter, "Simon son of John, do you truly love (**agape**) me more than these?" "Yes, Lord," he said, "you know that I love (**phileo**) you." Jesus said, "Feed my lambs." ¹⁶Again Jesus said, "Simon son of John, do you truly love (**agape**) me?" He answered, "Yes, Lord, you know that I love (**phileo**) you." Jesus said, "Take care of my sheep." ¹⁷The third time he said to him, "Simon son of John, do you love (**phileo**) me?" Peter was hurt because Jesus asked him the third time, "Do you love (**phileo**) me?" He said, "Lord, you know all things; you know that I love (**phileo**) you." Jesus said, "Feed my sheep."*

Some believe that John used the words agape and phileo interchangeably in this text. However, others argue that the words chosen by both Jesus and Peter are significant. In the first two questions, Jesus says Do you *agape* me? In other words, do you love me more than anything else? Do you love me in the highest and purest form that the word can express? Do you love me more then you love yourself, Peter? And Peter responds by saying "you know I *phileo* you," which is obviously not the same as the agape love Jesus spoke of in his first two questions. Then, Jesus changes his question and asks if Peter loves him as a brother. Peter is hurt, possibly because the implication here is that Jesus is saying "Do you at least love me as a friend?" Peter replies, You know we are friends, Jesus. Peter, however, was unable to say that his love for Christ was *agape*, and Jesus seems more concerned with honesty than with false declarations of love.

❧ Honestly, do you *agape* or *phileo* Jesus today? Explain how you came to that conclusion?

_____

_____

_____

_____

❧ Look up the following scriptures and see if you can identify whether the verse refers to **agape** or **phileo** love from your English translation. Write your answer out next to the verse. Even if you don't get them right, this exercise will help you see some more of the verses in the Bible that speak of love. Remember, you can go to **www.pastorpete.org** and check your answers. ✗

📖 Matthew 3:17 _____

📖 Matthew 5:43-44 _____

📖 Matthew 22:37-39 _____

📖 John 3:16: _____

📖 John 20:2 _____

📖 Romans 12:10 _____

📖 1 Peter 3:8-9 _____

Write out your memory verse in the space below. Try to do it completely from memory, then double-check yourself.

TAKE TIME TO PRAY

Love—Day Two

Memory Verse

John 3:16-17

Start today's study by writing out as much of your memory verse as you can in the space below. Then, look up the verse and make any corrections that are needed. Finally, read it three times from your Bible and pray before completing the following lesson.

_____

_____

_____

_____

*Y*esterday we looked at the technical side of love in the Bible as we examined the different ways it is expressed through the Greek language. For the remainder of our studies this week, we will look at some of the specific things that the Bible has to say concerning love. Start today by looking up 1 John 4:8-16 and answering the questions below.

> ❧ How did God show his love?

_____

_____

_____

❧ These verses say "whoever lives in love" also "lives in _____."
What does that mean to you?

_____

_____

These verses teach us that love is one of the characteristics of God's nature. At his core, God is holy, but that holiness is expressed through his love, justice (Ps 45:6, Isa 5:16), peace (1 Cor 14:33, 1 Thess 5:23), hope (Rom 15:13), kindness (Rom 11:22), grace (2 Cor 9:14; 13:14), mercy (Ps 51:1; 2 John 1:3), and many other things that all flow out of God's holiness. God is indeed love! His love is unconditional (agape) and he loved us long before we deserved it. He loved us even when we were still sinners (Rom 5:8). His love for us is nothing short of amazing!

Love is also eternal; it never ends, cannot die, and will last forever, according to the Bible. When Ann walked into my office in tears, I knew what she was about to say. She had been married to her husband for 57 years, and the previous Thursday we had laid him to rest. In our time before the service, I told Ann that the worst day was yet to come, and despite the pain, loneliness, and feelings of darkness that she had experienced in the two days since her husband passed, she had not yet faced the "worst day." After giving her a minute to collect herself, we prayed, and at the end of my prayer she blurted out, "Today is my worst day! It is the worst day of my life! I can't believe the love of my life is gone! I don't understand how 57 years of love can disappear so fast." "Is it really gone," I asked? "Do you love your husband less today then you did two weeks ago?" "No", she replied, "in fact I believe I love him more today than ever before, but... how... I just don't know, am I making that up? He is not even here anymore. How can that love remain and continue to grow?" With that, I opened my Bible to 1 Corinthians 13:13 and asked her if she would read it. She just stared at it for some time, and then she said, "Now I understand."

📖 What other things does this passage (1 Cor 13:13) say are eternal?

_____

_____

❧ Which of these three things is the greatest?

_____

_____

Love is also a defining mark for all of Christ's disciples. The world at-large might recognize us when we carry our Bibles, or when we kneel to pray, or by the t-shirt we are wearing, or maybe when we drive by them with a bumper sticker on our vehicle. While these and many other things do identify us as believers, they can't compare with love because it is the ultimate mark of Christ's disciples. We might not always have our Bibles, or be wearing the right clothes, or have a bumper sticker, but love goes with us wherever we are. Love can't be checked at the border like Bibles can. Love can't be stripped off our backs like clothing can. Love does not fade or wither like bumper stickers do. Love is a mark that we carry wherever we go. It can't be stopped, tamed, or snuffed out. Ultimately this thing called love is what defines us, and identifies us to the world around us.

📖 Write out John 13:35.

_____

_____

❧ Are you doing this?

_____

_____

❧ How would your church be different if this really happened?

_____

_____

❧ How would our world be different if this really happened?

_____

_____

📖 What does 1 John 3:14 say love is a sign of? ✖

_____

_____

Love is powerful and unstoppable. Because of true love, marriages are saved even after all hope seems lost. On the cross, love defeated all the evil forces of this world and the next. Love can't be contained, it can't be bottled up, and it can't be saved. For these reasons we should let it flow off of our tongues and out of our lives as freely as possible. We must open the tap and let it flow out into the world around us, where people long to sense and experience real love. Even the coldest, hardest, atheists long to be loved. Love is something that we have all been programmed to enjoy and crave. As believers we have it and we should let it flow!

Christ certainly did throughout his ministry. And through love, he calls us to do one of the most unnatural things we will ever do. He calls us to forgive and love our enemies. Why? Because true love is powerful and it is unstoppable!

📖 According to Matthew 5:43-48, why should we love our enemies?

_____

_____

_____

📖 Which memory verse dose Matthew 5:48 remind you of? Write that verse out from memory in the space below. ⚒

_____

_____

_____

Love is also a unifying force in the world. Love brings people together, and makes our relationships better and stronger. The more love we have in our churches, the more unity. The more love we have in our marriage, the more unity. The more love we have for our co-workers, the more unity we will have at work as well. There is no denying that love promotes unity. Churches that split, marriages that end, and families that are destroyed result from long periods without a key ingredient to sustain unity. This missing ingredient is called love. Where there is true love, unity is sure to follow.

📖 According to Colossians 3:12-16, what does love do?

_____

_____

❧ In what other things are we to clothe ourselves? ⚒

_____

_____

❧ After reading these verses, place a dot on the scale below indicating how well-clothed you think you are.

Naked _____ Well-Clothed

Write out your memory verse in the space below. Try to do it completely from memory, then double-check yourself.

TAKE TIME TO PRAY

Love—Day Three

Memory Verse

John 3:16-17

Start today's study by writing out as much of your memory verse as you can in the space below. Then, look up the verse and make any corrections that are needed. Finally, read it three times from your Bible and pray before completing the following lesson.

For the final two days of this study on love, we are going to examine what is perhaps the best-known passage on the subject. Paul's soaring description of love in the thirteenth chapter of First Corinthians is unmatched by any definition or description that has ever been offered still to this day. This is probably the most quoted chapter of scripture when it comes to weddings, and countless numbers of sermons have been preached and words written based on Paul's thoughts on this subject. So for the final two days of this study, you are going to be challenged to do something totally different. Instead of reading about what others say when it comes to love, the challenge is for you to seriously consider love in the context of your own life based on Paul's thoughts in First Corinthians 13. You should start by reading the entire chapter, then use the form below to describe how you have fulfilled or experienced each of the characteristics of love that is mentioned in the chapter. Take your time and seriously consider each aspect of love. It will encourage your spirit and enlighten your soul to see how well, or how poorly, you are doing when it comes to love.

📖 Start by reading 1 Corinthians 13:1-13, twice.

☐ First time
☐ Second time

❧ *Love is patient.*

- Describe a time when someone was lovingly patient with you.

_____

_____

_____

_____

_____

_____

- Describe a time when you were lovingly patient with someone else.

_____

_____

_____

_____

_____

_____

❧ *Love is kind.*

- Describe a time when someone was kind to you in a way that showed you the meaning of true love.

_____

_____

_____

_____

_____

- Describe a time when you were kind to someone else in a way that was only possible because of love.

_____

_____

_____

_____

❧ *It does not envy.*

- Describe a time when someone else could have been envious of you, but instead, they were just happy for you and their love for you increased even more.

_____

_____

_____

_____

- Describe a time when you were tempted to be envious of someone else, but chose not to be because of love.

_____

_____

_____

_____

❧ *It does not boast.*

- Describe a time when others could have boasted or bragged but they did not. How did that make you feel?

_____

_____

_____

_____

- Describe a time when you could have been boastful, but instead remained humble and through your humility expressed true love to someone else. Do you think they recognized it?

_____

_____

_____

_____

❧ *It is not proud.*

- Describe a time when someone else could have been prideful toward you, but instead they showed you what love was by remaining humble.

_____

_____

_____

_____

- Describe a time when you fought the temptation to be prideful in order to show others the true meaning of love.

_____

_____

_____

_____

❧ *It is not rude.*

- Describe a time when someone was rude to you. How did it make you feel?

_____

_____

_____

_____

• Describe a time when you were rude to someone else. How do you think it made them feel?

_____

_____

_____

_____

❧ End today's lesson by reading 1 Corinthians 13:1-13, twice.
  ☐ First time
  ☐ Second time

Write out your memory verse in the space below. Try to do it completely from memory, then double-check yourself.

_____

_____

_____

_____

TAKE TIME TO PRAY

Love—Day Four

Memory Verse

John 3:16-17

Start today's study by writing out as much of your memory verse as you can in the space below. Then, look up the verse and make any corrections that are needed. Finally, read it three times from your Bible and pray before completing the following lesson.

_____

_____

_____

_____

*Y*esterday, you started to examine closely what true love is by following Paul's outline in First Corinthians 13. Today you will continue to unpack the powerful principles of love that are mentioned in that chapter by thinking about the remaining eight characteristics of love. You should begin today's reading by reading the thirteen verses in this chapter twice to familiarize yourself with the text and prepare your heart to be impacted by its meaning.

📖 Start today's lesson by reading 1 Corinthians 13:1-13, twice.

☐ First time
☐ Second time

❧ *It is not self-seeking.*

- Describe a time when someone's "love" was self-seeking. Did you feel "loved" through their actions?

_____

_____

_____

_____

- Describe a time when you had ulterior motives that were hidden under the cover of "love." Why can love not be self-seeking?

_____

_____

_____

_____

❧ *It is not easily angered.*

- Describe a time when someone could have easily become angry with you but instead they loved you. Describe how that made you feel.

_____

_____

_____

_____

- Describe a time when you could have become angry with someone else but did not. How did that situation turn out?

_____

_____

_____

_____

❦ *It keeps no record of wrongs.*

- Describe a time when someone could have kept a record of your wrongs and used them against you but instead they forgave you and loved you.

_____

_____

_____

_____

- Describe a time when you decided to completely let a wrong go and just love someone instead.

_____

_____

_____

_____

❦ *Love does not delight in evil but rejoices with the truth.*

- What does this mean to you?

_____

_____

_____

_____

- Describe a time in the past when you have practiced this.

_____

_____

_____

_____

❧ *It always protects.*

- Describe a time when love protected you.

_____

_____

_____

_____

- Describe a time when your love protected someone else. Did they appreciate it?

_____

_____

_____

_____

❧ *Always trusts.*

- Describe a situation that required someone to trust you. Did you feel loved?

_____

_____

_____

_____

- Describe a situation that required you to trust someone else. How did this show them you loved them?

_____

_____

_____

_____

?? *Always hopes:*

- What does this mean to you?

_____

_____

_____

_____

- Describe a time when through your love you remained hopeful.

_____

_____

_____

_____

?? *Always perseveres.*

- Describe a time or situation when someone, through their love, stuck with you and proved that love always perseveres.

_____

_____

_____

_____

- Describe a time or situation when you persevered alongside someone else through the power of love.

_____

_____

_____

_____

❧ *Love never fails.*

- Do you believe this? Why, or why not?

_____

_____

_____

_____

❧ In the space below, write out your own soaring description of what love is. Don't try to copy Paul. Be original and creative as you describe what love is to you.

_____

_____

_____

_____

_____

📖 End today's lesson by reading 1 Corinthians 13:1-13, twice.

☐ First time
☐ Second time

Write out your memory verse in the space below. Try to do it completely from memory, then double-check yourself.

_____

_____

_____

_____

TAKE TIME TO PRAY

To review, use the space below to write all the memory verses you have learned so far, including this week's. You can also use this space for personal notes about this lesson.

Money—Day One

Memory Verse

John 1:16

Start today's study by writing out your memory verse in the space below. Then, read it three times from your Bible and take just a moment to pray before completing the following lesson.

There are really only three things you can do with money. You can spend it, save it, or give it away. When we do these three things following God's plan for our finances, life is so much better. Most people don't have a plan when it comes to money. As a result, most don't have any money. The goal of this week's lessons is not to make you into a millionaire or change all of your bad financial habits. Instead, we will take a basic look at what the Bible has to say about money. Whether you are rich, poor, or someplace in-between, these lessons will help everyone learn more and become better stewards of God's resources.

When my son was twenty-two-months old, we were walking down by the river early one morning at a conference center where I was speaking. My son loved rocks, especially the smooth ones down by the river. Holding three rocks in his small hands, he bent over to pick up another rock, and as he did he said "My rock!" In my son that morning I saw the common attitude of both children and adults when it comes to the things of this world. My son could not even speak a full sentence, but the greedy and selfish mindset was already a part of his life. Seeing what I perceived to be a teachable moment, I knelt down and said, "This is God's rock, Peter. We just get to enjoy it while we are here, but God made it. This is his rock." My son looked at me in silence and I could see the wheels spinning in his young mind. We continued to walk, saying nothing else about the matter, then Peter stopped at the next tree, looked at it, reached out and put his hand on the tree and said, "God's tree!" I said, "Yes, that is God's tree." Going a bit further we arrived at the dam in the river and through the clear water we watched the fish swim beneath our feet. Peter said "God's water?" "Yes," I replied, "God's fish?" "Yes, Peter, everything you see, smell, touch, hear, and taste is God's. Everything belongs to God." In five minutes, my son's selfish, self-centered, greedy attitude was transformed simply by helping him understand that everything belongs to God. If a twenty-two-month old child can learn this lesson, certainly we can as well.

When people come to me with financial issues, they are quick to want to assign blame. It's the wife who spends too much, or the husband who has an expensive hobby; it's the children's many wants and desires, or it's some circumstance that has caused the financial hardship. They immediately want to assign blame and be given a five-step program that will get them back on track. Blame and programs do little good, however, if the mindset of those affected is not transformed first. We must change our mindset when it comes to money.

Most people agree that we are supposed to give 10% to God through the tithe, and then they assume that the other 90% is ours to do with what we want. However, this selfish, greedy, unbiblical mindset is 100% our problem when it comes to money. The Bible teaches us the same lesson I was trying to teach my son: everything belongs to God. Not just 10%, or 20%—God owns everything. Every dollar we earn, our home, our vehicles, our clothes, even our lives, all belong to God. Look up the following verses and see how the Bible describes this concept.

📖 Deuteronomy 8:15-20

_____

_____

📖 Deuteronomy 10:12-14

_____

_____

📖 Psalms 50:8-15

_____

_____

📖 1 Chronicles 29:10-17

_____

_____

📖 Haggai 2:6-9

_____

_____

When we believe that anything we have is ours, we enter into an unhealthy and unbiblical mindset. This mindset always leads to selfishness, frustration, pain, and hardship. Before we can transform our finances, we must transform our mindset. We must understand that God is not concerned simply about what we do with 10% of his money. He calls us to be stewards of 100% of his money and we will be held accountable for all that we were given during our lifetime. When we enter into the proper mindset, we will spend, save, and give in a way that honors God, and as a result, others will be blessed and we will too.

    ❧ Before this lesson today, how did you view the things God has blessed you with? As his or yours?

_____

_____

    ❧ Is there anything you can think of in your possession that God has not given you?

_____

_____

    ❧ Is there anything you can think of that God could not take away from you?

_____

_____

    ❧ Why is keeping a biblical mindset about our possessions so difficult?

_____

_____

❧ What can we do to make sure we stay focused and have the proper mindset each and every day? Be specific.

_____

_____

_____

Write out your memory verse in the space below. Try to do it completely from memory, then double-check yourself.

_____

_____

_____

_____

TAKE TIME TO PRAY

Money—Day Two

Memory Verse

John 1:16

Start today's study by writing out as much of your memory verse as you can in the space below. Then, look up the verse and make any corrections that are needed. Finally, read it three times from your Bible and pray before completing the following lesson.

_____

_____

_____

_____

Yesterday, we said that there are only three things you can do with money: spend it, save it, and give it away. Today we are going to talk about spending, then we will tackle the other two over the next two days. While all three areas are important, we are going to look at them not based on the order of their importance, but instead on the priority we give each area. Interestingly, we place the most importance on spending, then saving, then finally giving. God's order would be the opposite: give, save, and then spend. Understandably, spending is the largest of the three areas for most families. Even if we did it God's way, by tithing 10% and then saving, spending would still account for 70 to 80% of a family's budget. As we learned yesterday, having the right mindset is the key to understanding our spending and our finances in general. With this in mind, take some time to answer the questions below before moving along in today's study.

❧ How would you explain the mindset we talked about yesterday to someone else?

_____

_____

❧ List the main things that you spend money on. Your list should be long.

_____

_____

_____

_____

When I was twenty-one years old, I had a money problem. Over the years I had accumulated a large amount of debt. College loans, a car payment, rent, vacations, electricity, cell phone bills, and all the other things had piled up and I was convinced that I had a money problem. Like most, I blamed my issues on a meager income. So I took on a third job, stocking shelves at a large retail store five mornings a week, from one a.m. to six a.m. Now I was working over eighty hours a week between three jobs and I was convinced my money issues would be solved. Despite working almost twelve hours a day, seven days a week, for almost six months, I was still having issues with money. There never seemed to be anything left and I could never get caught up. It was around this time that I heard a man on the radio named Dave Ramsey. While I was listening to other callers phone in, my problem was diagnosed. I did not have an income problem; I had a spending problem. Like most, I did not want to admit that I was a poor manager of the things God had given me, but the facts spoke for themselves and I knew something had to be done. So I started to read everything I could that the Bible had to say about money and it changed my life and my future family's life forever.

The statistics are clear: we have a major spending problem in America. Forty percent of American families spend more than they make. Because of our unhealthy and unbiblical spending habits, 96% of all Americans will be financially dependent on the government, family, or charity at retirement. Americans carry, on average, $8400 in credit card debt. If you were to make a 2% payment every month at an annual APR of 15%, it would take about thirty years to pay off that debt and it would include about $13,000 in interest.[25] Our misguided mindset about money, and more specifically about spending, has led us into a huge prob-

---

25 "Consumer Debt Statistics in America," http://www.progressiverelief.com/consumer-debt-statistics.html (accessed March 30, 2010).

lem with debt. When we don't spend wisely and biblically, we will always find ourselves in debt.

Debt will do many things *to* you, and it will do nothing *for* you! Some people say debt is a tool. I agree: it's a tool of the devil! The devil loves debt! That alone is reason enough to stay away from it, but there are other reasons we should avoid debt at all costs. For example, we should avoid debt because it demands too much from us. Look up Proverbs 22:7 and answer the question below.

    ✺   What does this verse say the borrower is?

_____

_____

_____

_____

Debt is very demanding. What does it demand? Well, for starters it demands your attention. Debt is like playing with a poisonous snake; you can do it and get away with it, if you pay real close attention. But as soon as you take your focus and attention away, you will get bit. I know a professional snake handler. He is an expert and has been practicing his trade for over twenty-five years. In that time, he has been bitten over fifteen times. It's not whether you will get bit, it's when! When we don't spend right, the debt we accumulate will demand our full and undivided attention and that takes us away from the things God wants us to focus on.

    📖   What does Philippians 4:8 say we should focus on? Is debt in the list?

_____

_____

_____

_____

Debt also demands our time. Of course, it demands our time to pay attention to it but it also demands our time to pay it off. All of those extra hours at work, and extra hours spent in an effort to catch up, could be used to further the kingdom of God. Instead, they are wasted focusing on debt.

Finally, debt demands our energy. It takes a lot of energy to deal with debt. Emotional, physical, and even spiritual energy is exerted in an effort to get caught up financially. Debt is just too demanding!

Debt is also distracting. Jesus says this in John 10:10: *The thief comes only to steal and kill and destroy; I have come that they may have life, and have it to the full*. But when I am focused on debt, I am distracted from the things God has for me. I lose sight of the full and abundant life he promised me. It distracts us from God's plan and purpose for our lives and causes us to focus on the lesser things of this world.

📖 What does Psalms 39:4-6 say about our lives? In the context of these verses why is the distraction of debt bad? ⛏

_____

_____

_____

_____

_____

Debt is also draining. Debt will just wear you out. All the demands and distractions take a great toll on us after a while. Proverbs 22:7 said *the borrower is slave to the lender*. Being a slave is draining. Slaves don't get to go home early, slaves don't take vacations, and slaves can't take three-day weekends. Those who are slaves to debt never get a break, and that debt will drain you of everything you have. The devil loves debt because through it he wears us out and drains us to the point that we can't be effective in God's kingdom.

No matter how good or bad your finances are today, you should avoid debt in the future at all costs. When it comes to spending, God never condones or encourages us to spend more than we have. If we follow that principle we will never find ourselves in the demanding, distracting, and draining situation that debt brings into our lives. If you are in debt today, I would highly recommend you use one of the resources listed at the end of today's lesson to get a better handle on your spending and your finances.

PRACTICAL ADVICE AND THINGS TO WATCH OUT FOR

As I told you at the beginning of this lesson, I know what it is to be in debt and struggling to just keep my head above water. But through lots of hard work, focus, discipline, prayer, and help from God, I no longer have any consumer debt that makes demands on my life, distracts me from my purpose, or drains me of my joy. This did not happen because I increased my income, but because I decreased my spending. I decided that I would spend God's money in God's way, and that changed my life forever! Through my own personal experiences and through counseling many families and individuals, I have found that there are some common debt traps that many people are not aware of. So the following is some advice on things you should try to avoid.

First, be careful about long-term debt. These are the large purchases we make in our lives. Things like cars, homes, boats, time-shares, and the like will eat you alive if you are not careful. Personally, I have seen people with seventy-year mortgages, and car payments that stretch for as long as seven years are not uncommon today. These long-term commitments to debt will be a burden for a significant amount of your life—be careful! When it comes to your vehicle it is better to use cash and buy a quality used vehicle than to make payments on something used or new. When you buy a new car or truck and drive it off the lot, it drops 20% in value. That's $5,000 on a $25,000 purchase! So unless you have so much money that you don't mind throwing $5,000 away, don't buy new! If you have that much money, then you should not need to borrow it to buy the new vehicle anyway. Some people say, "I buy new because used cars break down and cost me more money in the long run..." WRONG!!!!!! The average car payment is around $350 per month. That comes out to $4,200 each year. Do you know how much work you can do on a vehicle for $4,200? The truck I drive is over seven years old (in 2010) and has hundreds of thousands of miles on it. To date, I have never spent more than $600 in a single year on that truck. It is paid for; this means it pays me over $3,500 a year!

When it comes to buying a home, don't buy more then you can afford and definitely don't buy what the bank says you can afford. Unlike cars and other things, a home is an investment that with care will appreciate with time. Few people will ever be able to purchase a home with cash, but be careful when making a long-term debt commitment. Everyone wants a two-car garage, cathedral ceilings, and a house that's on a golf course or on a tract of land. But if you can't afford it, don't buy it! A good rule of thumb to keep you from buying a home you can't afford is as follows: If you can't put 20% down and afford the payments on a fifteen-year fixed loan, don't buy it.

Next, use paper, not plastic! You will spend less money on everything if you use cash instead of credit cards and debit cards. Allot money for things like groceries, dining out, and spending money. And when it's gone, it's gone! It is so easy to swipe a card and forget that there is money attached to it. If you have ever been on a cruise ship, you know that when you check in you are given a card. It is basically a credit card that is used to purchase anything you want on the ship. By design, you can't use cash on the ship. Why? Because they know you will spend more if all you have to do is swipe a card. People routinely run up bills over two, three, even four thousand dollars on these cards. When you use cash, you spend less. You will think twice before you hand over that $100 bill, I promise.

Finally, avoid impulse and emotional spending. I know a lady who shops on QVC almost daily. She buys so much stuff and most of it she never uses because it has been bought on impulse and she really does not need it. Garage sales are impulse areas as well. Be careful letting yourself think that it might not be there in an hour or after lunch. When you do this you will always spend more. If you don't have time to pray on it, sleep on it, and think on it, 99% of the time you should not buy it.

Spending is the biggest portion of most people's budget, so be careful when it comes to your spending. Never spend more then you make, avoid debt at all costs, and ask God to help guide you when it comes to spending. Remember, the proper mindset is essential when it comes to handling our spending God's way!

❧ What is the right mindset when it comes to money?

_____

_____

_____

_____

_____

RESOURCES TO CONSIDER

All of these can be found at **www.pastorpete.org**
Simply click on **Bookstore** and then **Finance**.

Dave Ramsey, *The Total Money Makeover*
Larry Burkett, *The World's Easiest Guide to Finances*
Dwight Nichols, *God's Plans for Your Finances*
David Bach, *The Automatic Millionaire* (it's not what you think)

Write out your memory verse in the space below. Try to do it completely from memory, then double-check yourself.

_____

_____

_____

_____

TAKE TIME TO PRAY

Money—Day Three

Memory Verse

John 1:16

Start today's study by writing out as much of your memory verse as you can in the space below. Then, look up the verse and make any corrections that are needed. Finally, read it three times from your Bible and pray before completing the following lesson.

_____

_____

_____

_____

*Y*esterday we talked about spending. Today we are going to look at what the Bible has to say about saving money. As we discovered yesterday, spending is the biggest part of anyone's budget and, unless you become a multi-millionaire or a billionaire, it will probably always be that way. But we must not let spending be all that we do with our money. We should also save some of it for tomorrow.

Most people don't save enough. While savings rates among families in America have fluctuated from 1% to as high as 8% over the past two decades, the truth is that most people are still not saving enough. One figure that seems to pop up over and over again, reflecting an accurate long-term savings picture for most people, is as follows: One-third of Americans are not saving anything at all. Another one-third are saving some, but not enough to reach their retirement goals, and the final one-third are saving enough to retire one day.[26] Statistics change so often that I am hesitant to include many in this section, but the fact of the matter is that an overwhelming number of people are depending on Social Security for their retirement plans. Take it from someone who speaks to seniors on a fixed income every week, DON'T COUNT ON THE GOVERNMENT WHEN IT COMES TO SAVINGS!!!! You need to take control of your own money and save some of it for the future. What does the Bible say? Read the following verses from the book of Proverbs and then write out what you think they are saying about saving.

📖 Proverbs 13:22

_____

_____

📖 Proverbs 21:20

_____

_____

📖 Proverbs 30:24-25

_____

_____

We all want to save, but can we really do it in today's world? The answer is YES, if we have the right mindset and understand the power of saving. It has been said that there are only a few different ways to acquire great wealth; you can win it, marry it, inherit it, earn it, find it, or save it. Most of us will never win the lottery; if that is your retirement strategy, you need to change your mind-set. Very few will marry into money or inherit a great sum of money. The median household income in the United States is around $50,000,[27] so let's face it: most of us will never earn great sums of money either. You might find a treasure map in your attic that leads you to millions in pirate gold, or find a huge gold nugget in a river while hiking, or discover the largest diamond ever found in a public diamond mine, but I doubt it! So if winning it, marrying it, inheriting it, earning it, and finding it are out, then that just leaves saving it. And this is actually a lot faster and easier than most people think. Let me explain.

---

26   "Two-thirds of Americans don't save enough," Mortgage Rates Credit Cards Refinance Home CD Rates by Bankrate.com. http://www.bankrate.com/brm/news/retirement/oct_07_retirement_poll_results_a1.asp (accessed April 01, 2010), p. 1.

27   "US Census Press Releases," Census Bureau Home Page. http://www.census.gov/Press-Release/www/releases/archives/income_wealth/012528.html (accessed April 01, 2010).

Most people can save $5 a day, right? Sure you can. It will take some sacrifice but it can be done. My wife and I made some financial decisions years ago that save us way more than $5 a day. For example, we bought a $20 pair of hair clippers and she cuts my hair. This saves our family about $130 each year. We also started using cloth diapers for our children. The initial investment was around $300, but it saves us over $2,000 for each child over the course of the time they are in diapers. We generally drink water when we go out to eat. Not only is this better for our health, it also saves us a few dollars each time we dine out. By shopping around for the cheapest electricity (which is allowed in Texas), we saved about $50 a month. By getting out of debt and destroying our credit cards, we saved 15% a month in interest payments. And the list goes on, but you get the point. If you really want to, you can save $5, $10, or even $20 a day by making small adjustments in your lifestyle. Will this really matter? It seems like such a small amount, right? Well, let's do the math.[28]

If you saved $5 a day or $150 a month and put that away in some kind of IRA or similar investment fund, that earned, on average 10% over the lifetime of the account, here is what it would look like:

YEAR	AMOUNT
1	$1,885
2	$3,967
5	$11,616
10	$30,727
15	$62,171
30	$339,073
40	$948,611

That's almost a million dollars! And all you have to do is save small amounts of money over a long period of time! Everyone can do this! What if you saved $10 a day, or $300 a month?

YEAR	AMOUNT
1	$3,770
2	$7,934
5	$23,231
10	$61,453
15	$124,341
30	$678,146
40	$1,897,224

28   The tables provided in this chapter come from David Bach, *The Automatic Millionaire: A Powerful One-Step Plan to Live and Finish Rich* (New York: Broadway Books, 2004), 44-45.

That pack of cigarettes is not only hurting your health, it is stealing your future as well. The same can be said of soda, candy, and donuts. Recently, in one of the financial courses that is offered at our church, we had a family give a testimony about donuts and soda. After tracking their expenses, they realized that as a family they spent just over $350 each month on donuts in the morning on the way to school and drinks and snacks on the way home each day. That is a two-million dollar issue. Just think about that for a minute. Or that $10 lunch you have every day instead of bringing something to work is costing you millions over the course of your life. We are talking about almost two million dollars over the course of a lifetime by saving just a few dollars a day. You can do this, with just a little discipline and effort. But let's say you go crazy and you really get serious about this savings stuff. Let's say you decide as a family to save $20 a day or $600 each month. This is possible if you are willing to do the work to get out of debt and be serious when it comes to your spending. If you did this, here is what your savings chart would look like.

YEAR	AMOUNT
1	$7,539
2	$15,868
5	$46,462
10	$122,907
15	$248,682
30	$1,356,293
40	$3,794,448

So, how do we make this happen? How can we save money to ensure that we have something for tomorrow? As we have discussed already, it starts with the right mind-set. We must understand that saving is something God wants us to do. We must not become too focused on saving or we will mess up the other two areas—spending and giving. Balance is the key to managing money. We should spend some, save some, and give some! You should start saving something today. Even if it's just $1 a day or $30 a month, save something!!! You have to get your spending under control before you can save like you really want to. Getting out of debt is vital when it comes to saving money. You should get out of debt ASAP. Then you will really be able to save.

If you really want to save money, then I suggest you read David Bach's book *The Automatic Millionaire*. While I don't agree with everything David says in his book, in particular his negative view of budgets, the method he talks about in his book is valuable and has worked for my family in combination with other methods that are taught by other experts in the field. It's not a get-rich-quick book; instead, he shows you the beauty of automation when it comes to savings. Make savings automatic by setting up a bank withdrawal or automatic transfer to happen on or around each payday. That way you don't forget to save.

It's never too late to start, but the sooner you start, the better. Teach your children and your grandchildren the power of saving a little each day and you can give them the tools they need to become wealthy. They can do it simply by saving it a few dollars at a time, rather than by taking a chance on winning it, marrying it, inheriting it, earning it, or finding it. Finish today's lesson by answering the questions below.

❧ Are you satisfied with your savings today?

_____

_____

_____

_____

❧ Do you think you will be financially secure when you retire? Do you want to be?

_____

_____

_____

_____

❧ What are you currently spending money on that you could do with out? How could getting rid of these things help you save $5 to $20 a day? List them out.

_____

_____

_____

_____

❧ Who can you talk to about creating a financial savings plan?

_____

_____

_____

_____

Write out your memory verse in the space below. Try to do it completely from memory, then double-check yourself.

TAKE TIME TO PRAY

Money—Day Four

Memory Verse

John 1:16

Start today's study by writing out as much of your memory verse as you can in the space below. Then, look up the verse and make any corrections that are needed. Finally, read it three times from your Bible and pray before completing the following lesson.

_____

_____

_____

_____

Today, you will conclude our short study on money by looking at what the Bible has to say about giving. It should be noted here, at the start of the lesson, that like love and real joy, giving is something that is impossible to explain or comprehend. It can only be experienced. You can hear testimony after testimony about how giving has changed people's lives, but until you actually take the step of faith and do it God's way, it is impossible to understand the transformative power of giving. There is just something that is supernaturally unexplainable when it comes to tithing and giving back to God and his kingdom. With this in mind, we will attempt to unpack this subject today, but before we do, it is important to understand two key terms that will be used throughout the study.

KEY TERMS

1. **Tithing:** Full 10% of all income.

2. **Giving:** Anything you give above and beyond your tithe.

I have actively been involved in full-time ministry for well over a decade. During that time, many statistics have changed, but the numbers on tithing have not. Most available research reports that the number of modern day disciples who tithe (10%) fluctuates at between 5 and 7% from year to year.[29] Therefore we can conclude that 90-95% of Christians—who claim to follow Christ—are not tithing. The question is, Why?

People don't tithe for several reasons. The reason many don't tithe is because they can't afford to. When your spending and saving practices are out of balance, this leaves no room for tithing or giving. Many people in America today are simply too far behind to tithe because of their poor spending habits. However, the solution to their problem (spending) is found in what they have decided they will never be able to do (tithe). Why does the Bible talk about tithing? God could have funded the church in many different ways other than calling those who belong to it to tithe 10%, right? So why did God institute the tithe? Part of the answer is to break the materialistic, self-centered, self-absorbed, lifestyle we are naturally drawn to. Each time I tithe or give, I am willingly saying that someone else is more important than me. However, when we keep it all for ourselves, we only enhance the selfishness and materialism in our lives and we tend over time to become more and more self-absorbed and less and less concerned with others.

The second reason people don't give is because they don't feel that it is biblical. Some argue that there is no biblical mandate or command to give, and others argue that because there is no clear black-and-white direction given in the New Testament specifically on the subject of tithing, we are no longer called to tithe under the new covenant. Common sense, however, quickly rules out this argument. For example, we are told not to "kill" in the Ten Commandments (the old covenant). Does this mean that because we are under the new covenant today, and no longer under the old covenant, we can go around killing people? Certainly not! When you understand scripture in its full context and as a whole, this makes perfect sense, and it's the same for tithing and giving as well.

Let's examine the origin of the tithe and giving in the Bible and see what we can conclude as far as these two arguments are concerned. The first time the Bible mentions the tithe is in Genesis 14:18-20, when Abraham gives a tithe to the priest Melchizedek, but the first mention of a tenth being given directly to

---

29 "New Study Shows Trends in Tithing and Donating," The Barna Group—Barna Update. http://www.barna.org/barna-update/article/18-congregations/41-new-study-shows-trends-in-tithing-and-donating?q=tithe (accessed April 03, 2010).

God is found in Genesis 28:20-22. Take a minute to read those verses and answer the questions below.

🙐 Who gives this tithe to God?

_____

_____

📖 What else does he do for God in these verses? What do the next three verses have in common with Genesis 28:20-22? ✗

_____

_____

📖 Deuteronomy 12:4-7:

_____

_____

📖 Nehemiah 10:34-39:

_____

_____

📖 Matthew 23:23:

_____

_____

Tithing from the beginning in the Old Testament all the way through the New Testament and up until this very day has never been about paying or appeasing God. It is a part of the way we worship and honor the Lord. Jesus was upset in Matthew 23 because the Pharisees and teachers of the Law gave a tenth out of pride instead of humility. It was not about worshiping God; it was about impressing others. We find a similar situation in Luke 18:12, when the religious man brags at the temple about fasting twice a week and giving a tenth of all he earns. But he does not go home justified. When we make tithing about us, we miss the point and it loses its spiritual significance and power in our lives. Only when our tithing and giving become a part of our worship will we be able to fully experience their eternal rewards. Tithing is not an event that happens when we get paid; it is a part of our lifestyle of worship that we lead as modern day disciples of Jesus Christ.

📖 What did Jesus say about giving in Matthew 6:2-4? Why? ⚒

_____

_____

As we have seen, tithing is Biblical and the principles of both giving and tithing can be found in both the Old and New Testaments. However, some preachers and churches in the modern age have taken tithing out of its proper place as a part of worship, and they have placed so much focus on it outside of the context of worship that they have indeed made a biblical concept and principle unbiblical, because they have perverted it for their own benefit. True believers don't tithe because they have to; they tithe because they want to. Tithing is about worship. It is a part of our worship, and true believers want to worship God, so tithing and giving come naturally to those who long to worship.

📖 Read 2 Corinthians 9:6-9, and describe Paul's philosophy on sowing and reaping.

_____

_____

_____

🕊 From these verses, does it appear that we are required to give? ⚒

_____

_____

_____

Tithing is not just a part of our worship; it is also a part of God's plan for humanity. As we learned in Week Three, the church is the method that God has chosen to reach out and spread the good news of Christ to the entire world. It is impossible to imagine how this could be possible without any money at all. When believers worship through their tithes, they are also helping spread the gospel. Some argue that too much of that money goes to pay preachers their million-dollar-a-year salaries and to build worship arenas that seat 15,000 people. Honestly, how many preachers do you know who are millionaires, and how many churches out there have fancy extravagant facilities? The truth is that many ministers work a second job to get by, and 99.8% of the rest earn a very modest income. Furthermore, most churches are modestly sized and decorated. Certainly there are preachers and churches that abuse the resources God brings into their storehouse, but the overwhelming majority does not. When we rob

God of the tithe he deserves as a part of our worship, we rob ourselves and the kingdom as well.

📖 Write out your memory verses Matthew 28:19-20, and Mark 16:15 in the space below.

_____

_____

_____

_____

📖 Do you think the church can accomplish this mission faster with or without money? Explain

_____

_____

_____

_____

📖 Now look up Malachi 3:8-11. What are we supposed to do with our tithes and offerings? Why?

_____

_____

_____

So far we have focused primarily on tithing and bringing one-tenth of all we have to God. But the Bible also speaks highly of giving, as well. Once we have brought our tithe to God, we are then encouraged to consider and pray about giving. We might give to help a neighbor or a family member. We might give a special offering to a missionary or a building program. We could give to an orphanage or a nonprofit organization or to any other good work that God lays on our hearts. Giving is about worship, too. When I am obedient in giving over and beyond my tithe, I bless the heart of God through my obedience. We should, however, never let our giving take priority over tithing.

Before we close this study on money, let's examine a few myths about tithing and giving. To do this, we will look at what the Bible has to say about each of the following myths. You have probably heard someone say these in some form or fashion, or perhaps you are guilty of saying them or thinking them yourself. As you read these myths, look up the verses that are mentioned as well and write down what the Bible says about each myth.

1. Only rich people should tithe or give.
    📖 2 Corinthians 8:2

    _____

    _____

    _____

2. We should just give what we can and not worry about tithing.
    📖 2 Corinthians 8:3-4 ⚒

    _____

    _____

    _____

3. If I had more, I would give more.
    📖 Matthew 6:33 ⚒

    _____

    _____

    _____

4. If I tithe, I won't have enough to live on.
    📖 Luke 6:38 ⚒

    _____

    _____

    _____

5. God has not really given me anything that is worth a full tithe.
    📖 John 1:16, 3:16

    _____

    _____

    _____

How should we tithe and give? First, we should give immediately. We should give God his tithe from the first fruits of our labor. If you wait till the end of the month, you are not likely to succeed in the long term when it comes to tithing. When we wait till the end of the month, we are telling God that we lack the faith and the discipline to trust him with our finances. Tithing and giving is about worship and obedience: we do both in faith.

Second, you should give regularly. Some like to wait and give one big check at the end of the quarter or year. The better solution is to tithe each time you get paid. If you are paid weekly, tithe each Sunday; if you get paid bi-monthly or monthly, then tithe on the following Sunday when you arrive at church. If you know you are going to miss due to a vacation or business trip, mail it in or drop it by the church office. Why would you want to withhold your worship through tithing and giving for a week or a month? If you don't tithe regularly, you most likely will not tithe at all. If you can, automate your giving and tithing. Many churches have online giving available that allows the worshipper to set up reoccurring transactions to ensure that God gets the first fruits of your labor and you never forget to worship God through your tithe. If your church does not have a system to automate your tithing, your bank surely will have some kind of online banking tool that will make this possible. When you set up your tithing and giving to automatically be delivered to the church, you no longer have to worry about spending your tithe or forgetting to write the check on Sunday morning. Instead, you can know for certain that your worship through giving has been fulfilled. This is similar to what we learned yesterday when it comes to automating some kind of a savings plan.

On Day One, we learned that most people are failing with money because of the wrong mind-set when it comes to money. In general, we use God's money in the following order. First we spend it, then if there is any left we save it, and finally if there is enough we give it away. God's plan for His money is exactly the opposite, and when we use his plan there is always enough. God's plan works like this. First, give your money away through tithing and giving. Next you should save some money. Then you wisely spend what is left. This really works. When you follow God's plan, you always have enough to give, save, and spend. Granted you might have to adjust your spending some, but that is better than adjusting your giving and savings. Try managing God's money in God's way for three full months and I promise you will not regret it.

There are only three things you can do with money. Spend, save, and give it away. The first two things are earthly and they will only last for a short while. The third thing you can do with God's money is eternal and will pay dividends forever. Each time you get paid, you should tithe first, then pay yourself (save), then spend what is left with the proper mind-set. This will ensure that you keep the proper balance and perspective when it comes to money. The secret is making sure you are doing all three things God's way instead of your way. When we give, save, and spend God's money in the balanced and biblical way, as we are taught in the Bible, money becomes a blessing not only to ourselves but to others as well.

Write out your memory verse in the space below. Try to do it completely from memory, then double-check yourself.

TAKE TIME TO PRAY

To review, use the space below to write all the memory verses you have learned so far, including this week's. You can also use this space for personal notes about this lesson.

_____

_____

_____

_____

_____

_____

_____

_____

_____

_____

_____

_____

_____

_____

_____

_____

_____

_____

_____

New Life—Day One

Memory Verse

John 10:10

Start today's study by writing out your memory verse in the space below. Then, read it three times from your Bible and take just a moment to pray before completing the following lesson.

---

*I*n volume one of *The Absolute Basics of Christianity,* we studied the assurance of our eternal salvation in Week One. We also covered the basics of important topics such as baptism, church, discipleship, evangelism, forgiveness, gifts, heaven and hell, the I Am (God and Jesus), joy, the kingdom of God, love, and money. For the first part of this second volume, we will begin by looking at the new life we have in Christ. This new life encompasses all that we have previously learned in volume one and all that we will learn in the coming weeks as well.

The concept of new life can be confusing, to be sure. Take for example the story of Nicodemus in John 3. He was confused when Christ said he must be born again. *"How can a man be born when he is old?"* Nicodemus asked. *"Surely he cannot enter a second time into his mother's womb to be born!"* (John 3:4) While most people in today's society would not ask such a question, many are still as confused as Nicodemus was when it comes to our new life in Christ. So this week we are going to talk about some of the changes that come with our new life in Christ.

The words "new life" only appear together as a phrase twice in the New Testament.[30] A simple search will also show that the word "new" appears fifty eight times. The word "life," however, is found 234 times in the New Testament. The Greek word for "life" (ζωή, zoe) that is used in both passages to indicate "new life" is only found 135 times in the Greek New Testament. Despite only having two direct references to this idea of "new life" we will later see that the Biblical concept of "new life" is firmly rooted in scripture. However, to begin the study you should examine these two particular passages that speak of new life specifically. They are similar, yet different from each other in several ways. As you look at them, make notes about what they mean and the different contexts in which they are used. Don't just read them. Think about them and attempt to understand and unpack them.

📖 Acts 5:17-23 ⚒

_____

_____

_____

📖 Romans 6:1-7 ⚒

_____

_____

_____

❧ After reading these verses, what do you think we should do with our "new life"? In the space below, write out what the phrase new life means to you. How would you explain it to a nonbeliever?

_____

_____

_____

_____

When I meet with families prior to performing a funeral service, I try to ask a series of questions about the deceased's life so that I can have a good understand-

---

30   In the New International Version of the Bible

ing of who they were and what they believed. There are two particular answers that grieve my soul when I ask about the spiritual life of the deceased. The first is "He did not know or profess Christ." Since Jesus is the only way to the Father (John 14:6), and ultimately to heaven, this means that the individual has no hope of eternal salvation. Obviously this answer is one that causes much concern and heartache. The second is equally concerning and grievous. Many times the family says something like "He was very private about his faith. We know that he knew Jesus; in fact, he was baptized 62 years ago. But he did not really talk about it much because he thought that religion was a private affair between him and Jesus." I often find myself doing everything I can not to scream, "If it is so private, why did Jesus do so much in public? Why does he call us to GO and tell others!? Why does Romans 10:9 say to believe in your heart *and* confess with your MOUTH?" There is nothing private about being a disciple of Christ. We live our lives in full view of the unbelieving world to show them that there is a better hope and a superior way to navigate through life. His name is Jesus and he brings new life! We should tell everyone we can about this "new life" we have in Christ.

The passage found in Acts is the first of three (Acts 12:6-11; 16:26-29) miraculous prison breaks in the book of Acts. The apostles are specifically told to go and use this "new life" as a means to tell others about Christ. Like these early believers we too are called to go and tell as many as possible about this new life we have in Christ Jesus. When ordinary men and women present the simple message of the gospel, extraordinary things happen. You are ready today to start telling others the good news of Jesus Christ. New life can only be found in him, and like the apostles we are called to "Go, and stand in the temple courts, to tell the people the full message of this new life." (Acts 5:20)

While the passage in Acts speaks primarily to the practical point of telling others about this new life, Romans 6 speaks to the spiritual point of a new eternal life through Jesus Christ. Our new life that is made possible only through the blood of Christ gives us a reason to tell others and celebrate our eternal salvation.

- Why do you think the church in general does not celebrate this new life more? Why don't believers tell others about their new life in Christ? ⚒

___

___

- How would you tell someone who did not know Christ about this new life? What are the four parts of sharing your testimony? (volume one, Week Five)

___

___

___

To finish today's lesson, look up and read the following passages. Think about them in the context of "new life" and, as you did with Acts 5:17-23 and Romans 6:1-7, search for the meaning in the text and consider what God's word is trying to teach you about new life.

📖 Romans 8:1-7 🎬

_____

_____

📖 John 3:15-16 ⚒

_____

_____

📖 John 11:21-27 ⚒

_____

_____

Write out your memory verse in the space below. Try to do it completely from memory, then double-check yourself.

TAKE TIME TO PRAY

New Life—Day Two

Memory Verse

John 10:10

Start today's study by writing out as much of your memory verse as you can in the space below. Then, look up the verse and make any corrections that are needed. Finally, read it three times from your Bible and take just a moment to pray before completing the following lesson.

---

*Y*esterday we examined some of the basic aspects of the "new life" we have in Christ. Today we will turn our focus toward some more specific things that happen when we enter into the full and abundant new life that Christ offers. For example, our new life should be fruitful. As Christians we are called to be productive and to bear much fruit, but what does this actually mean? What does it look like? And how does it happen? Today we will attempt to answer these questions.

To live a fruitful life means that you are producing something through your faith. Fruit indicates spiritual growth, progress, and reproduction. When we live a focused life and we make it a point to interact with God and others on a regular basis, we grow spiritually, and that leads to spiritual maturity and spiritual fruit that can be seen. Over the years, believers should see their faith progress as well. If you are the same today as you were yesterday, or worse yet, five years ago, there is a problem. Spiritual fruit is a sign that you are living a healthy spiritual life as you progress in your faith. Finally, the signs of spiritual fruit in your life indicates that you are also reproducing. God's plan for humanity has always been for people just like you to tell others and bring them into the faith. When we share our faith, we are participating in the process of reproducing ourselves. Even if those we share with don't respond right away, we can be assured that as we plant and water the seeds, ultimately they will sprout and grow. The bottom line is that all healthy plants produce fruit. However, if you starve them of vital nutrients, sunlight, or water, they will fail to grow, progress, and they will never reproduce. It is not any different for Christians and the fruit we produce is a defining mark for all Christians.

 📖 Look up Matthew 7:15-20. Who does Jesus say you will be able to recognize by their fruit?

_____

_____

 📖 Now read the following verses from John 15 and identify at least one lesson from each passage of scripture as it relates to living a fruitful life.

 • John 15:1-4

_____

_____

 • John 15:5-8

_____

_____

 • John 15:16-17

_____

_____

Now that you have a basic understanding of what it means to live a fruitful life, it is time to examine what this life actually looks like. There are many verses in the Bible that, when combined and understood together, give us an accurate picture of what this kind of life should resemble. However, for the sake of time and space in this basic study, we will only examine three of these passages. Many people think that the fruit of the Spirit is only defined in Galatians 5 because that particular passage actually says *But the fruit of the Spirit is...* The fruitful life that we are equipped and called to live is actually much more extensive than what is mentioned in the passage in Galatians, as you will learn with the following exercise.

📖 Look up Galatians 5:22-26, 2 Peter 1:5-8, and Romans 12:9-18, then list the different things each refers to as qualities we should possess as modern day disciples of Christ. Finally, circle or highlight any that appear in more than one text. Keep in mind that they will probably not be word for word, but rather, concepts that carry over from one text to the other.

Galatians 5:22-26	2 Peter 1:5-8	Romans 12:9-18

❧ Now look at each one of the things listed in the chart, and in the space below, write out how or why you are better at them today than before you knew Christ. You should pick 3 to 5 of the things above to focus on for this assignment.

_____

_____

_____

_____

_____

❧ Of all of the things mentioned earlier in the chart, which five are easiest for you? How does that relate to your spiritual gifts that we discussed in chapter seven of the first volume of *The Absolute Basics of Christianity*?

_____

_____

_____

_____

_____

The final question we must answer is how? How do we receive the ability to produce this kind of fruit? After all, isn't it possible to be kind, considerate, and loving outside of Christ? Most nonbelievers have these traits too, right? After all most people are "good people." While this may be true, there is something different about the fruit of the Spirit—that is, it comes from God, and thus it propels the believer to a new level of kindness, love, grace, mercy, and compassion. Earlier you read verses from John 15, in which Jesus makes it abundantly clear that none of these things are possible unless we are willing to "remain in him." The book of Romans explains it like this.

> So, my brothers, you also died to the law through the body of Christ that you might belong to another, to him who was raised from the dead, in order that we might bear fruit to God. ⁵For when we were controlled by the sinful nature, the sinful passions aroused by the law were at work in our bodies, so that we bore fruit for death. ⁶But now, by dying to what once bound us, we have been released from the law so that we serve in the new way of the Spirit, and not in the old way of the written code.
>
> Romans 7:4-6

Like most people, before you were saved you were likely a "good person." But it was the law that made you good. You were nice to people because you were taught that being nice was the right thing to do. You loved people because they loved you; you were patient with people because you knew you had to be in order to be accepted. The fruit of the Spirit is different, because it comes to those who believe through the blood of Christ. We no longer do it because of the "law"; we do it because it is who we are. This is how we are able to forgive and even pray for our enemies, as Christ commands. We are able to love those who hate us and bless those who curse us. It is not because we are better mannered, or stronger willed; it is because we have been transformed by the blood of Christ Jesus. We have been released from that old law, and we now serve in the new way of the Spirit! The fruitful life is a wonderful and powerful life when it is obtained, fully embraced, and experienced in the life of the modern day disciple.

❧ In closing today, reflect on your own life. Are you living a fruitful life?

_____

_____

Write out your memory verse in the space below. Try to do it completely from memory, then double-check yourself.

TAKE TIME TO PRAY

New Life—Day Three

Memory Verse

John 10:10

Start today's study by writing out as much of your memory verse as you can in the space below. Then, look up the verse and make any corrections that are needed. Finally, read it three times from your Bible and take just a moment to pray before completing the following lesson.

So far this week, we have said that our new life is about living a fruitful life through Jesus Christ. Today we are going to talk about the importance of living a faithful life. Faithfulness is a desirable trait. We want our spouses, children, employer, employees, church, government, and everyone else in general to be faithful. Naturally we expect that they will be faithful and do what they say they will do. Despite good intentions and the best-laid plans, we have all experienced the pain and frustration that comes with unfaithfulness. The fact is that we live in a very unfaithful world. Almost half of all marriages in America end in divorce. Most are a result of some kind of unfaithfulness. In recent years, scandals in the church at-large have involved financial mismanagement, embezzlement, and sexual misconduct, just to name a few. Most people work for companies that will let them go at the first sign of financial trouble because we live in a world that only sees the bottom line. Equally, many employees are quick to jump ship at the first opportunity. We find that more and more children are growing up without fathers, that broken promises from politicians is the norm, and the list can go on and on. The fact is that we live in a world that radiates unfaithfulness. And as a result we live in a world of dissatisfaction, frustration, disappointment, despair, and pain. The new life, the full and abundant life that Christ offers in John 10:10, will only be realized when we learn to live faithful lives.

It would be easy to get wrapped up in some of the specific things in which we should be faithful—things like church attendance, prayer, giving, missions and ministry, marriage; and the list could easily cover many more topics. Instead of bogging down in details, however, let's look at three broader areas that will help us be faithful in these specific areas of life.

The first is learning to be faithful where you are. You must learn this lesson if you want to find the full and abundant life. Contentment is one of the keys to living life as a follower of Jesus Christ. This does not mean that you can't try to improve your situation in life; it simply means that you learn to accept where God has placed you. The full and abundant life is not found in a promotion, new car, new home, or better education. It's right in front of you! It's today, it's right now, it's here. Don't waste it! Learn to be faithful where you are. After all, if you can't be faithful here, what makes you think you will be faithful anywhere at all?

Let's briefly examine the life of King Josiah from the book of 2 Kings. Josiah became king at the age of eight, according to 2 Kings 22:1. This young boy inherits a kingdom that, as far as God is concerned, is in ruins. His father and grandfather were not interested in leading the people the way God had commanded. Instead, it was about money, fame, and power for his ancestors. He did not inherit a perfect kingdom but Josiah decided that he wanted to lead the people in a way that honored God. After some years passed, Josiah decided to send a priest to inquire of a prophet about what would happen to his kingdom. He wanted to know if all his hard work as king would pay off. Read the report he got from the prophet in 2 Kings 22:15-17 and answer the questions below.

> ❧ Did he get good news or bad news from the prophet? What did he say would happen to Josiah's kingdom?

_____

_____

_____

_____

_____

✣ What would you have done at this point after hearing this message from God?

_____

_____

_____

_____

📖 Now read how Josiah responded in 2 Kings 23:3. What did he decide to do?

_____

_____

_____

_____

Now that is an example of faithfulness. This young king said, "I am going to be faithful and lead these people toward God despite knowing in the end that God is going to destroy it all." He could just have easily said "Forget it. Why should I work hard and make all these sacrifices and put up with all these struggles? If you are going to destroy it all, I will just live it up!" Instead, he decided to live a faithful life. So what happened? Well, God was true to His word and everything was ultimately destroyed. But look at 2 Kings 23:25 and see what the Bible records of the life of Josiah.

📖 Fill in the blanks below from 2 Kings 23:25

Neither _____ nor _____ Josiah was there a king

like him who _____ to the LORD as he did—with _____

his heart and with _____ his soul and with _____

his strength, in accordance with all the Law of Moses.

Josiah knew something that few Christians understand today. He understood that being successful and being faithful are not necessarily one in the same. You can be successful without being faithful. And you can be faithful and not be successful. We place too much emphasis on success, when we should be focusing on living faithful lives. To the world, Josiah was a failure because his kingdom was destroyed. But God says there was never any other king like him. If you want to have the full and abundant life that Jesus speaks of in John 10:10, stop chasing after success and start running hard after faithfulness. Learn to be faithful where you are and you will have the life that few find.

Next, we need to learn to be faithful with what we have. Far too many Christians think that if they only had more, they would be happier. As a minister I speak to people from all walks of life, and I can safely say that money, fame, power, and status will not make you happy. In fact, some of the saddest, most depressed people I have ever met are the same people that many Christians pray they will be like one day, not because they are faithful, but instead because they are people who "have things." The beauty of the new life we have in Christ is that it is not contingent upon anything other than Christ. We don't need money or other material things to experience the full and abundant life. You must learn to be faithful with what you have.

 📕 Look at the woman in Luke 21:1-4. What did she have? What did she do with it? Would you say she was faithful?

_____

_____

_____

_____

When I think of people like George Muller, Charles Spurgeon, Mother Teresa, Billy Graham, and the Apostle Paul, I don't think of people who had everything they wanted. I think of people who were faithful with what they had and God blessed them right where they were with what they had. They lived the full and abundant life because they were faithful with what they had. There may be people with more talent, money, power, or fame than you, or people who "just got dealt a better deck" than you did, as they say. But as far as the full and abundant life is concerned, that does not matter. All that matters is that you are faithful with what you have.

The final area in which we must be faithful is the fire. We live in a culture that says we should not have to go through hard times or suffer any in the fire. The problem is that this is not what the Bible teaches. It is easy to be faithful on the mountain top when things are going great, everyone is healthy, the bank account is full, and the kids are bringing home straight A's. But what do you do when life happens and things heat up? Are you faithful or faithless? Do you run *to* God or *from* God? When the fire gets hot, do you let God mold you and refine you further or do you withdraw and seek shelter from the flames? Learning to be faithful in the fires of life is key to living the full and abundant life each and every day.

Most Christians desire to be a piece of fine jewelry that can be worn and proudly shown off to all of the world, but do you realize what it takes to make that gold band on your finger or the pendant on your necklace? That fine piece of jewelry was once a dirty piece of metal that was mined from the earth. It was then heated up and refined to burn out all of its impurities. Gold must be heated up to 1945[31] degrees Fahrenheit before it will begin to melt so that it can be purified and molded. We all want to be that beautiful piece of jewelry but we refuse to go through the fire. The truth of the matter is that if we refuse the fire and are unwilling to be faithful in the fire, we will never be all that God intends, or experience the full and abundant life that he promises.

📖 Does Matthew 7:13-14 sound like an easy life?

_____

_____

_____

_____

📖 According to Isaiah 43:1-3, does God promise that we will not have to go through the fire, or that we will not burn up in the fire? What's the difference? What does that mean to you? How will this change the way you react when life heats up next? ⚒

_____

_____

_____

_____

_____

_____

📖 Can you list the three things we must learn to be faithful to in order to experience the full and abundant life?

_____

_____

_____

_____

---

31 http://www.kitco.com/jewelry/meltingpoints.html.

Write out your memory verse in the space below. Try to do it completely from memory, then double-check yourself.

_____

_____

_____

_____

TAKE TIME TO PRAY

New Life—Day Four

Memory Verse

John 10:10

Start today's study by writing out as much of your memory verse as you can in the space below. Then, look up the verse and make any corrections that are needed. Finally, read it three times from your Bible and take just a moment to pray before completing the following lesson.

The final lesson in this study on new life will revolve around the issue of focus. Being fruitful, and faithful is important but without focus long-term success as a believer is simply not possible. There is no denying that with our new life in Christ comes a new focus on Christ. It is no longer all about us; instead, it is all about him. In Christ we don't make decisions based on what we want; instead, we pray and then move in the direction that God calls us to move, whether it makes sense or not. This tends to be fairly simple and straight-forward at first. However, over time, for some reason or another we lose our focus and we start to fall back into the old life. Do you remember when you first came to know Jesus Christ as your Lord and Savior? You were on top of the world and ready to tell anyone and everyone about all that God had done for you. You were excited to serve at church and participate in all that God was doing in your community. Inevitably, that always seems to change and that early excitement fades and, while we continue to follow Christ, we start to follow at a distance.

   📖 Look up and read Galatians 5:7. Have you ever experienced this? Explain

_____

_____

_____

_____

When my wife and I brought our first child home from the hospital, we entered into a new chapter of life. As we prepared to leave the hospital, we triple-checked the car seat. I checked the tires on the truck and made sure everything was in tip-top shape for our forty-five-minute ride home. As we drove home I had both hands firmly on the wheel and I cruised along at a mind blowing fifty-miles-an-hour. I looked twice as hard at every red light and stop sign. My cell phone rang three times but I ignored it and refused to pick it up. When we got home, I made sure all of the electrical outlets had their covers on them after I got my wife and child settled. Then I proceeded to do many more strange things. Why did I drive slower, pay more attention, and make sure those outlets were covered? After all, a three-day-old infant is not going to walk over and stick something in the electrical socket, right? It seems silly now, but my new life as a father brought a new focus that I had never known before.

It is the same for those who find new life in Christ. There will be a new focus and a new intensity about life. You find yourself doing things you never did before. Your friends and family start to notice that you have changed. Why? Because with a new life in Christ comes a new focus.

   📖 Write out your memory verse (John 10:10) again in the space below.

_____

_____

_____

_____

   ✤ How does this life sound to you?

_____

_____

_____

❧ What are the differences between the life Jesus brings and the old life you once lived that was ruled by the thief in this verse?

_____

_____

_____

❧ What are some things the thief stole from you in the past?

_____

_____

_____

❧ Think back to when you first became a believer. Did you experience a new focus in life? Explain, and give examples in the space below.

_____

_____

_____

❧ How do we receive new life? Write out your memory verses from Romans 10:9 and John 14:6 in the space below. (These verses are from volume one)

_____

_____

_____

_____

_____

For long-term success when it comes to the new life you have in Christ, you need to focus on at least three things. The first is your spiritual maturity. It is imperative that you grow, mature, and develop into the person God has called you to be. As a modern day disciple, you must be intentionally focused on your spiritual maturity because it will not happen unless you work at it. Becoming mature in your faith will require dedication, work, and focus. You should do the following things to keep your spiritual maturity in focus and on course.

1. **Interact with God.** Read your Bible, pray daily, and interact with God. Don't just read, and don't just pray; communicate with God. Listen, meditate, memorize, analyze, and reflect on the things that God is saying and doing in your life.

2. **Interact with others.** You should be involved in your local church and participate in ministry and missions opportunities. Being with your local congregation for worship each week should also be a high priority in your life. When we gather together to magnify God, and when we come together as the body of Christ, we are more likely to remain focused.

📖 Look up the following verses and place a G next to the verses that have to do with interacting with God, and an O next to the verses that have to do with interacting with others. 🛠

- Matthew 28:19-20 _____

- Mark 16:15 _____

- 1 Corinthians 12:25-27 _____

- Ephesians 6:18 _____

- 2 Timothy 3:16-17 _____

- Philemon 6 _____

Next, we must also focus on spiritual relationships. The one true God that we worship has always been and will always be a God of relationships. From the Garden of Eden to this very day, he longs for real relationships with his people. As his children, we should long to have healthy, biblical, lasting, and fulfilling relationships with other people, too. We must be focused on building up these relationships if we want to have long-term success in staying focused. Other people can hold us accountable, keep us on track, or help us get back on track when we stray. They build us up and encourage us when we are down. When you have great relationships with other believers, life is much better. Without healthy, meaningful, spiritual relationships, the full and abundant life that Christ promised will remain out of reach. While he was here on this earth, Christ focused heavily on relationships as he built a team of people to carry on the ministry after he was gone. One of the most fulfilling aspects of our new life in Christ is being able to enjoy spiritual relationships with other believers. We must focus on our relationships.

📖 What does Proverbs 27:17 say about relationships?

_____

_____

According to Hebrews 10:23-25, what are the benefits of having strong re-lationships with other believers?

_____

_____

_____

Finally, to stay focused over the long term as it relates to our new life in Christ, we must focus on our spiritual destiny. In other words, focus on the finish line. Spiritual maturity and spiritual relationships are like the steps in the race we are running. We must focus on each step of the race; we must focus on what is right in front of us or we will trip and fall. However, any great long-distance runner knows that focusing on the finish line is important as well. We don't know where the finish line is in life but we can be sure that we will all one day arrive there, and we can focus on running our race in such a way as to receive the prize upon its completion. Staying focused on the finish line will help us keep going when the race gets hard, when relationships break down or spiritual maturity seems out of reach. Staying focused on the finish line will help us press on when temptations and trials threaten to break us. We must stay focused on our spiritual destiny.

What did Paul say he was straining toward in Philippians 3:13-15?

_____

_____

_____

Describe a time when staying focused on your end goal helped you push through and reach it.

_____

_____

_____

_____

Naturally we tend to focus on negative things in life, but when this happens we are sure to lose sight of the important things that we have gained in our new life with Christ. Your new life in Christ has brought a new focus. Keeping this focus is very important if you desire to enjoy the full and abundant life that Christ offers us in John 10:10.

📖 Look up Philippians 4:8-9 and list all of the things that Paul says we should focus on.

_____

_____

_____

❧ Do we focus enough on these things?

_____

_____

❧ What do we tend to focus on in life?

_____

_____

Your new life should show signs of spiritual fruit as you grow and mature. Your faithfulness and dedication to God and others will increase as your faith grows more and more each day as well. The modern day disciple however must always strive to remain focused. Avoid people and activities that impede your focus, instead we must surround ourselves with other believers who will make every effort to help us remain focused on the purpose and plan God has for our lives. The new life we have received through Christ Jesus was not for us alone. This new life is a gift that we should not only cherish, but that we must share with the world as well.

Write out your memory verse in the space below. Try to do it completely from memory, then double-check yourself.

_____

_____

_____

_____

TAKE TIME TO PRAY

MEMORY VERSE REVIEW

To review, use the space below to write all the memory verses you have learned
so far, including this week's. You can also use this space for personal notes about
this lesson.

_____

_____

_____

_____

_____

_____

_____

_____

_____

_____

_____

_____

_____

_____

_____

_____

_____

_____

_____

Obedience—Day One

Memory Verse

1 John 2:5-6

Start today's study by writing out your memory verse in the space below. Then, read it three times from your Bible and take just a moment to pray before completing the following lesson.

_____

_____

_____

_____

In week four of *The Absolute Basics of Christianity* we learned about discipleship and memorized 1 John 2:6. This week we will add verse five to memory while we discover what it means to be obedient as disciples of Christ Jesus. The Bible speaks a great deal about obedience. Total obedience to God is necessary if we desire to live the full and abundant life that Christ offers us. The truth of the matter is we cannot claim to be Christians and then live our lives as we please and refuse to obey God. Disobedience always leads to sin and many believers today are suffering a great deal simply because they refuse to obey. Until we grasp what it means to be totally obedient to God, we will never reach our full potential in Christ.

📖 Write out your memory verse for this week, 1 John 2:5-6.

_____

_____

_____

_____

❧ What does this verse tell you about obedience?

_____

_____

When I was growing up, I always wanted my parents to answer the question, WHY? Why do I have to do it this way? Why do I have to clean my room? Why do I have to be home at ten? Why can't I have what I want? Why? And the answer to my question never seemed to be sufficient. My parents generally said, "Because I said so..." Now as an adult, I realize that this answer from my parents was sufficient to stand on its own, but as a child it only frustrated me. Today when my parents say something like "because I said so" the answer is sufficient, simply because as I have matured I have also learned that my parents are generally right, and they always have my best interest in mind. Many people have the same issue with obeying God. "Why should I do it?" they ask. To be certain, because God said so should be enough, and as we mature in our faith it will at some point become sufficient as an answer once we learn that we can trust and rely on God in every situation. But until then, we naturally want to know why we should obey. So let's look at a few reasons that may help us answer the question "Why should we obey?"

❧ According to your memory verse for this week, why should we obey?

_____

_____

Obedience is a sign of love. It shows that we trust, respect and love whoever gives the command. When a child obeys a parent, it shows that the child trusts, respects, and loves them. When children don't obey, it is a sign that they don't trust, respect, and love their parents. Almost all parents find themselves in situations, especially in the Terrible 2s and the teenage years, where children reject obedience on a consistent basis. At the heart of the problem are trust, respect, and love. Think about teenagers for a moment. Why are these years full of disobedience? In part it is because, during this time in children's lives, they become increasingly critical and skeptical about everything in the world. What they once blindly trusted now must be proven and verified within themselves before it is accepted. They also begin to identify more with others their own age and they start to respect their peers more than their elders. Furthermore, when they were younger, mom and dad hung the moon; now they start to see that mom and dad are not perfect and they lose some respect that previously was unquestioned. Finally, we arrive at the issue of love. It's not that teenagers no longer love their parents. Rather, the problem is that they now love themselves more. They get a bad case of "me-itis" and it becomes all about them. It's not that they love you less; it is that they love themselves more. These three things combine and can result in many years of disobedience.

As Christians we have the same problems. While we may say in Bible study and at church on Sunday that we trust God, the truth of the matter is that we really don't. We don't trust him enough to "tithe" as he calls us to. We don't trust that he will answer our prayers; we don't believe that he can heal our marriages; we don't trust that he will meet our needs, or comfort our broken hearts. We just don't trust him. We don't respect God in the proper way either. Few truly fear God and respect his authority. And if we are honest, we love ourselves more than we love God. That is not to say we don't love God at all, but we love ourselves more than God. We can see this in the way we spend our money, time, and energy. Read the following verses and describe what they say about obedience being a sign of love.

📖 John 14:15

_____

_____

📖 2 John 1:4-6

_____

_____

Our total obedience to God is also a sign that we know him. When we really understand who God is and what he has done for each of us, we will obey him; when we understand how powerful, mighty, and holy he is, we will desire to obey him. When we truly understand how much he loves us, we can't help but obey him. Our obedience is proof to the world that we understand and know who God is and who it is that we serve.

📖 Based on what 1 John 2:3-4 says, do you think you really know who God is?

_____

_____

_____

As modern day disciples, we should obey God because it shows that we love him and that we know him. But there is a final reason we should choose to obey him. Our obedience is the best thing we can give him. It doesn't matter how much money you have, you could never pay God back for all that he has done for you (John 1:16). No matter how many years you live and how many great things you do for the kingdom, they will never compare or even come close to comparing to what God has done for you. The best thing we can do is to obey him all the days of our lives. This is the greatest gift we can give to God. Close today's lesson by looking up the following passages and reflecting on the verses and questions below.

📖 According to 1 Samuel 15:17-25, what did Saul do wrong? What is God most concerned with? ⚔

_____

_____

📖 Look up Proverbs 21:1-3 and write out verse 3.

_____

_____

_____

📖 According to Mark 12:29-33, what is more important than "all burnt offerings and sacrifices?"

_____

_____

🕊 Can you think of anything that God desires more than obedience?

_____

_____

🕊 Are you living your life in a way that is 100% obedient to God? What are you holding back? What are you keeping for yourself? List these things out and then turn them over to God today!

_____

_____

_____

Write out your memory verse in the space below. Try to do it completely from memory, then double-check yourself.

TAKE TIME TO PRAY

Obedience—Day Two

Memory Verse

1 John 2:5-6

Start today's study by writing out as much of your memory verse as you can in the space below. Then, look up the verse and make any corrections that are needed. Finally, read it three times from your Bible and take just a moment to pray before completing the following lesson.

_____

_____

_____

_____

Yesterday, we started our study on obedience by looking at three reasons why we should be obedient to God. Today, we will look at a few more things that should motivate our obedience to God. Tomorrow we will examine some examples, both positive and negative, from God's word on the issue of obedience. Start today's study by looking up the following passages and figure out what they all have in common in the context of obedience. �֎

📖 Matthew 8:27

_____

_____

📖 Mark 1:25-28

_____

_____

📖 Luke 19:37-40

_____

_____

❧ Now write out your memory verse from Week Two in volume one of *The Absolute Basic's of Christianity* (Matt 28:19-20). Circle the word obey.

_____

_____

_____

_____

_____

_____

_____

As believers, we are called to teach others to obey. How can we do this if we have not learned the lessons of obedience ourselves? How can we teach others to do something we are not doing? Imagine walking into a fitness center to lose weight and requesting a personal trainer's assistance. What would you do if the trainer who was assigned to assist you in losing weight was hundreds of pounds overweight herself? Would you accept her advice? Of course not! Many in the world refuse the advice, counsel, and good intentions of believers because they know we are not practicing what we are preaching. We can't teach others about something we are not currently practicing ourselves. We must learn to be obedient so that we can fulfill the Great Commission and teach others to obey as well.

❧ How can the church fulfill the Great Commission if we are unwilling to be obedient to God? Is there any way?

_____

_____

_____

❧ How do you think your church, community, and the lost world in general would be different if Christians really obeyed God?

_____

_____

_____

When we obey God and do the things he asks us to, we are blessed and life is easier, better, and more fulfilling than if we disobey and attempt to do things alone. Growing up, especially in my teens, like most people I attempted to do things my way whenever I could get away with it. Looking back on those years now, I think about all of the pain, hardship, and suffering that I could have avoided if I had only listened to my parents and the other adults that I disobeyed. Because of my disobedience during those years, I wasted a great deal of time and many opportunities that I can never get back. In the same way, I fear that many Christians will one day look back from heaven on their lives and see how many blessings they missed as a result of their disobedience. Life is much better when we choose to obey God.

📖 According to Luke 11:27-28, who is blessed?

_____

_____

❧ List out as many of the commands that God gives us as believers as you can in the space below.

_____

_____

_____

❧ How many of these things would make your life worse if you did them? 🎬

_____

_____

❧ Looking at these commands, how do you think your life would be better if you obeyed God?

_____

_____

᪣ What does Jesus say in Matthew 11:28-30? Do you think our obedience has anything to do with this? Explain.

_____

_____

_____

We are also rewarded for our obedience. Like any great father, our Father in heaven rewards us for our obedience. But we must obey completely. Too many times, we try to obey part of the command and ignore the other part. Like our own children, we try to do as little as possible to get credit for completing the task. When I was a child and my mother asked me to clean my room, I would stuff my dirty clothes in the space between the bed and the wall, I would hurriedly push my toys into the closest, and I would sweep the dirt under the bed rather then picking it up with the dust pan and taking it to the trash. Sometimes I would get away with this cleaning strategy and receive my reward. However, in a few short days I would be out of clothes, my closet doors would not close as my toys bulged out, and I could no longer hide under my bed during hide-and-seek without emerging covered in filth. Inevitably my mother would see the signs, or find out otherwise, that while it appeared that I was obedient in fulfilling her request, indeed I was at best only partially obedient. Partial obedience is equal to full disobedience. Spiritually speaking, we know that our Father in heaven sees all things and we cannot hide our disobedience from him with partial obedience. We must settle for nothing less than complete obedience, for that is what he desires. Then we will be rewarded. Read the following verses and describe the kind of reward that was received as a result of the characters' obedience.

📖 1 Kings 3:10-14

_____

_____

📖 Proverbs 3:1-10

_____

_____

📖 Proverbs 16:7

_____

_____

📖 John 8:49-51 ⚒

_____

_____

📖 John 14:20-21

_____

_____

❧ Finish today's study by thinking about the following question: Why do you think being totally obedient is so hard?

_____

_____

_____

_____

Write out your memory verse in the space below. Try to do it completely from memory, then double-check yourself.

_____

_____

_____

_____

TAKE TIME TO PRAY

Obedience—Day Three

Memory Verse

1 John 2:5-6

Start today's study by writing out as much of your memory verse as you can in the space below. Then, look up the verse and make any corrections that are needed. Finally, read it three times from your Bible and take just a moment to pray before completing the following lesson.

_____

_____

_____

_____

For the next two days of our study on obedience, we are going to look at some specific examples from the Bible about the effects of obedience and disobedience. The Bible speaks a great deal about the topic of obedience but we can only learn so much by looking at obedience as a topic of scripture. We must now go deeper and see how it affects the lives of those in the Bible and how it affects us today as well. Start today's study by looking at the story that is shared in Luke 5:1-10 and answer the questions below.

❧ Were they obedient or disobedient?

_____

_____

❧ What was the result of their obedience or disobedience?

_____

_____

❧ How was their faith affected by their obedience or disobedience?

_____

_____

❧ How might this apply to us today as modern day disciples? 🎬

_____

_____

_____

We also see many examples of disobedience in the Bible. The main lesson we must learn about disobedience is that our disobedience will always be accompanied by consequences. The Bible says this in Numbers 32:23: *You may be sure that your sin will find you out.* We might be able to fool our friends, family, church, pastor, or boss, but we will never be able to fool God. When we are disobedient, he knows it and it will one day be brought into the light for all to see. We see an example of this in Joshua 7. God has commanded his people to destroy everyone and everything. However, the silver, gold, and other possessions of the people they conquered proved to be too tempting to pass up. So a very clever young man thought he could disobey God and get away with it. However, in Joshua 7:11, God says this, *Israel has sinned; they have violated my covenant, which I commanded them to keep. They have taken some of the devoted things; they have stolen, they have lied, they have put them with their own possessions.* Disobedience always brings consequences, and those are revealed in Joshua 7:16-26. Read that passage and answer the questions below.

❧ Were they obedient or disobedient?

_____

_____

❧ What was the result of their obedience or disobedience?

_____

_____

ᘍ How was their faith affected by their obedience or disobedience?

_____

_____

ᘍ How might this apply to us today as modern day disciples?

_____

_____

The next passage you will examine comes from the gospel of John. This happens near the end of Jesus' ministry, on the last night he would spend with his disciples before being arrested, tried, beaten, and ultimately killed on the cross. As Jesus spent time with those he loved, he displayed one of the most telling and amazing things of his entire ministry. However, there was one disciple who was unwilling to submit and obey Christ as he attempted to serve his disciples. Read the passage found in John 13:2-10 and answer the questions below.

ᘍ Who is Jesus speaking to when he says, "Unless I wash you, you have no part with me."

_____

_____

ᘍ Was this disciple obedient or disobedient?

_____

_____

ᘍ What did the disciple decide to do?

_____

_____

ᘍ How do you think his faith was affected by this event?

_____

_____

ᘍ How might this apply to us today as modern day disciples?

_____

_____

Being obedient to Christ and to the will of God is impossible if we are unwilling to make Christ the center of our lives. We must be willing to become less in order that he might become more. Jesus shows us what this attitude looks like as he prays in the garden just before they come to arrest him. Read the following scriptures and answer the questions that go with each set of verses.

   📖 Read Luke 22:39-44. What was the attitude of Jesus in these verses?

_____

_____

_____

   ❧ Who was he focused on?

_____

_____

_____

   📖 Now read Matthew 16:21-25. What was the attitude of Peter like in these verses?

_____

_____

_____

   ❧ What did Jesus say was Peter's problem? Is this still a problem for believers today? ⚒

_____

_____

_____

   ❧ Who was Peter focused on?

_____

_____

_____

❧ After reading these two passages, how important do you think focus is when it comes to obedience?

_____

_____

_____

❧ Is your focus in the right place? How is that affecting your obedience to Christ?

_____

_____

_____

Write out your memory verse in the space below. Try to do it completely from memory, then double-check yourself.

_____

_____

_____

_____

TAKE TIME TO PRAY

Obedience—Day Four

Memory Verse

1 John 2:5-6

Start today's study by writing out as much of your memory verse as you can in the space below. Then, look up the verse and make any corrections that are needed. Finally, read it three times from your Bible and take just a moment to pray before completing the following lesson.

_____

_____

_____

_____

Today, we will conclude our week focusing on being obedient to God. Obedience is key to the life of any believer because it is impossible to please or serve God unless we learn how to be totally obedient to the will of our Father. Yesterday, we looked at some examples of those who were, and were not, obedient to God. Today, we will examine some additional scriptures that will once again show us the value of obedience. Start today's study by looking at the life of Jonah. Look up and read Jonah 1:1-17, then read Jonah 3:1-5 as well.

❧ Was Jonah obedient or disobedient? Explain.

_____

_____

❦ Who was Jonah focused on?

□ Himself

□ God

❦ What was the result of Jonah's disobedience?

_____

_____

❦ What was the result of Jonah's obedience?

_____

_____

❦ How do you think Jonah's faith was affected by this event? What do you think he learned?

_____

_____

❦ How might this apply to modern day disciples?

_____

_____

Next, we will look at the encounter Philip had with the eunuch in Acts 8:26-40. Unlike Jonah, Phillip is obedient to God and open to sensing how the Spirit is moving in his life. Read this passage in Acts 8:26-40 and answer the questions below.

❦ What differences do you see between Jonah and Philip as it relates to obedience?

_____

_____

_____

❦ How do you think an experience like this would affect your faith?

_____

_____

ᚹ Do you think that God still speaks to us, like he did to Philip, through the Spirit? ✺

_____

_____

Finally, we will look at Paul's wonderful description of Christ's obedience in Philippians 2:1-11. After you read those verses, answer the questions below.

ᚹ What do you think was the reason Christ remained totally obedient throughout his ministry?

_____

_____

_____

ᚹ How has Christ's obedience affected each of us? How would our eternal lives be different had he chosen to be disobedient?

_____

_____

_____

ᚹ After doing this study on obedience, why do you think it is so difficult to be totally obedient to God?

_____

_____

_____

ᚹ How will your life be different as a result of this week's lesson? What will you change, and what will you watch out for in your own life?

_____

_____

_____

_____

꙳ Finally, what areas of your life need the most attention when it comes to obedience? What has God told you to do that you are currently not doing? List the steps necessary to change your disobedience into full obedience.

_____

_____

_____

_____

Obedience will never be easy, but it is necessary for anyone who dares to follow Christ. We cannot claim to be Christ's followers and refuse or disobey the orders of Christ. As believers, we must follow his instructions to the letter, despite what we think, what we want, or how we feel. Being obedient starts with understanding that God is in control and we are not. Until we are willing to fully submit our lives and place them under God's control, total obedience will be impossible. Anything less than total obedience is complete disobedience in the eyes of God. We cannot be partially compliant and expect to receive or be the blessing that God intends.

Write out your memory verse in the space below. Try to do it completely from memory, then double-check yourself.

_____

_____

_____

_____

TAKE TIME TO PRAY

To review, use the space below to write all the memory verses you have learned so far, including this week's. You can also use this space for personal notes about this lesson.

_____

_____

_____

_____

_____

_____

_____

_____

_____

_____

_____

_____

_____

_____

_____

_____

_____

Prayer—Day One

Memory Verse

1 Thessalonians 5:16-18

Start today's study by writing out your memory verse in the space below. Then, read it three times from your Bible and take just a moment to pray before completing the following lesson.

_____

_____

_____

_____

F. B. Meyer once said, "The greatest tragedy of life is not unanswered prayer, but unoffered prayer." Prayer is powerful; in fact, it is the most powerful tool we have as believers, yet many times we fail to unleash this incredible weapon of faith. If we prayed more, we would accomplish more than we could ever dream of. But the problem is that for one reason or another, we simply fail to pray. For this week's study you should focus on more than the scriptures that you are required to look up and the verse you are asked to memorize. Over the next four days, you should focus not on learning about prayer, but instead on actually praying. Make prayer a priority for the coming week and I promise you will not be disappointed.

There are many different models and methods that can be used to teach or explain prayer to others. When I was a new believer, a friend told me about the ACTS acronym that guides my prayer life to this day. In my opinion, what is most appealing about this method is that it is scalable. In other words, as you grow as a Christian and as your prayer life matures, this method grows as well. The ACTS acronym is easy to remember and it does not tell you how to pray, but instead guides you through your daily prayers. ACTS stands for:

*A*doration

*C*onfession

*T*hanksgiving

*S*upplication

While you certainly do not have to do these four things in any particular order, I would encourage you to start with adoration as often as possible. Of these four things, adoration is the one we tend to overlook most often. If we put it off until the end of our prayer, we are likely to forget it all together or simply become too involved in one of the other three areas. Therefore we should do it first so that we are certain to include it in our prayers. What is adoration, though? Here are several definitions of the word:

1. In the strictest sense, it's an act of religion offered to God in acknowledgment of His supreme perfection and dominion, and of the creature's dependence upon Him; in a lesser sense, the reverence shown to any person or object possessing inherently, or by association, a sacred character or a high degree of moral excellence.[32]

2. Someone once said that it is the supreme act of worship.

3. Profound love or regard.[33]

4. The act of paying honor, as to a divine being; worship. Reverent homage. Fervent and devoted love.[34]

⊱ Below write your own definition of the word adoration based on what you know so far.

_____

_____

_____

---

32 "Catholic Encyclopedia: Adoration," New Advent. http://www.newadvent.org/cathen/01151a. htm (accessed April 27, 2010).

33 "Adoration," The Free Dictionary, http://www.thefreedictionary.com/adoration (accessed April 27, 2010).

34 "Adoration," Dictionary.com, http://dictionary.reference.com/browse/adoration (accessed April 27, 2010).

Adoration is about God not you! It has nothing to do with your circumstances, wants, needs, desires, troubles, temptations, or trials. More specifically, it is about praising God and glorifying him. Some find this concept to be easy to remember by saying "We are adorning God with our praise." This sounds like a simple task but you will find that it is difficult to leave yourself out of your prayers. For example, read the statements below and select the one that exhibits adoration in the purest sense of the word. Explain why the other statement is not adoration. ✗

1. Thank you for being mighty to save.
2. Thank you for saving me from my sins.

1. God I am amazed at your wonderful creation.
2. God your creation is amazing.

1. Lord, I need your help...
2. Lord, your strength, might, and power are limitless

Finally, before moving on to the next part of the ACTS acronym, look up the following two verses that serve as great examples of what adoration actually is. Then write out some of your own short statements of adoration.

📖 Psalms 145:3

- Who can fathom His greatness?

_____

_____

_____

_____

📖 Psalms 147:1-5

- What do you think about verse four?

_____

_____

_____

_____

❧ To make sure you understand this concept of adoration, take some time to think about and write down your own statements of adoration in the space below. Try to do at least three. When you are done, pause for a minute and use them to adorn God with praise through prayer.

_____

_____

_____

_____

_____

The final three things are fairly self-explanatory and we tend to do them more often than adoration. Therefore, we will spend less time examining their meanings. The C stands for Confession.

❧ Define in your own words what confession means in the context of prayer.

_____

_____

_____

📖 According to Psalms 66:18, why is it important for us to confess our sins?

_____

_____

_____

❧ What do you think happens if we forget to confess a sin? Or what happens if we die before we are able to confess a sin? Will our eternal salvation be secure? Explain. ✗

_____

_____

_____

Next, we should spend some time giving thanks to God. Thanksgiving is when we get to thank God for the things he has done for us specifically.

Earlier, you read some statements that illustrated what adoration sounds like in our prayers. The other statement in each pair was a statement of thanksgiving. There is nothing wrong with thanksgiving; in fact, it should be a major part of our prayer life. But adoration should be as well. Go back and review those statements one more time and see if you can see the difference between thanksgiving and adoration once again.

❧ Write out your memory verse below.

_____

_____

_____

_____

❧ Now write out your memory verse from Week Ten, "Joy," in volume one of *The Absolute Basics of Christianity*, Philippians 4:4.

_____

_____

_____

_____

❧ According to your memory verse, when should we give thanks?

_____

_____

📖 According to Philippians 4:4, when should we rejoice?

_____

_____

❧ How would your life be different if you did these two things regularly?

_____

_____

_____

_____

�＆ Write out your definition of thanksgiving in the context of prayer. How is this different from adoration?

_____

_____

_____

Finally, supplication is when the worshipper comes to God and makes requests. These requests might be personal or they might be intercessory prayers on behalf of others. The worshiper might pray for good health, or for help in overcoming an obstacle in life, or one might pray that a family member or friend comes through an operation, or that a co-worker might accept Jesus as their Lord and Savior. Generally, we are good at supplication. Most people spend the majority of their prayer time making requests of God and asking him to meet their needs. However, when our prayer life is balanced with a healthy dose of "adoration," "confession," "thanksgiving," and "supplication," our times of prayer go to an entirely different level. Those who desire to worship God through their prayers should be engaged in all four of these areas.

📖 What does Philippians 4:6 tell us to do when it comes to prayer?

_____

_____

📖 Look up John 15:7. Does it seem as though Jesus is discouraging us from asking God for things? Explain.

_____

_____

_____

_____

📖 In the context of prayer, what does Moses do in Exodus 32:30-34?

_____

_____

📖 What is Paul's prayer in Romans 10:1?

_____

_____

❧ Fill in the ACTS acronym below and explain what each letter stands for in your own words.

- **A**_____

  _____

  _____

- **C**_____

  _____

  _____

- **T**_____

  _____

  _____

- **S**_____

  _____

  _____

Close today's lesson by practicing what you have learned about prayer so far. As you pray, be intentional about being engaged in all four areas of the ACTS prayer model. Prayer is powerful, but only if we do it!

Write out your memory verse in the space below. Try to do it completely from memory, then double-check yourself.

TAKE TIME TO PRAY

Prayer—Day Two

Memory Verse

1 Thessalonians 5:16-18

Start today's study by writing out as much of your memory verse as you can in the space below. Then, look up the verse and make any corrections that are needed. Finally, read it three times from your Bible and take just a moment to pray before completing the following lesson.

_____

_____

_____

_____

*Y*esterday we began our study on prayer by looking at the acronym ACTS as a basic model for prayer. Remember that doing these things in order is not as important as doing all four of these things when we pray. Our prayer life should be consistent, and it must be balanced. Using the ACTS model on a regular basis will help develop both consistency and balance in your prayer life as a modern day disciple.

❧ What does ACTS stand for? Write out a short description and an example for each letter below.

• **A**_____

_____

_____

- **C**_____

  _____

  _____

- **T**_____

  _____

  _____

- **S**_____

  _____

  _____

To make sure that you have a great understanding of what ACTS prayers looks and sounds like, your assignment for today is to look up the scriptures below and carefully examine some of the prayers found in the Bible. As you read these prayers, your goal is to identify how the worshiper engaged God through prayer as it relates to the ACTS model. Remember that they probably will not be in that exact order. These prayers will also contain things that may not fit into any of the ACTS categories. Make sure you read each prayer several times to ensure that you have adequately identified as many of the ACTS categories as possible. Take good notes so that you can reference these prayers in your small group time.

📖 Nehemiah 1:1-11. This is a great prayer and while some of the ACTS are easy to find, a few are more difficult. ⚒

- **A**_____

  _____

  _____

  _____

- **C**_____

  _____

  _____

  _____

- **T**_____

  _____

  _____

  _____

- **S**_____

  _____

  _____

  _____

What other things do you see in this prayer?

_____

_____

_____

What did you learn from this prayer that could apply to your prayer life today?

_____

_____

_____

John 17:1-26. This is a huge prayer from the lips of Christ. There are many examples of each of the ACTS. ✘

- **A**_____

  _____

  _____

  _____

- **C**_____

  _____

_____

_____

- **T**_____

_____

_____

_____

- **S**_____

_____

_____

_____

❧ What other things do you see in this prayer?

_____

_____

❧ What did you learn from this prayer that could apply to your prayer life today?

_____

_____

📖 Genesis 32:9-12. ⚒

- **A**_____

_____

_____

_____

- **C**_____

_____

_____

_____

- **T**_____

  _____

  _____

  _____

- **S**_____

  _____

  _____

  _____

❧ What other things do you see in this prayer?

_____

_____

_____

❧ What did you learn from this prayer that could apply to your prayer life today?

_____

_____

_____

_____

📖 Psalms 51:1-17. ⚒

- **A**_____

  _____

  _____

  _____

- **C**_____

  _____

_____

_____

- **T**_____

_____

_____

_____

- **S**_____

_____

_____

_____

❧ What other things do you see in this prayer?

_____

_____

❧ What did you learn from this prayer that could apply to your prayer life today?

_____

_____

_____

These four prayers are only a sample of the many prayers in the Bible that exhibit the ACTS model. These men prayed long before the ACTS acronym was coined and made popular. They did not pray from a model; they prayed from their hearts to a God they knew personally. The ACTS model for prayer is just a guide, and we must not get so caught up in making sure that we have equal doses of adoration, confession, thanksgiving, and supplication that we forget what prayer is. Prayer is about communicating with God. It is about speaking to and hearing from the Creator of the universe. Let the ACTS model guide your spirit, but do not let it consume you as you pray. Over time you will find that these four things will become second nature and you will naturally do them in random orders and in varying amounts, depending on how God is moving in your life.

Write out your memory verse in the space below. Try to do it completely from memory, then double-check yourself.

TAKE TIME TO PRAY

Prayer—Day Three

Memory Verse

1 Thessalonians 5:16-18

Start today's study by writing out as much of your memory verse as you can in the space below. Then, look up the verse and make any corrections that are needed. Finally, read it three times from your Bible and take just a moment to pray before completing the following lesson.

In previous lessons we have started with the basics of a subject or topic, then moved on to the issue of "how to." This week, however, it was more important that you understood the aspect of how to pray and start using the ACTS model first. Now we can turn our attention to some of the basics, and indeed, the finer details about prayer.

Christians in general agree that we should all pray. Most believers, if they were honest, would also admit that they should pray more. Many people pray once or twice a day and those prayers in general last only a few brief minutes, or at times, seconds. Most people spend the majority of their prayer time on the S and C of the ACTS model. Occasionally they will venture into the T area, and we almost never truly practice the A. To put it bluntly, our prayers are more about us than they are anything else. This has happened because prayer requires one thing that we cannot make, invent, save, or control. It requires our time and we never seem to have enough of it. When we try to fit our prayers into a certain amount of time at the dinner table, just before we fall asleep, or as we drive to work going eighty miles-an-hour and praying we hit all the green lights so we won't be late, we just don't have much room for anything but ourselves in our prayers. Our natural instinct is to take care of our own needs first and then, if there is time, we will get to the other aspects of prayer, but there never seems to be enough time. It is similar to the concept we discussed in Week Thirteen on money. We naturally try to manage our money by spending first, saving second, and then giving third, and we wonder why there is never enough. There is never enough because we are not doing it in the right order. When we give first, save second, and spend third there is always enough. When it comes to prayer we should start in the same place we do with our money—not with ourselves (spending) but instead with God. Then, we should pray for others, and finally, conclude with our own needs. I have found this to be a great way to ensure that I take the time that God deserves when it comes to prayer.

ek Can you list what ACTS stands for?

_____

_____

_____

_____

ek How would you explain each letter to a friend or family member?

_____

_____

_____

_____

ek Prior to this week's study, how did you spend your prayer time? Rank each of the areas of the ACTS model below. Place the percentage that you estimate you prayed in each area below. Your total should add up to 100%.

A _____ C _____ T _____ S _____

A common question about prayer is when we should we do it. Look up the following scriptures, and in the space provided, write out what they say about when we should pray

📖 Ephesians 6:18

_____

_____

📖 1 Thessalonians 5:16-18

_____

_____

📖 James 5:13

_____

_____

📖 Philippians 4:6

_____

_____

📖 Colossians 4:2

_____

_____

📖 Luke 18:1

_____

_____

Tragically, we have been successful in making prayer nothing more than an event in our day. It is an event in our worship services at our dinner tables, and at our children's bedsides. We live our lives all day long and then at certain times we pray. We can then check it off the list and move on with other events in our day. Prayer was never intended to be an event; instead, when it is properly understood, it is a way of being for the modern day disciple. Prayer is not something we do as much as something we are. We are children of God, so naturally we should talk to him throughout the day, just like we would our own children. Our children are not check-boxes in our day, or an event on the agenda (at least they shouldn't be); they are a part of us. Raising children is a lifestyle, not an event. Prayer is a lifestyle as well.

❧ Honestly, has your prayer life in the past been an event or a lifestyle? What has it been for the last month?

_____

_____

_____

❧ What do you want it to be: a lifestyle or an event? If change is needed, how do you plan to accomplish the change? What steps do you need to take to ensure that you live a lifestyle of prayer?

_____

_____

_____

I was recently asked an interesting question about prayer. "Pastor, why don't I ever feel like I hear God when I pray?" "How long do you generally pray" I asked. "On average maybe three to five minutes a few times a day," the man said. I responded, "Of that three to five minutes in prayer, how long do you listen?" The man looked at the floor, and said "Good point." We have made prayer all about us, when it should be all about God. Because it is all about us, we talk, and when we are done, we leave. Then we wonder why we never hear from God. The answer is simple: it's because we never listen. It has been said that God gave us one mouth and two ears so we would be reminded to listen twice as much as we talk. But who has the time to listen? When we rush our prayers, we virtually never listen. I have found that the sweetest moments in my day come as I sit in silence, waiting for God's voice to pierce my heart and speak to my soul. Stillness and silence are wonderful things that most of us never enjoy, but they are necessary if we are going to hear from God.

📖 Look up and read Matthew 14:23, Matthew 26:36, Luke 6:12, John 6:15-16. What do you notice that all of these verses have in common?

_____

_____

❧ Why do you think Jesus did this?

_____

_____

Close the lesson today with prayer. Use the ACTS model that we discussed in Days One and Two but take your time as you pray. Make it a point to pause and listen—not for seconds, but instead for minutes. This will be difficult at first and the enemy will attempt to cloud your mind and heart with many things. Don't give up; stay focused and be patient. God desires to hear from us when we pray, but he also desires to speak to us. When our desire to hear from him equals his desire to hear from us, we find ourselves in the sweet lifestyle of praying without ceasing.

Write out your memory verse in the space below. Try to do it completely from memory, then double-check yourself.

TAKE TIME TO PRAY

Prayer—Day Four

Memory Verse

1 Thessalonians 5:16-18

Start today's study by writing out as much of your memory verse as you can in the space below. Then, look up the verse and make any corrections that are needed. Finally, read it three times from your Bible and take just a moment to pray before completing the following lesson.

So far this week, we have looked at the ACTS model that can be used to guide our personal prayer life. Yesterday we talked about when we should pray, as well as the emphasis on "listening" that must accompany our prayers. To finish our study on prayer, we will tackle the question, "Why should I pray?"

The first reason that the modern day disciple should pray is because it is necessary. There is nothing more important than prayer in the life of a believer. Our power, strength, understanding, wisdom, and patience all come from prayer. When we fail to pray, we fail at all we attempt in this life. Having an active and fulfilling prayer life takes time but we cannot afford to *not* spend time in prayer. It is vital to the life of a believer. Martin Luther was as busy as any Christian, yet he said, "I have so much business I cannot get on without spending three hours daily in prayer."[35] John Wesley said, "God does nothing but in answer to prayer." He backed up his conviction by devoting two hours daily to that sacred exercise.[36] Prayer is vitally important for those who desire to be used by God. It is of utmost importance that we do not neglect the honor of spending our lives consumed in prayer.

Some people contend that prayer is not vital for believers because God has already decided what the outcome will be for any situation. So if it can't be changed, why pray? Furthermore, why should we pray if God already knows what we are thinking and feeling? Look up the following scriptures and you decide what the Bible has to say about these two questions.

📖 Exodus 32:9-14

____

____

📖 Jonah 3:1-10

____

____

Paul contends in both First and Second Corinthians that we are "God's fellow workers" (1 Cor 3:9; 2 Cor 6:1). The Hebrew word used in the passage in Exodus and Jonah is *nacham*, which can also mean "to change one's mind." When we examine the prayers that people like David, Nehemiah, Abraham, Paul, Peter, and Jesus prayed, it is easy to see that they prayed with the expectations that their prayers carried the possibility of making a difference. We must be careful not to assume that just because we pray, God will change everything. However, we can be assured that God hears and considers our prayers. To this point, Robert Foster writes, "This comes as a genuine liberation to many of us, but it also sets tremendous responsibility before us. We are working with God to determine the future! Certain things will happen in history if we pray rightly. We are to change the world by prayer. What more motivation do we need to learn this loftiest human exercise?"[37]

📖 Read Matthew 7:7-11. According to these verses, why do you think we should pray? ⚒

____

____

35 Richard J. Foster, *Celebration of Discipline: The Path to Spiritual Growth*, 3rd ed. (Harper San Francisco, 1998), 34.

36 Ibid., 34

37 Ibid., 35.

📖 Read 1 Timothy 2:1-8. According to these verses, why should we pray? ⚒

_____

_____

📖 According to 1 John 5:13-15, why should we pray? ⚒

_____

_____

📖 According to Jeremiah 33:1-3, why should we pray? ⚒

_____

_____

The modern day disciple should pray for all of the above reasons. However the main reason we pray is because we want to. The follower of Christ longs to be in constant communication with Jesus. It is a privilege and an honor to be able to communicate with the Creator of the universe through prayer. Those who understand the power of prayer will never waste a single moment that could be spent praying.

Write out your memory verse in the space below. Try to do it completely from memory then double-check yourself.

_____

_____

_____

_____

TAKE TIME TO PRAY

To review, use the space below to write all the memory verses you have learned so far, including this week's. You can also use this space for personal notes about this lesson.

_____

_____

_____

_____

_____

_____

_____

_____

_____

_____

_____

_____

_____

_____

_____

_____

_____

Quiet Time—Day One

Memory Verse

Psalms 23:1-3

Start today's study by writing out your memory verse in the space below. Then, read it three times from your Bible and take just a moment to pray before completing the following lesson.

This week's study is going to be unlike any other study in *The Absolute Basics of Christianity*. You will not be asked to look up and examine scriptures this week based on the topic for the week. Instead, you will be required to pull together everything you have learned from the past seventeen weeks and put it into action by practicing a quiet time for the next four days. Each day will begin with a simple lesson that you should read before moving on to the scripture and prayer journal, which will follow on the next two pages. Each lesson will require twenty-five to forty minutes to complete. You should do your best to ensure that you will have uninterrupted time for these four lessons.

The term "quiet time" can sound a bit simplistic and perhaps "cheesy" at first. However, setting time aside each day to spend with God in silence will help you mature and grow as a believer. Last week, as we studied the importance of prayer, we learned that Jesus took many opportunities during his earthly ministry to get away from the crowds and in many cases, the disciples, to spend "quiet time" with his Father in heaven. If it was important to Jesus, it should be important to us as well.

The devil will do all he can to distract you from spending time alone in the stillness of God's presence. He knows that it is in these times, alone with God, that you will be transformed, encouraged, strengthened, and moved by the still small voice of the almighty God. For this reason you need to *set* four things to increase your chances of success in having a regular quiet time.

1. **Set a time.** Select a time each day to meet with God. Choose a time when you are most likely to be alert and prepared to meet with God. Do not give God the leftovers of your day; give him the best. Set a time and stick to it!

2. **Set a place.** Find a place that is free from distractions. Turn off your cell phone and computer and anything else that might distract you. Find a quiet secluded place for your quiet times.

3. **Set a goal.** Set a goal to spend a certain amount of time with God each day. This time should increase as you mature in your faith. You will find that you desire to spend more and more time with God as you grow. Set a goal and stick with it, even if you don't hear him speaking and have nothing left to say. Stay and enjoy the sweet stillness of resting in his holy presence.

4. **Set your mind.** You must make up your mind that no matter what, you will meet God in this place and this time, and will meet this goal every day. As you grow and this becomes a part of your lifestyle, it will be much more difficult for the devil to distract you, but for now you must set your mind and do this every day, no matter what!

Now that you have set these four things, you are ready to start your first guided quiet time with God. This week you will be reading the book of Philippians. Start each day with a short prayer, and then read the chapter that is assigned for the day at least once. It would be best if you took time to read the chapter twice. Once you have read the chapter, fill in each box in the scripture journal. If you have difficulty filling in a box, go back and read the scripture again, or pray and then consider the question again.

Close your study by spending some time in prayer. It is recommended that you devote a minimum of ten minutes to prayer for each study. No matter how long you pray do your best to spend at least half of the time simply listening to God. Conclude your study by filling in the prayer journal.

SCRIPTURE JOURNAL

Book Name: **Philippians**   Chapter: __1__   Date: _____

Cross References	How do these verses apply to your life today?
	What promises are in these verses?
Key Verses	*What commands are in these verses for you to follow?*
Key Words/Concepts	*After reading these verses what do you most need to work on or change?*
	Other notes, thoughts or ideas...

PRAYER JOURNAL

Today I prayed:

- A _____
- C _____
- T _____
- S _____

God has answered the following prayers:

_____

_____

As I silenced my thoughts and mind, I heard or sensed God saying:

_____

_____

After praying I feel like I need to take the following specific action:

_____

_____

Before I prayed I was feeling...

_____

_____

After praying I feel...

_____

_____

Other notes or thoughts about today:

_____

_____

_____

Write out your memory verse in the space below. Try to do it completely from memory, then double-check yourself.

Quiet Time—Day Two

Memory Verse

Psalms 23:1-3

Start today's study by writing out as much of your memory verse as you can in the space below. Then, look up the verse and make any corrections that are needed. Finally, read it three times from your Bible and take just a moment to pray before completing the following lesson.

_____

_____

_____

_____

*B*eing prepared to meet with God is critical when it comes to having a successful quiet time. Take the story of Moses at the burning bush, for example. God calls out to Moses and commands him not to come any closer until he removes his sandals. *Do not come any closer*, God said. *Take off your sandals, for the place where you are standing is holy ground* (Exod 3:5). This ground was holy because God's presence was there. We know that God is with us and he has an active presence in our lives despite our physical location. So in a sense, every square inch of the earth is holy ground. God commanded Moses to remove his sandals due to the way that Moses was rushing into the presence of God. We see in this encounter that it is only after Moses pauses to remove his sandals that he fully comprehends that he is in the presence of God. At this point, he places his face on the ground and worships.

How often do we rush into God's holy presence? In our busy, hectic, crazy world, we seldom have the time to stop and remove our sandals. As a result we forget how special, how intimate, and how amazing it is to be in the presence of the one and only holy God. When we take the time to pause and truly consider that when we pray and read God's word we are actually in his holy presence, then and only then do we actually understand the power of these brief moments in our day. When we take the time to prepare and enter into his presence with our hearts in order, we are certain to get so close to the living God that we can feel the warmth of his holy breath filling our soul. How sweet it is!

SCRIPTURE JOURNAL

Book Name: **Philippians**   Chapter: **2**   Date: _____

Cross References	How do these verses apply to your life today?
	What promises are in these verses?
Key Verses	What commands are in these verses for you to follow?
Key Words/Concepts	After reading these verses what do you most need to work on or change?
	Other notes, thoughts or ideas...

PRAYER JOURNAL

Today I prayed:

- A _____

- C _____

- T _____

- S _____

God has answered the following prayers:

_____

_____

As I silenced my thoughts and mind, I heard or sensed God saying:

_____

_____

After praying I feel like I need to take the following specific action:

_____

_____

Before I prayed I was feeling...

_____

_____

After praying I feel...

_____

_____

Other notes or thoughts about today:

_____

_____

_____

Write out your memory verse in the space below. Try to do it completely from memory, then double-check yourself.

Quiet Time—Day Three

Memory Verse

Psalms 23:1-3

Start today's study by writing out as much of your memory verse as you can in the space below. Then, look up the verse and make any corrections that are needed. Finally, read it three times from your Bible and take just a moment to pray before completing the following lesson.

_____

_____

_____

_____

People often remark, "Why should I spend quiet times with God? After all, I already know him, and I am going to heaven. My day is just too busy, and time is too short to give up thirty minutes to pause, read my Bible, and pray." As a pastor, my day is as busy as the next guy's. There are endless amounts of administrative tasks, meetings, reports and budgets to review, staff issues, families in need, events to organize, hospital visits to make, phone calls and emails to return, and the list goes on. But I have learned that the most valuable time in my day are the moments I spend in the stillness with God. There are three specific reasons why spending time alone with God is valuable to me:

First, it charges me up. When I have finished spending time alone with God, I always fill refreshed and fully charged. Even when God rebukes or corrects me, I come away with a new sense of purpose and clear direction that encourages me and fills my cup. Only when my cup is overflowing with the grace and goodness of God can I really meet all the demands of the day and be a blessing to others. Time with God charges my soul and gives me strength for the day.

The second thing it does is to challenge me. As I read God's word, I am challenged to be a better husband, father, friend, minister, and follower of Christ. There is a challenge on every page of God's word and when I humbly consider those challenges and apply them to my life, I grow and mature in my faith. When I am challenged spiritually, I remain alert, sharp, and ready for whatever the enemy might throw my way.

The final thing that time alone with God does for me is to bring about change in my life. God's written word is useful to remind me of how much farther I have to go as a believer. As I pray and encounter God through the Spirit, I am challenged to change as well. When you come into the presence of God it is so overwhelming you cannot help being changed.

Spending time alone with God does take time; it does require sacrifice, discipline, and dedication. But anyone who has attempted it and stayed with it will tell you it is worth it!

SCRIPTURE JOURNAL

Book Name: __*Philippians*__   Chapter: __**3**__ Date: _____

Cross References	How do these verses apply to your life today?
	What promises are in these verses?
Key Verses	*What commands are in these verses for you to follow?*
Key Words/Concepts	*After reading these verses what do you most need to work on or change?*
	Other notes, thoughts or ideas...

PRAYER JOURNAL

Today I prayed:

- A _____

- C _____

- T _____

- S _____

God has answered the following prayers:

_____

_____

As I silenced my thoughts and mind, I heard or sensed God saying:

_____

_____

After praying I feel like I need to take the following specific action:

_____

_____

Before I prayed I was feeling...

_____

_____

After praying I feel...

_____

_____

Other notes or thoughts about today:

_____

_____

_____

Write out your memory verse in the space below. Try to do it completely from memory, then double-check yourself.

Quiet Time—Day Four

Memory Verse

Psalms 23:1-3

Start today's study by writing out as much of your memory verse as you can in the space below. Then, look up the verse and make any corrections that are needed. Finally, read it three times from your Bible and take just a moment to pray before completing the following lesson.

Today you will finish this part of our study on spending quiet times with God by reading Philippians 4. Before you do that however, you should take some time to answer the following questions and be prepared to discuss them in your next small group or Bible study session. If you are not in a small group study, you should find a committed believer and discuss your answers with them.

    ৳ What did you find most difficult about this week's study? What was the best or easiest part of the study?

_____

_____

_____

ᵛ What prayers did God answer in your life this week?

_____

_____

_____

_____

_____

ᵛ What did you learn from God's word this week? Be specific.

_____

_____

_____

_____

ᵛ What book of the Bible do you plan to read next for your quiet times?

_____

_____

_____

_____

ᵛ How has this week's study helped you grow in your faith as a believer?

_____

_____

_____

_____

_____

SCRIPTURE JOURNAL

Book Name: **Philippians**   Chapter: **4**   Date: _____

Cross References	How do these verses apply to your life today?
	What promises are in these verses?
Key Verses	What commands are in these verses for you to follow?
Key Words/Concepts	After reading these verses what do you most need to work on or change?
	Other notes, thoughts or ideas...

PRAYER JOURNAL

Today I prayed:

- A _____
- C _____
- T _____
- S _____

God has answered the following prayers:

_____

_____

As I silenced my thoughts and mind, I heard or sensed God saying:

_____

_____

After praying I feel like I need to take the following specific action:

_____

_____

Before I prayed I was feeling...

_____

_____

After praying I feel...

_____

_____

Other notes or thoughts about today:

_____

_____

_____

Write out your memory verse in the space below. Try to do it completely from memory, then double-check yourself.

To review, use the space below to write all the memory verses you have learned so far, including this week's. You can also use this space for personal notes about this lesson.

_____

_____

_____

_____

_____

_____

_____

_____

_____

_____

_____

_____

_____

_____

_____

_____

_____

_____

_____

Revelation—Day One

Memory Verse

2 Timothy 3:16-17

Start today's study by writing out your memory verse in the space below. Then, read it three times from your Bible and take just a moment to pray before completing the following lesson.

---

*B*ecause humankind is finite and God is infinite, we cannot know or fellowship with him unless he reveals himself to us.[38] Our task this week is to outline the way in which the God of the universe has revealed himself to humanity. Like many other topics that we have studied in *The Absolute Basics of Christianity*, the revelation of God could easily be an entire study on its own. Therefore we are forced to focus our attention over the next four days on the basics of God's divine revelation. In order to do this, we will focus our attention on the Bible. God's holy word is one of the most significant ways he has chosen to reveal himself to humanity.

We will begin our study with some basic facts about the Bible. The book we call the Bible is actually composed of sixty-six individual books. These books are

---

38 Millard J. Erickson, *Introducing Christian Doctrine,* ed. L. Arnold Hustad (Grand Rapids, MI: Baker Academic, 2001), 43.

divided into the Old Testament and New Testament. The Old Testament contains thirty-nine books and the New Testament contains the remaining twenty-seven books of the Bible. There are 1,189 chapters in the Bible: 929 in the Old Testament, and 260 in the New Testament. Take a few minutes to look up and write down all sixty-six books of the Bible in the space below. You can find a complete list of all sixty-six books in the Table of Contents located near the front of your Bible.

1. _____

2. _____

3. _____

4. _____

5. _____

6. _____

7. _____

8. _____

9. _____

10. _____

11. _____

12. _____

13. _____

14. _____

15. _____

16. _____

17. _____

18. _____

19. _____

20. _____

21. _____

22. _____

23. _____

24. _____

25. _____

26. _____

27. _____

28. _____

29. _____

30. _____

31. _____

32. _____

33. _____

34. _____

35. _____

36. _____

37. _____

38. _____

39. _____

40. _____

41. _____   54. _____

42. _____   55. _____

43. _____   56. _____

44. _____   57. _____

45. _____   58. _____

46. _____   59. _____

47. _____   60. _____

48. _____   61. _____

49. _____   62. _____

50. _____   63. _____

51. _____   64. _____

52. _____   65. _____

53. _____   66. _____

  Ș Mark any books of the Bible in your list above that you have never heard of before, or are very unfamiliar with. Take some time later to familiarize yourself with these books of the Bible.

_____

_____

_____

While the following figures are somewhat debatable, most people believe that the Bible was written over a 1,500-year time span and some forty individual writers composed the individual books that make up the official canon we have today. God used people from all walks of life and varying backgrounds to reveal himself to humanity. Some were kings, others peasants; there were philosophers and fisherman, statesmen and poets, scholars and slaves. Furthermore, some of the books of the Bible were written from within the walls of lavish palaces, and others from the cell of a prison or dungeon. Other books were penned in the wilderness, and still others while on the road during missionary journeys. Some were written in times of war, others in times of peace. The diversity and creativity of our God can clearly be seen in the way he chose to reveal himself to humanity by using so many different people from such varying backgrounds to give us the book we know as the Bible.

The natural question, then, that many people are led to ask is, "Can we trust the Bible? After all, it was written by so many different people over such a long period of time, how can we know for certain that it is trustworthy?" Some have gone so far as to find the smallest of errors in the Bible and use that to point to its untrustworthiness. For example, in the Book of 2 Chronicles 4:2, the Bible states: *²He made the sea of cast metal, circular in shape, measuring ten cubits from rim to rim and five cubits high. It took a line of thirty cubits to measure around it.* However, in the modern era we have discovered that the circumference of a circle is pi (3.14159). Therefore, the biblical account here is not scientifically accurate to the decimal. The Bible was not intended to be a science or math book, or a book on the laws of physics. The Bible is the Spirit's book,[39] and it is intended to reveal spiritual things to humanity. When it comes to complex mathematical equations, you might be able to reach into the pages of God's word and find some issues with accuracy. However, when it comes to the complex spiritual issues of your soul, you will find no issues at all. God's word is fully reliable and trustworthy on all matters that involve humanity's separation from their Creator and how humanity, despite being in a hopeless situation, can be restored through the Blood of Christ.

In tomorrow's study, we will start to look at some specific ways in which we should be experiencing the word of God to gain the full power of God's revelation to humanity. Conclude today's study by answering the questions below.

> ❧ Can you list the four things that your memory verse says the word of God is useful for?

_____

_____

_____

> ❧ Have you ever doubted the trustworthiness of the Bible? Why? Be specific.

_____

_____

_____

_____

---

39 Stanley J. Grenz, *Theology for the Community of God* (Nashville: Broadman & Holman, 1994), 524.

Write out your memory verse in the space below. Try to do it completely from memory, then double-check yourself.

_____

_____

_____

_____

TAKE TIME TO PRAY

Revelation—Day Two

Memory Verse

2 Timothy 3:16-17

Start today's study by writing out as much of your memory verse as you can in the space below. Then, look up the verse and make any corrections that are needed. Finally, read it three times from your Bible and take just a moment to pray before completing the following lesson.

wo weeks ago we studied prayer. In that study, we learned that many of us fail to hear God's voice because we fail to stop and listen. While that is often the root of the problem, there is another major issue that many of us face when it comes to hearing from the Spirit of God. We don't know what his voice sounds like. Even when we stop and listen, we might still miss the voice of God's Spirit simply because we don't know what God sounds like when he speaks.

I can be in a room with thousands of people and somehow I am still able to distinguish the sound of certain voices. My wife, son, mother, father, or any one of my three brothers stands out in the noise and confusion of a large room of people. Why? Because I know the sound of their voices. The tone, pitch, and words they use are so familiar to me that I can easily distinguish them from all the others in a crowded room. The world we live in is crowded, loud, confusing, and busy. If we don't know what the voice of God sounds like, no matter how long we stop and listen it is unlikely that we will be able to distinguish his heavenly whispers in our lives.

📖 Read John 10:27. What does Jesus say his sheep do?

_____

_____

🕊 Can you do this without knowing what his voice sounds like?

_____

_____

It is easy to understand how Christ's twelve disciples would have been able to know the voice of God because Christ lived with them for three years. They walked down many miles of road together. They heard Jesus preach and teach. They sat around the campfire at night with one another. They heard him pray on many occasions. But what about us? How are we supposed to know what the voice of God sounds like? The answer is that we learn the sound of his voice by experiencing his written word in our lives. From the Bible we can learn what the voice of God sounds like.

There are many different ways to experience God's word, and the committed Christian should make every effort to engage the Spirit through as many possible experiences as possible. We should read, hear, study, meditate, and memorize God's word. If we commit to doing these five things, we are certain to be able to tune our spiritual ears into the sound of God's voice.

There are several different ways you can read the Bible. The first method some use is the "flick and point" method. This method simply involves you opening the pages of the Bible randomly, closing your eyes, and pointing to a place on the page to begin reading. Admittedly, I myself use this method at times when I have a few minutes—as I sit in the hospital waiting room, when I have a few spare minutes during lunch, or when I find it difficult to fall asleep at night. There is no wrong way to read the Bible. I believe it is so powerful that you could read it backwards and it would speak to you. However, if "flick and point" is your primary method of selecting your scripture readings, it is unlikely that you will grow a great deal in your understanding of the Bible, or read the Bible on a regular basis.

Others choose a "general systematic" method to scripture reading. They might use a daily Bible or some kind of Bible reading plan to go from Genesis to Revelation in a year. A daily chronological Bible can be a great tool that allows you not only to read the Bible in a year but also to gain a better understanding of the order in which events take place in the Bible. Some might read the New Testament from Matthew to Revelation in ninety days. You could read all of the books of the law, the prophecies, or the epistles of Paul in a systematic way over a certain period of time. This method can be highly effective. However, the best experience with this method will only happen with an individual who already has a strong, disciplined habit of reading God's word. If you try to start in Genesis and read through Revelation in a year as your first exercise with God's word, in general you will find success very difficult.

The method I use the most, and with which I have seen the greatest success rate in the lives of others, is what I call the "specific systematic approach." In this method the individual believer takes a small portion of scripture or even a small book of the Bible and reads it every day for a certain period of time. For example, you might read the entire book of Philippians at least once a day for a month. This book contains four chapters and can be read in about fifteen minutes. Once you have met your goal with Philippians, you might move on to 1 Timothy or James for a month. Larger books can be broken down into smaller sections—for example, Matthew 1-5 or Acts 15-20. As you read the same chapters day after day, it is very powerful to experience how the Spirit moves as you better understand that portion of scripture. Look up the following verses that deal with the importance of reading God's word and answer the questions below.

> ❧ Of the above methods, which one are you currently using as you read God's word?

_____

_____

> ❧ Which method will you commit to using for the next month? What will you read?

_____

_____

> 📖 In 1 Timothy 4:13, what does Paul tell Timothy to do?

_____

_____

> 📖 According to 2 Timothy 2:15, why do you think it is important to read the Bible?

_____

_____

📖 Read Proverbs 2:1-15. According to this passage, why should we read the Bible?

_____

_____

📖 Read 1 Kings 19:11-13. Who hears from God in this passage? Do you think it was their first time to hear God's voice (see 19:9)? How did this person know when to hide under the cloak? ⚒

_____

_____

_____

The method you use to read God's word is less important than the fact that you must read it every day. Through God's word we begin to understand what God does and does not say to those he loves. We clearly see the language he used to communicate with believers in the past. And through reading God's word, whenever we hear that still small voice, we are then able to quickly discern whether it is from God or not. If we don't know what God's voice sounds like, however, it is unlikely that we will experience its power on a regular basis.

Write out your memory verse in the space below. Try to do it completely from memory, then double-check yourself.

_____

_____

_____

_____

TAKE TIME TO PRAY

Revelation—Day Three

Memory Verse

2 Timothy 3:16-17

Start today's study by writing out as much of your memory verse as you can in the space below. Then, look up the verse and make any corrections that are needed. Finally, read it three times from your Bible and take just a moment to pray before completing the following lesson.

_____

_____

_____

_____

*Y*esterday, we talked about the importance of reading God's word. There are several other ways that we can experience the power of the Bible as well. For example, we can hear his word. In the space below, list all the ways you can think of that involve hearing God's word.

    ❧ How can we hear God's word?

_____

_____

_____

📖 According to Romans 10:17, why is hearing God's word important?

_____

_____

_____

The ability to hear God's word allows us to experience what we have read in a different way. Chuck had been reading the Bible regularly for over thirty years. As a result he was a respected Bible teacher in the church. Despite adamantly disagreeing with the idea, Chuck, along with many others in the church, had committed to listen through the New Testament over a period of time. In the deacons' meeting he stood up and said, "I just think it is a waste of time! Real Christians read the Bible; lazy Christians listen to it!" Forty short days later, Chuck stood up and in tears admitted how wrong he had been. By listening to the word of God being read audibly, he had heard things and experienced the power of God's voice in unimaginable ways. He was so convinced that he suggested the church make listening through the New Testament a yearly challenge. With radios and CD players in virtually every vehicle, and Mp3 players on many phones, there is no reason we can't take a few minutes each day to listen to the word of God. Listening to God's word evokes a different emotion and level of understanding that we simply can't experience if we only read it.

We should also take time to study God's word. Studying the word of God takes time and you may or may not be able to do it every day. Regardless of how often you do it, you should commit to regularly study the word of God. When you study God's word, you take time to read commentaries, analyze the meanings of words, or study specific topics or people in the Bible. In other words, you dive into the depths of the Bible and attempt to uncover the deeper truths that are contained in its pages. Rather than waiting for Sunday to roll around so the preacher can spoon feed you, take time to study God's word yourself on a regular basis.

📖 Look up and read 2 Timothy 2:15. Why is studying the Bible important?

_____

_____

_____

🐾 Would you say that you can do what the last six words of this verse say?

_____

_____

_____

The next thing we should do with God's Word is to memorize it. When we take the time to memorize God's word, it not only changes us but it changes the world as well. It helps us gain confidence as we share and defend our faith. It allows us the freedom to impact the lives of others, even when we don't have our Bibles in hand. Memorizing scripture gives us the ability to speak words of encouragement and life into others at any moment in time. It also gives us the ammunition that is necessary to beat the enemy when he attacks us in our own lives. Memorization is not easy and it does not happen quickly, and as a result, many Christians have given up or flat out refuse to memorize God's word. However, with time, patience, and practice, you can memorize God's word.

- At this point in the study, you have memorized eighteen different passages including this week's. On another sheet of paper, without looking at any notes or your Bible, write all eighteen verses out to review. Bring this to your next class to share with others as well.

- How well did you do with the assignment above? How does that make you feel?

_____

_____

Finally you should meditate on the scriptures. Meditation is the discipline of taking time to think and ponder on certain verses or topics in the Bible. For example, I might just spend time thinking about the greatness of God, without any commentaries or other study aids and with my Bible closed.. Or you might ponder the significance of a specific word or verse in the Bible, clearing your mind and listening for God's voice to clarify the topic or subject in question. When we study the Bible we are attempting to learn from others. When we meditate, we are attempting to learn directly from God.

- What does Joshua 1:8 say that we should do with the word of God? When should we do it?

_____

_____

- If we do this, what will the result be? What do you think that means? �֍

_____

_____

_____

Write out your memory verse in the space below. Try to do it completely from memory, then double-check yourself.

TAKE TIME TO PRAY

Revelation—Day Four

Memory Verse

2 Timothy 3:16-17

Start today's study by writing out as much of your memory verse as you can in the space below. Then, look up the verse and make any corrections that are needed. Finally, read it three times from your Bible and take just a moment to pray before completing the following lesson.

For our final lesson on God's revelation to humankind through the Bible, we are going to closely examine what the Bible is useful for. The memory verse you have been assigned this week is one of the most powerful verses in the New Testament. It speaks of both the reliability and usability of God's holy word.

📖 According to 2 Timothy 3:16-17, what is scripture useful for?

1. _____

2. _____

3. _____

4. _____

Before we thoroughly examine the usefulness of scripture, we must first understand the significance of the phrase *All scripture is God-breathed*. The adjective used here is *theopneustos* which is a combination of two other Greek words: *theos* ("God") and *pneo* ("breathe"). This is one of the greatest texts in the New Testament describing the inspiration, or the "God-breathed" aspect, of the Bible.[40] Although the Bible doesn't spell out the mechanics of how God inspired the writers, it makes clear that the ultimate source was God himself.[41] Because every word that is contained within the pages of the Bible was directly revealed from God himself, it is therefore the most trustworthy source of inspiration and guidance for all Christians. "The Bible is our standard for testing everything else that claims to be true. It is our safeguard against false teaching and our source of guidance for how we should live. It is our only source of knowledge about how we can be saved." [42] Within its pages we find, peace, comfort, assurance, wisdom, power, safety, love, grace, mercy, and countless other constant reminders of the intimate relationship that God desires to have with his children.

    📖 Look up and read 2 Peter 1:19-21. What must we understand according to these verses?

_____

_____

_____

    ✿ Who carried the biblical writers along, according to this passage? Does this increase or decrease your confidence in the reliability of the Bible?

_____

_____

_____

Hebrews 4:12-13 says, *For the word of God is living and active. Sharper than any double-edged sword, it penetrates even to dividing soul and spirit, joints and marrow; it judges the thoughts and attitudes of the heart.* [13]*Nothing in all creation is hidden from God's sight. Everything is uncovered and laid bare*

---

40   Kenneth L. Barker and John R. Kohlenberger, eds., *Zondervan NIV Bible Commentary,* Accordance electronic ed. (Grand Rapids, MI: Zondervan, 1994), n.p.

41   Philip Yancey and Tom Stafford, eds., *The NIV Student Bible,* revised ed., Accordance electronic ed. (Grand Rapids, MI: Zondervan, 2002), n.p.

42   *Life Application Study Bible,* Accordance electronic ed. (Carol Stream, IL: Tyndale House Publishers, 2004), n.p.

before the eyes of him to whom we must give account. Sometimes people claim that the Bible is no longer useful, as 2 Timothy 3:16-17 suggests, because it is too old-fashioned or because it was not written with our culture and contemporary problems in mind. This could not be further from the truth. God's word is living and active in the lives of believers. It is as sharp and powerful today as it was the day the words were penned. Therefore, it is as useful to the modern day disciple as it was a generation ago or even a thousand years ago. These are the words that God himself brought to life and wrote through men and women throughout the ages for believers to be able to benefit from for all time. God's word is indeed useful.

Paul goes on to describe four specific things that God's word is useful for. First, he says it is useful for *teaching*. The Greek word used for teaching is *didaskalia*. This word does not refer to the process or method of teaching but to its content. In this context, as in most others in the New Testament, *didaskalia* refers specifically and exclusively to divine instruction, or doctrine, given to believers through God's word, which included not only the Hebrew Scriptures (Old Testament) and the teaching of Jesus during his incarnation but also the inspired teaching of the apostles and New Testament authors.[43] The content of the Bible is given to believers to benefit our lives and help us learn how to navigate the narrow and sometimes rough road that we follow as Christians. It speaks to every area of life, and from the pages of God's word the modern believer can learn the things that are necessary to run the race that has been marked out for us.

The Bible is also there to *rebuke* us if need be. The English word rebuke expresses sharp disapproval or criticism of someone or a specific action. Paul's choice of words here was no different. He used the word *elegmos*. The Louw and Nida Greek dictionary gives the following definition of this word, "To state that someone has done wrong, with the implication that there is adequate proof of such wrongdoing."[44] Another common translation is "reproof" (see ESVS, KJV, NASB). This word implies that there is sufficient evidence for the rebuke to take place, and that the correction is made in an attempt to better the individual who is being rebuked. God does not use his word to call attention to our wrongdoing through a strong rebuke for the fun of it. Instead, it is done in an attempt to refine us and mold us into what we have been created to be.

📖 Write out your memory verse from 1 Peter 1:15-16.

_____

_____

_____

---

43 John MacArthur, *2 Timothy,* The MacArthur New Testament Commentary. Accordance electronic ed. (Chicago: Moody Press, 1995), 154.

44 Johannes P. Louw and Eugene A. Nida, *Greek–English Lexicon of the New Testament Based on Semantic Domains,* (New York: United Bible Societies), n.p.

ક્ર Is this possible without some kind of correction and periodic rebuke's in life? Why or why not?

_____

_____

_____

ક્ર Have you ever rebuked a child, co-worker, friend, or employee in love? Did you do it to help them or hurt them?

_____

_____

_____

ક્ર Explain a time or situation when God's word rebuked you. Be as specific as possible.

_____

_____

_____

Paul goes on to say that God's holy word is useful for *correcting* as well. John MacArthur says the following in his commentary on this passage. "*Epanorthœsis* (correction) is used only here in the New Testament and refers to the restoration of something to its original and proper condition. In secular Greek literature it was used of setting upright an object that had fallen down and of helping a person back on his feet after stumbling. After exposing and condemning false belief and sinful conduct in believers, Scripture then builds them up through its divine correction. Correction is Scripture's positive provision for those who accept its negative reproof."[45]

Some have argued that rebuking and correcting are one in the same. However, they clearly are not. You can be rebuked, but refuse God's positive correction in your life. Believers might be convicted of their sin through the power of God's word, and then cease to allow it to move on to the next step, which is correction. It is important not only that we embrace the rebuke, but that we allow God's word to continue its work of correcting our lives as well.

---

45 John MacArthur, *2 Timothy,* MacArthur New Testament Commentary. Accordance electronic ed. (Chicago: Moody Press, 1995), 160.

Finally, the writer states that God's word is useful for *training*. The word used here was originally used to describe the way that parents trained their children (see Eph 6:4). God's word trains us in how to live both inwardly in our relationship to him as well as outwardly in our relationships with other people. It gives specific instruction and advice that builds all believers up and trains them for their journey through life. As a parent, you train your children day-by-day, week-by-week, and lesson-by-lesson. It is a slow, steady, consistent, long process to adequately train children in the way they should go. However difficult the process might be, the reward is greater. It is the same way with our training in the scriptures. It takes time, effort, energy, consistency, patience, and a great deal of dedication. However, over a lifetime, the result of the training we receive not only changes our lives but the world as well.

📖 Write out 2 Timothy 3:16-17 again in the space below. What is the overall purpose for the word of God in a believer's life?

_____

_____

_____

_____

In 2 Timothy, Paul says, *"I give you this charge: Preach the word; be prepared in season and out of season; correct, rebuke and encourage—with great patience and careful instruction"* (2 Tim 4:1-2). It is impossible to do this unless we have first submitted our own lives to God's word and allowed it to shape and mold us into an accurate reflection of who Christ has called us to be. God's word will teach, rebuke, correct, and train us when we submit our lives to it. However, the larger purpose is so that we may be thoroughly equipped for every good work. There is no magic prayer that will equip us. Great sermons alone cannot accomplish this task. Reading wonderful Christian books or listening to Christian radio is not God's main plan for equipping the saints. While all of these things and many more play some role, it is ultimately God's word that equips the believer. There simply is no substitute for the word of God.

🏃 How has God's word equipped you?

_____

_____

_____

❧ Is there anything in life that you feel the Bible is unable to equip you for? If so, what is it?

_____

_____

_____

Write out your memory verse in the space below. Try to do it completely from memory, then double-check yourself.

_____

_____

_____

_____

TAKE TIME TO PRAY

To review, use the space below to write all the memory verses you have learned so far, including this week's. You can also use this space for personal notes about this lesson.

_____

_____

_____

_____

_____

_____

_____

_____

_____

_____

_____

_____

_____

_____

_____

_____

_____

_____

Spirit—Day One

Memory Verse

John 15:4

Start today's study by writing out your memory verse in the space below. Then, read it three times from your Bible and take just a moment to pray before completing the following lesson.

In Week Nine of *The Absolute Basics of Christianity,* we took a basic look at who both God and Jesus Christ are. This week we will attempt to uncover the truth about the Holy Spirit. In next week's study, we will bring all three together as we look at the Trinity.

The Holy Spirit is the most confusing and overwhelming aspect of the Holy Trinity.[46] The concept of the Spirit is perplexing for several reasons. First, we have far less to which to compare the Spirit in the earthly world that we live in. God is accurately referred to and described as "the Father." In the same way, Jesus is generally described as "the Son." These descriptions help us picture and

---

46 We will discuss the Holy Trinity in more detail next week. For this week's study, you only need to know and understand that the Trinity refers to God the Father, Jesus the Son, and the Holy Spirit working together as one.

understand the general and basic characteristics of both God and Christ. The Spirit, however, is much more difficult to explain because we have nothing on earth to compare it to. The most likely thing to compare the Spirit to is a ghost, and sometimes the Holy Spirit is referred to as the Holy Ghost. The problem is that people are afraid of ghosts, or perhaps they don't believe in ghosts, so as a result our negative view of ghosts leads to an unfavorable view of the Spirit of God as well.

The Bible is also less descriptive when it comes to revealing who and what the Spirit is. This is primarily due to the fact that God's unique role in the history of humanity is well-documented in the Old Testament. Jesus' role is revealed in the New Testament as he came to earth and accomplished his purpose for humankind. But the Spirit's principal role in the history of humanity does not take place in either the Old or New Testament. Instead, it is happening right now. As we will see in our study, the Holy Spirit is mentioned, and indeed very active, in both the Old and New Testaments. However, the primary mission of the Spirit is being lived out as we await the return of our Savior.

The Hebrew word used for spirit in the Old Testament is *ruach*. This word carries the idea of "wind" or "breath." Those living in the time of the Old Testament placed great significance on a person's breath. As long as a person was breathing, he was alive; when he failed to breathe he was dead. One does not need to go to medical school to understand that with the absence of breath, there is no life. Therefore, the *ruach* was the "breath" that enlivened all creatures on planet Earth. Grenz says this of this concept of the *ruach,* "when God removes the Spirit, creatures die, but when he sends his Spirit, the earth is renewed (Ps 104:29-30; Isa 32:15)... All living creatures, therefore, owe their existence to the work of God's Spirit." [47] One modern day definition of Spirit is "an animating or vital principle held to give life to physical organisms"[48] Despite all of the evidence that the Spirit of God is at the center of all life, we rarely understand or think of the Spirit in these terms today.

    📖 Look up the following verses to determine what those in the Old Testament thought about the role of the Spirit in giving and preserving human life.

       •   Genesis 6:3

_____

_____

_____

---

47 Stanley J. Grenz, *Theology for the Community of God* (Nashville, TN: Broadman & Holman, 1994), 472.

48 "Spirit ," Merriam-Webster Online. http://www.merriam-webster.com/netdict/spirit (accessed May 11, 2010).

- Job 27:3

_____

_____

_____

- Job 34:14-15

_____

_____

_____

📖 With this concept in mind, read Psalms 51:11. What is the significance of the writer's request as it relates to the work of the Holy Spirit? ✕

_____

_____

_____

✺ Do you think the Spirit is still a life-giving agent today? Explain your answer and use Bible verses if possible.

_____

_____

_____

As we stated previously in this lesson, another major problem with understanding the working and role of the Holy Spirit comes from our lack of evidence or ability to compare it directly to something we have experienced with our physical senses. As a result, many commonly think of the Holy Spirit as a ghost, or a mystical spiritual force that roams the earth. While we desire to experience the love of the Father's hands and the grace and mercy that came from the blood of Christ through the nails that pierced his hands, most assume that the Spirit does not even have hands. In other words, many just don't know what to believe about the Spirit because the idea of a Holy Spirit, or Holy Ghost, sounds strange at best and absolutely creepy and frightening at its worst. We view the Father and Son as persons but the Spirit is nothing more than a "thing." The Bible, however, is clear that the Holy Spirit is much more than a "thing." In the coming days we will examine the person of the Holy Spirit, including the work of the Spirit and some of the characteristics that the Spirit possesses. However, you can start to understand

and build your foundation for the personhood of the Spirit by looking up the following verses. In these verses things are done to the Spirit that simply cannot be done to an impersonal "thing." Look each verse up and do your best to identify the different things that are done to the Holy Spirit. 🛠

📖 Mark 3:28-30

____

____

📖 Acts 5:3-9

____

____

📖 Acts 7:51-53

____

____

📖 Ephesians 4:29-32

____

____

Write out your memory verse in the space below. Try to do it completely from memory, then double-check yourself.

____

____

____

____

TAKE TIME TO PRAY

Spirit—Day Two

Memory Verse

John 15:4

Start today's study by writing out as much of your memory verse as you can in the space below. Then, look up the verse and make any corrections that are needed. Finally, read it three times from your Bible and take just a moment to pray before completing the following lesson.

---

*Y*esterday we took a basic look at what the term "Spirit" actually means and how people in the biblical period would have understood the term. We then concluded the study by examining some of the different interactions that humans had with the Holy Spirit that help prove not only that the Holy Spirit is real, but that the Spirit is an authentic person with qualities much like our own. Today, we will start looking at what the Holy Spirit actually does. We will begin by examining the Spirit's role in the Old and New Testaments. Tomorrow, we will examine the role of the Holy Spirit in the life of believers today.

Yesterday we said that God the Father played his major role with humanity in the Old Testament. Jesus Christ the Son came and fulfilled his primary mission in the New Testament. And the Holy Spirit's chief role is happening right now in the present, in and through the life of modern day disciples just like you. However, all three persons of the Holy Trinity play a part in all three eras of human History. We see God at work in the New Testament and today as well. We see Jesus at work in the Old Testament and he is still active today. In the same way, we see the Spirit at work in the Old Testament and New Testament.

In the Old Testament, we see the Spirit do many things and fulfill many different roles. Below you will find a list of some of the things that the Spirit did during the time of the Old Testament. You will also see a series of verses. You should look up each verse or passage and decide which role you see the Spirit playing. ✘

1. _____ Genesis 1:2

2. _____ Ezekiel 2:1-4

3. _____ Exodus 31:1-5

4. _____ Ezekiel 8:1-5

5. _____ Genesis 41:34-42

a) Revealing God's message

b) Creation

c) Imparting skills

Because the Holy Spirit did not take a primary role in the Old Testament, the Spirit also did not indwell all believers, but instead only indwelt selected persons temporarily for divine service or for a specific purpose and time. It is clear that the Spirit was present during the Old Testament period. However, the activities and involvement of the Spirit were very selective as were the activities and involvement of Jesus Christ. Look up the following verse to illustrate this point and make notes to which you can quickly refer during your next small group session.

📖 1 Samuel 10:9-13

_____

_____

The Holy Spirit was also active during the New Testament period as Christ and the disciples and early apostles delivered the gospel to the world. We will limit our study somewhat today by only looking at a few verses from the New Testament that show the Spirit's involvement, because in tomorrow's lesson, as we uncover the role of the Spirit in our lives, we will examine verses from the New Testament that link the Biblical era to the modern day as far as the Spirit is concerned. For now, look up the following verses and write out the role that the Holy Spirit played in each instance.

📖 Matt 3:16-17

_____

_____

📖 Luke 1:30-38

_____

_____

📖 Luke 4:1-4

_____

_____

📖 Luke 4:13-15

_____

_____

📖 Luke 10:21 ✖

_____

_____

Today we discovered that the Spirit played a limited but vital role both in the Old and New Testament. Tomorrow we will examine the main purpose of the Holy Spirit and how that affects our lives in the present day.

Write out your memory verse in the space below. Try to do it completely from memory, then double-check yourself.

_____

_____

_____

_____

TAKE TIME TO PRAY

Spirit—Day Three

Memory Verse

John 15:4

Start today's study by writing out as much of your memory verse as you can in the space below. Then, look up the verse and make any corrections that are needed. Finally, read it three times from your Bible and take just a moment to pray before completing the following lesson.

---

n the book of Acts, the coming of the Spirit marked the inauguration of a new era, the age of the mission of the church.[49] God marked the beginning of the Old Testament era with the birth or creation of the world in Genesis 1. The birth of Christ ushered in the second era in the New Testament, and the pouring out of the Holy Spirit on all believers brought about the beginning of the third and modern era in which we live. It is interesting that each of the three members of the Trinity plays the primary role in marking the beginning of the era in which they are most actively involved. This helps to reinforce the idea or concept that all three persons

---

49 Stanley J. Grenz, *Theology for the Community of God* (Nashville, TN: Broadman & Holman, 1994), 497.

of the Trinity are active in each era, but one person of the Trinity is the principal being for each time period.

There is some debate over when the Spirit actually came to all believers. We will not explore all the different angles of this issue, both for the sake of time and because this study is designed to give the reader only a basic foundational knowledge of the issues. However, the issue is important and significant enough to give some attention to. Read the following passages, noting how they are similar and different, and be prepared to discuss them in your next small group meeting.

📖 John 20:19-23

_____

_____

_____

📖 Acts 2:1-12

_____

_____

_____

Some believe that the Holy Spirit first came to humanity in John 20, while others contend that it is not until after Jesus ascends into heaven and at the time of Pentecost that the Holy Spirit comes to dwell in the hearts of all believers. There are no firm and steadfast answers to the debate. But what does it matter? Praise God the Spirit is here! We are not alone; our helper has arrived and we are safe and secure thanks to the Spirit of God. It seems entirely possible that Jesus introduced his closest and most faithful disciples to the Spirit shortly after his resurrection in an effort to help them during their time of despair, fear, and loneliness, as they battled the hopeless thoughts of life without Christ. Then in Acts 2, at just the right time in history, the Spirit came to all who believed. The timing is far less significant than the arrival of the Spirit himself.

So what does the Spirit do? What is his objective or mission? Grenz writes, "Ultimately the goal of the Spirit is to glorify the Father through the Son, by bringing God's reign to completion and this by consummating the establishment of the eschatological community... His task is to affect the ultimate goal of God's program for creation."[50] The Spirit is at work in the church and the lives of those who make up the church. He is moving in such a way as to build, sustain, guide, protect, and grow the kingdom of God. It is impossible to comprehend all that this means,

---

50 Ibid., 490.

but we do gain some understanding of this process from the pages of scripture. Look up the following verses, and identify the specific work with which the Spirit is involved in each passage.

📖 John 3:2-9

_____

_____

📖 John 14:25-27

_____

_____

📖 John 16:5-14

_____

_____

📖 Romans 8:26-27

_____

_____

📖 1 Corinthians 12:8-11

_____

_____

📖 Galatians 5:16-26

_____

_____

The Holy Spirit plays a major role in both the revelation and illumination of scripture. Grenz correctly writes, "He both authors and speaks through the Bible, which is ultimately the Spirit's book."[51] It is through the Spirit that God was able to use humans to pen his holy words and reveal to humanity the book we call the Bible. Likewise, it is through the Spirit that we are able to discern, understand, and comprehend the meaning and significance of those words that were revealed

---

51   Ibid., 495.

through the Spirit of God. Without the Spirit as our guide, we would have no hope of discerning God's will for our lives through his holy word.

📖 According to 2 Corinthians 3:14-17, what does the Spirit do?

_____

_____

📖 Have you ever realized this before? How important to you is this?

_____

_____

📖 How would you explain the Holy Spirit to a nonbeliever or skeptic?

_____

_____

Write out your memory verse in the space below. Try to do it completely from memory, then double-check yourself.

_____

_____

_____

_____

TAKE TIME TO PRAY

Spirit—Day Four

Memory Verse

John 15:4

Start today's study by writing out as much of your memory verse as you can in the space below. Then, look up the verse and make any corrections that are needed. Finally, read it three times from your Bible and take just a moment to pray before completing the following lesson.

---

*M*illard Erickson correctly states that "being filled with the Spirit is not so much a matter of our getting more of the Spirit as it is a matter of his possessing more of our lives."[52] Yesterday, we examined John 20:19-23, and Acts 2:1-12 in an effort to understand when the Spirit comes into our lives. We concluded that the exact moment that the era of the Spirit began was far less important than the assurance of his presence in our lives. The Bible clearly teaches that the Spirit is at work in the lives of all believers. So why does it seem that he is more at work in the lives of some and less in the lives of others? Does the Spirit of God play favorites? Is there some secret prayer or deed that some people know about and

---

52 Millard J. Erickson, *Introducing Christian Doctrine*, ed. L. Arnold Hustad (Grand Rapids, Mich.: Baker Academic, 2001), 284.

others have not yet been able to find? In reality, the reason some seem to possess more of the Spirit is totally due to their obedience.

As we previously discovered in *The Absolute Basics of Christianity*, being obedient and submitting our lives to Christ is the highest goal for all disciples. When we withhold parts of our lives and refuse to follow the commands and directions of our Lord, we should not be surprised to find that others who are totally committed and fully devoted are more aware of what the Spirit is doing in their lives and in the world around them. It's not that they have any more of the Spirit than you have; instead, they have simply been willing to give the Spirit of God a greater role in their lives. Until we are willing to fully trust and obey the Spirit of God, it will be impossible to experience his overwhelming power in our lives. Obedience is the key if we desire to be directed and guided by the Spirit of God. Look up and read John 14:15-19, and then answer the questions below.

    What does Jesus say his disciples will do if they love him?

_____

_____

    Who is the counselor that Jesus says God will send?

_____

_____

    Why do you think it is impossible for the world to see or know the Spirit of truth?

_____

_____

    Now look up Romans 8:9-17. Where does the Spirit of God live? What does this passage teach us about the previous question?

_____

_____

_____

Both of these passages help us understand that we don't get "some" of the Spirit when we confess Christ as our Lord and Savior and then receive the rest later. Instead, when we become children of God we get all of the Spirit of God. The Spirit lives inside of each of us and tapping into its fullest potential depends on our willingness to submit our lives completely to the work of the Spirit.

We have no need to fear the role of the Spirit in our lives. Instead, we should embrace his holy presence and make every attempt to become in tune with who the Spirit is and what he does. He was sent into our lives to be a blessing for the modern day disciple, just as Christ was sent to be a blessing to the world during the first century. Yesterday, you were asked to look up the following verses and identify the specific work of the Holy Spirit in each passage. In the space below, take some time to consider each verse again, and this time write out how each of these traits of the Holy Spirit might benefit you as a believer today. Write down specific examples of ways you have seen the Holy Spirit working in these areas of your life.

📖 John 3:2-9

_____

_____

📖 John 14:25-27

_____

_____

📖 John 16:5-14

_____

_____

📖 Romans 8:26-27

_____

_____

📖 1 Corinthians 12:8-11

_____

_____

📖 Galatians 5:16-26

_____

_____

When we stop to think about it for just a few moments, it is easy to see how the Holy Spirit guides us, speaks to us, anoints us with our spiritual gifts, intercedes for us, and protects us. We are blessed to have the presence of the Holy Spirit in our lives. We should celebrate and praise God for giving us such a wonderful and amazing gift. At the same time, we should make every effort to get to know the Spirit of God on a personal level, just as we have with God the Father and Christ the Son. May we continually give our lives totally to the Spirit and allow him to work both inside of us and through us as we walk on this planet.

Write out your memory verse in the space below. Try to do it completely from memory, then double-check yourself.

TAKE TIME TO PRAY

To review, use the space below to write all the memory verses you have learned so far, including this week's. You can also use this space for personal notes about this lesson.

_____

_____

_____

_____

_____

_____

_____

_____

_____

_____

_____

_____

_____

_____

_____

_____

_____

_____

_____

Trinity—Day One

Memory Verse

John 14:23

Start today's study by writing out your memory verse in the space below. Then, read it three times from your Bible and take just a moment to pray before completing the following lesson.

The doctrine of the Holy Trinity is one of the most complex and confusing doctrines in the Christian faith. On the surface this idea might seem simple; however, when we start to consider the implications of three persons being one, we are quickly faced with many difficult and mysterious issues that will never be fully understood on this side of heaven. Because of its complexity, some readers might question why it would be included in a workbook that is aimed at "The Absolute Basics of Christianity." Others might ask why we should spend a week studying something we will never be able to comprehend or understand. The reason we are going to examine this complex doctrine is because it is one of the most unique and essential doctrines we have in the Christian faith. And while we will never fully comprehend the doctrine itself, in studying the issues surrounding the Trinity we begin to understand its significance to our past, present, and future. When we look closely at the Trinity, we learn more about our Creator as well as his Son, the Holy

Spirit, and ourselves. While you certainly will not be able to fully understand the Trinity by the end of this week's study, you should be able to do the following things:

1. You will be able to better explain the Trinity to others.
2. You will have a good understanding of the historical background that surrounds the doctrine of the Trinity.
3. You will have a strong biblical view of the Trinity.

No other religion in the world makes a claim as bold and astonishing as the Christian faith. Not only does our faith claim to have a Savior who lived on earth, suffered, died, and then rose from the grave to save our souls, we also have a God who is said to be three in one. In volume one *of The Absolute Basics of Christianity*, we learned about God the Father and Jesus Christ the Son. Last week we learned about the third person of the Trinity, the promised Holy Spirit, who lives with us today. This week we will study how all three of these persons make up the Trinity. The doctrine of the Trinity states that these three individual beings are indeed one, as well. The word "trinity" is not found any place in the Bible. So how or why did this complex doctrine find its way into the Christian faith if it is not explicitly defined and explained in the Bible? Today we will attempt to lay a solid foundation supporting the case for the doctrine of the Trinity by examining the basic historical evidence that surrounds this issue. In the coming days, we will take time to unpack what the Bible has to say on the subject, but to fully understand the biblical context of the Trinity we must first understand how this doctrine came to be such a major part of our religion.

The issue originally arose because the ancient Hebrews worshipped in a strict monotheistic way. That is to say, they worshipped only one God. While the Hebrews were not the only ones to practice monotheism during this period of human history, there was a great deal of both idol worship and the worship of multiple gods among the ancient societies. The Hebrew people were very serious and strict in their worship of one and only one God. In Deuteronomy 6, we find what the Hebrews called the *Shema*. Take some time and read Deuteronomy 6:4-9 carefully and answer the questions below.

📖 Write out the part of the verse that relates to the Hebrews' monotheistic worship.

_____

_____

📖 List the things they are called to do in verses 5 through 9.

_____

_____

📖 Just for fun and a greater understanding of other religions, see if you can identify the monotheistic (one God) religions versus the polytheistic religions (multiple gods). Place the letter M by the religions that are monotheistic, and a P by the religions that are polytheistic. ✗

- Buddhism   _____

- Hinduism   _____

- Islam   _____

- Shinto   _____

- Druze   _____

- Sikhism   _____

The problem arose when Christ, and later the Holy Spirit, were introduced into the Christian faith. "Viewing themselves as the continuation of the people of faith, the early Christians resolutely maintained the tradition of monotheism they inherited from the Old Testament. The God they worshiped, these believers asserted, is the one and only true God, the God of the patriarchs. The early Christians continued the Jewish worship of one God. But they also knew that this God had revealed himself in Jesus, the head of the church and the Lord of all creation."[53]

With the life, death, burial, and resurrection of Christ and the arrival of the Holy Spirit into the lives of believers, the early church and first generation of Christians, who vigorously and passionately held to the idea of there being only one true God, were forced to attempt to explain their Christian experience with the three persons of the Trinity and their understanding of monotheistic worship at the same time.

It was not until the council of Nicene in 325 A.D. that we see the first official attempt by the church to explain the Trinity. While the council acknowledged the presence and activity of the Holy Spirit, they only identified God the Father and Jesus the Son as being one in their creed. This, however, would be revised in 381 A.D. at the first Council of Constantinople. It was here for the first time that we find a definitive statement about the Trinity. In the chart below you will find the Nicene Creed of 325 next to the revised creed of 381. Many interesting changes were made over the intervening fifty-six year period, showing how the theology of the early church was evolving and taking shape. You should spend some time examining this chart,[54] focusing mainly on the sections that deal with the issue of the Trinity.

---

53   Stanley J. Grenz, *Theology for the Community of God* (Nashville, TN: Broadman & Holman, 1994), 71.

54   "Nicene Creed," Wikipedia, the Free Encyclopedia, Comparison between Creed of 325 and Creed of 381, http://en.wikipedia.org/wiki/Nicene_Creed#cite_note-15 (accessed May 25, 2010).

Nicene 325	Constantinople 381
We believe in one God, the Father Almighty, Maker of all things visible and invisible.	We believe in one God, the Father Almighty, Maker *of heaven and earth, and* of all things visible and invisible.
And in one Lord Jesus Christ, the Son of God, begotten of the Father [the only-begotten; that is, of the essence of the Father, God of God], Light of Light, very God of very God, begotten, not made, being of one substance with the Father;	And in one Lord Jesus Christ, the only-begotten Son of God, *begotten of the Father before all worlds*, Light of Light, very God of very God, begotten, not made, being of one substance with the Father;
By whom all things were made [both in heaven and on earth];	By whom all things were made;
Who for us men, and for our salvation, came down and was incarnate and was made man;	Who for us men, and for our salvation, came down from heaven, and was incarnate *by the Holy Ghost of the Virgin Mary*, and was made man;
He suffered, and the third day he rose again, ascended into heaven;	*He was crucified for us under Pontius Pilate*, and suffered, *and was buried*, and the third day he rose again, *according to the Scriptures, and* ascended into heaven, *and sitteth on the right hand of the Father*;
From thence he shall come to judge the quick and the dead.	From thence he shall come again, *with glory*, to judge the quick and the dead;
	whose kingdom shall have no end.
And in the Holy Ghost.	And in the Holy Ghost, *the Lord and Giver of life, who proceedeth from the Father, who with the Father and the Son together is worshiped and glorified, who spake by the prophets.*
	In one holy catholic and apostolic Church; we acknowledge one baptism for the remission of sins; we look for the resurrection of the dead, and the life of the world to come. Amen.
[But those who say: 'There was a time when he was not;' and 'He was not before he was made;' and 'He was made out of nothing,' or 'He is of another substance' or 'essence,' or 'The Son of God is created,' or 'changeable,' or 'alterable'—they are condemned by the holy catholic and apostolic Church.]	

   ⅊ What other things strike you as you read these two creeds from the early church?

_____

_____

   ⅊ Why do you think the concept of the Trinity has become so widely accepted today despite the fact that Christianity still remains strictly monotheistic? Prior to this study, had you ever questioned the Trinity based on the monotheistic argument?

_____

_____

_____

_____

   ⅊ What would you tell someone who said "Due to the Trinity, the Christian faith actually worships three gods and is polytheistic?"

_____

_____

Tomorrow, we will start to unpack the evidence we find in the Bible about the tri-union between the Father, Son, and Spirit. The mystery and confusion around this topic is great. However, with a solid understanding of the history and the biblical evidence, the modern day disciple will be well-equipped to better explain the faith. The Holy Trinity is crucial for Christians because within the Trinity we find the three centerpieces of our faith: God, Jesus, and the Holy Spirit.

Write out your memory verse in the space below. Try to do it completely from memory, then double-check yourself.

_____

_____

_____

_____

TAKE TIME TO PRAY

Trinity—Day Two

Memory Verse

John 14:23

Start today's study by writing out as much of your memory verse as you can in the space below. Then, look up the verse and make any corrections that are needed. Finally, read it three times from your Bible and take just a moment to pray before completing the following lesson.

---

*Y*esterday, we gained a basic understanding of the history of the doctrine of the Trinity in the Christian faith. In the next two lessons we will look at what the Bible has to say about the Trinity. This is a particularly difficult task because, as we learned yesterday, there are no verses in the Bible that explicitly explain the doctrine of the Trinity. There are, however, many verses that lead Christians to acknowledge the doctrine of the Trinity and, as we will learn today, there is enough evidence to support this theological concept.

Some would argue that 1 John 5:7 (KJV), which reads, "For there are three that bear record in heaven, the Father, the Word, and the Holy Ghost...," is a direct reference to the Holy Trinity. However, when we examine the Greek texts we find no record of this verse reading this way prior to the sixteenth century. Modern textual study has yielded the nearly unanimous consensus that these words were not part of the original document penned by the apostle.[55] Erickson writes, pertaining to this verse, that "Here is apparently, a clear and succinct statement of the three-in-oneness. Unfortunately however, the textual basis is so weak that some recent translations (e.g., NIV) include this statement only in an italicized footnote, and others omit it altogether (e.g., RSV). If there is a biblical basis for the Trinity it must be sought elsewhere."[56] If we read 1 John 5:6-9 from the earliest Greek manuscripts, we find that it refers to Jesus Christ as both the "water" and "blood." Therefore, this biblical reference only accounts for two persons of the Trinity, not all three. However, even without a single scripture that explicitly links all three persons of the Trinity together as one, the case is strong and conclusive that there is such a thing as the Trinity.

📖 Write out your memory verse from Week Two (Matt 28:19-20). What do these verses say about the Trinity? Read the verses closely to see if you can notice anything significant.

_____

_____

_____

These verses list all three persons of the Trinity together in a single verse: "... baptizing them in the name of the Father and of the Son and of the Holy Spirit..." (Matthew 28:19). However, there must be more if we are going to make a case for the Holy Trinity. The significance is found in the word "name." This word is singular both in the English text we have in our hands today and in the original Greek manuscripts. It seems strange that the author would write "name" singular when referring to three persons, unless the original author and audience understood that God was, in some mysterious way, three distinct persons united in one tri-union. Look up 2 Corinthians 13:14, where we see another example.

❧ What quality does the Apostle Paul attribute to Jesus in this verse?

_____

_____

❧ What quality does the Apostle Paul attribute to God in this verse?

_____

_____

55 Stanley J. Grenz, *Theology for the Ccommunity of God* (Nashville, TNenn.: Broadman & Holman, 1994), 69.

56 Millard J. Erickson, *Introducing Christian Doctrine,* ed. L. Arnold Hustad (Grand Rapids, MI: Baker Academic, 2001), 109–110.

❧ What quality does Paul attribute to the Holy Spirit in this verse?

_____

_____

Here again is a linkage of the three names in unity and apparent equality.[57] Paul ends his second letter to the Corinthian church by praying that all three persons of the Trinity would be with the people of this church. He makes no distinction in rank, status, or importance when it comes to the Father, Son, or Spirit. Paul again connects Christ and God in Philippians 2:5-11. Read those verses and answer the questions below.

❧ What does the Trinity have to do with our "attitude"?

_____

_____

📖 Explain what verse 6 means to you.

_____

_____

On more than a single occasion, Jesus himself also refers to being one with the Father. Look up the following verses and answer the questions below.

📖 What does Jesus say in John 5:16-25 in regard to the Holy Trinity?

_____

_____

📖 Look up and read John 10:25-40. Who is trying to kill Jesus? Why?

_____

_____

❧ Do you think his statement in verse 30 helped him subdue and calm the crowd that was preparing to kill him? Why, or why not?

_____

_____

---

57 Ibid., 110.

The NIV commentary offers the following explanation of John 10:30: "I and the Father" preserves the separate individuality of the two Persons in the Godhead; the word "one" (GK G1651) asserts unity of nature or equality (cf. 1 Cor 3:8). The Jews were quick to apprehend this statement and reacted by preparing to stone Jesus for blasphemy because he, a man, had asserted that he was one with God. For them Jesus' language did not mean simply agreement of thought or purpose but carried a metaphysical implication of deity."[58]

It is highly unlikely that Jesus would have carelessly said these words. He believed that he was united to God in total and complete unity. Had Christ wanted to calm the crowd or attempt to escape to save his life, he would never have made such a claim. But this was the truth and it seems that Jesus wanted to leave a record or account of such a claim, perhaps so that future generations could have solid evidence from his own lips that such a thing as the Trinity existed. While he does not explain the Trinity, or give mention to the Holy Spirit specifically, there seems to be a logical reason for his vagueness.

First, this encounter was not about teaching a group of his disciples about the doctrine of the Trinity. Rather, it was a very rough encounter that he had with a very antagonistic group of people who had already made up their minds when it came to Christ. They were in total opposition to both Christ and his ministry. This is made clear in verse 31: *Again the Jews picked up stones to stone him.* The verb that is translated "picked up" in the English language literally means to carry. Knowledge of some biblical history helps us to expand this point even further. It is extremely unlikely that there would have been enough loose stones on Solomon's Colonnade, for it was smoothly paved. But the temple nearby, which would have been under construction during this time, would have had many loose stones around it that could have been used to stone Christ. So it seems that this group (or at least some) came with the intention of killing Christ even prior to his statement.

But why would Christ not mention the Spirit? As you will recall from last week's study, the Spirit did not come and indwell believers until after the resurrection of Christ and his ascension into heaven. People would not have understood any reference to the Spirit, so it seems that Christ simply refers to God the Father, whom the Jews in the audience would have been extremely familiar with.

Tomorrow we will look at even more scriptures that refer to or give insight about the Holy Trinity. As you conclude this lesson, reflect on the following questions to prepare for tomorrows study.

❧ What new things have you learned about the Trinity so far in our study?

_____

_____

---

58 Kenneth L. Barker and John R. Kohlenberger, eds., *Zondervan NIV Bible Commentary. Accordance electronic ed.* (Grand Rapids, MI: Zondervan, 1994), n.p.

❧ Have you ever doubted the existence of the Trinity? Why?

_____

_____

❧ Why do you think the Trinity is so hard to comprehend?

_____

_____

❧ Why do you think the Bible is not very specific on the subject of the Trinity?

_____

_____

❧ How would you explain the concept of the Trinity to someone else?

_____

_____

_____

_____

Write out your memory verse in the space below. Try to do it completely from memory, then double-check yourself.

TAKE TIME TO PRAY

Trinity—Day Three

Memory Verse

John 14:23

Start today's study by writing out as much of your memory verse as you can in the space below. Then, look up the verse and make any corrections that are needed. Finally, read it three times from your Bible and take just a moment to pray before completing the following lesson.

_____

_____

_____

_____

*I*n Day Two, we examined some of the scriptures that help explain the doctrine of the Trinity. Today you will be asked to look up several different passages from the gospel of John. This gospel gives us the best and most specific instruction when it comes to this complex and overwhelming issue.

Before we examine these scriptures, it is imperative that we attempt to understand some of the imagery that has been used to describe what the Trinity is and how it works. As we learned in the first day of our study, this complex doctrine has been debated and discussed ever since the arrival of Christ and the Holy Spirit caused confusion in the lives of the monotheistic Hebrews. While each of the following explanations of the Trinity has weaknesses, it is important to understand some of the main arguments that you may encounter as you try to explain this concept to others.

THE ABSOLUTE BASICS OF CHRISTIANITY

One of the most popular analogies is that the Trinity is like water. The analogy states that water can be liquid, gas, or solid, but it's still water—thereby explaining how one thing can actually be three. Even when water is in its gaseous (steam) or solid state (ice), it is essentially still water. While this analogy may give us something to which to compare the Trinity, it is flawed, like all other earthly comparisons, for water cannot exist in all three states at the same time. If you have a certain amount of water, it can only exist as liquid, gas, or solid at any given time. The Holy Trinity on, the other hand, mysteriously exists as one and three at the same time.

There is also an analogy using the common household egg as its example. The egg is said to consist of the yolk, white, and shell, and these three then make up the whole egg. Again, while this analogy might help us understand the Trinity on some level, it falls short because it leads to what is known as "Tritheism." This is "the belief that there are three distinct, powerful gods, who form a triad. Generally three gods are envisioned as having separate powers and separate supreme beings or spheres of influence but working together."[59] The problem here is that the focus is placed too much on the individuality of the three parts of the Trinity and too little on the unity of the three.

Others have compared the Trinity to a tree. They say that a tree is made up of roots, trunk, and branches. Still others have likened the Trinity to a pair of jeans because they are singular at the top and plural at the bottom, thus forming the basis for the Trinity. There are hundreds of other earthly analogies that have been used in an attempt to explain this heavenly mystery. In his book *Theology for the Community of God*, Grenz writes. "All such analogies are reminders that the imprint of the triune God may be found in creation, as Augustine suggested. But nevertheless, nothing in creation is totally analogous to the one God who is the three-in-one."[60]

> ❧ Despite knowing that we can never fully explain the Trinity with earthly analogies, what other imagery can you think of that might be used to help others comprehend this difficult concept? What are the flaws in these analogies?

_____

_____

_____

_____

---

59 "Tritheism," *Wikipedia, the Free Encyclopedia.* http://en.wikipedia.org/wiki/Tritheism (accessed May 27, 2010).

60 Stanley J. Grenz, *Theology for the Community of God* (Nashville, TN: Broadman & Holman, 1994), 92.

The remainder of today's study should be spent looking up the following verses and examining their significance as it relates to the concept of the Trinity. Make detailed notes that will allow you to discuss these verses in your next small group time. Take your time as you read, and pray over the power of these passages.

📖 John 14:16-26

_____

_____

_____

📖 John 16:13-15

_____

_____

_____

📖 John 20:21-22

_____

_____

_____

📖 1 John 4:2-14

_____

_____

_____

While we will never be able to fully understand the concept of the Holy Trinity our efforts to uncover the biblical truth for this topic is valuable. Through our study we learn about the history, evidence and issues that surround this important piece of our theology. The Trinity is unique to Christianity and all believers should be thankful for it's existence in our lives even if we don't understand many of it's details.

Write out your memory verse in the space below. Try to do it completely from memory, then double-check yourself.

TAKE TIME TO PRAY

Trinity—Day Four

Memory Verse

John 14:23

Start today's study by writing out as much of your memory verse as you can in the space below. Then, look up the verse and make any corrections that are needed. Finally, read it three times from your Bible and take just a moment to pray before completing the following lesson.

---

*O*ver the past twenty weeks in *The Absolute Basics of Christianity,* many different topics have been presented and discussed. The goal of this study has been to help you formulate a faith that is active and living, rather than accumulating knowledge for the sake of knowledge. Today's assignment is for you to write out your own creed, or statement, of what you believe as a Christian. In the first lesson this week, you read the Nicene Creed as well as the changes that were made at the Council of Constantinople in 381 A.D. This was essentially a statement of faith by the church. Today you will write your own statement of faith based on all you have learned and come to believe over the past twenty weeks. For this assignment you will probably need to go back and review past lessons and topics that we have discussed. Take your time and cite your memory verses and other scripture as often as possible. Be prepared to share all or part of your statement of faith in your next small group meeting.

I have included a basic form below to guide you as you develop your personal Christian creed. You are free to add to this list but your creed should include what you believe about the following topics. Start by writing out what you believe about each area below, then combine them into one single statement of faith.

❧ What I believe about God

_____

_____

_____

_____

_____

❧ What I believe about Jesus

_____

_____

_____

_____

❧ What I believe about the Holy Spirit

_____

_____

_____

_____

❧ What I believe about the Holy Trinity

_____

_____

_____

_____

∂€ What I believe about God's church

_____

_____

_____

_____

∂€ What I believe about the Bible

_____

_____

_____

_____

∂€ What I believe about being a disciple of Christ

_____

_____

_____

_____

∂€ Write out your full statement of faith below or on another sheet of paper.

_____

_____

_____

_____

_____

_____

_____

_____

_____

Write out your memory verse in the space below. Try to do it completely from memory, then double-check yourself.

TAKE TIME TO PRAY

To review, use the space below to write all the memory verses you have learned so far, including this week's. You can also use this space for personal notes about this lesson.

_____

_____

_____

_____

_____

_____

_____

_____

_____

_____

_____

_____

_____

_____

_____

_____

_____

_____

_____

Unity—Day One

Memory Verse

Hebrews 10:24

Start today's study by writing out your memory verse in the space below. Then, read it three times from your Bible and take just a moment to pray before completing the following lesson.

_____

_____

_____

_____

When you hear the word "unity," what do you think of? You might think of a strong marriage or a successful sports team. We all think of different things when we hear this word. When I hear the word unity, one word always comes to my mind: SPARTAN! You might be familiar with the movie *300* that depicted the Spartan warriors' ability to fight as a unit in the battle of Thermopylae. Those 300 men held at bay the largest, most powerful army the world had ever known for days, all because of one thing. They knew how to fight as a unit. They had unity. They were unified in every move and every thrust of the spear. They were a unit in all they did. Just like today, this unity did not come easily for the Spartans.

Spartan boys were taken from their parents at the age of seven, and put into military training. They were placed in barracks with other boys their age. Those boys would become the men they would fight with until age sixty, when they were allowed to retire. They cared for each other's wounds, worked together, and trained together so that each warrior knew what the others were doing. They trained constantly with the same group of young boys, becoming teenagers and then men together.

At around age thirteen, the boys were taken from their barracks and given one pair of clothes. They were given no shoes or food and then, with only the instruction to "survive," they were sent out. For an entire year the boys had to survive alone. If they survived this year (and many did not), they would continue their training. Then at around age twenty, they were given their first official military orders and saw combat. For thirteen years these boys trained and lived as a unit and they were an incredible fighting force.

It was not until age thirty that the men were considered worthy to marry, reproduce, and live away from their barracks. Those who were still living at this point had spent twenty-three years with their brothers in arms. This created a unified fighting force the likes of which has never been reproduced. These men would often go home only to work the fields, sire children, and make sure things were in order. They would then return to their fighting units to train and live with their comrades.

The Spartans were known around the world to be one of the deadliest and most effective fighting forces. Sparta was not a big country but it was a country with a big reputation, and no one wanted to mess with the Spartans if it was avoidable.

The Spartans teach us at least two things about unity. The first is that achieving unity is not easy and does not happen quickly. As we will learn later, our unity comes from and through our Lord Jesus Christ, so in a sense it has already been achieved for us. However, this true and easy unity can only be found in a perfect world that is void of sin. The world in which we operate, however, is far from perfect. It is full of people who become prideful, jealous, and vicious at times. Sadly, humanity has become increasingly wicked and hurtful toward each other. The sinful world in which we live as God's people makes unity difficult at best and next to impossible at worst. Like the Spartans, we will have to work hard for many days, weeks, months, and years to become a people who can operate in total unity. Unity is hard, very time-consuming, and requires work.

The second thing the Spartans teach us is that unity is more than a word or an idea. Unity is a tool and a mighty force that God can use if we do the work and take the time to achieve it in his church and our families. We will never know how many kings and kingdoms thought of invading Sparta and chose to abandon their plans simply because of the unity of the Spartan army. You see, once real unity has been achieved, oftentimes unity in and of itself will be enough to ward off the enemy from launching his attack. If your church, for example, is unified, the enemy might turn his sights and attention to a weaker and less unified group rather than pressing the attack against a cohesive group that he knows will defeat him. A unified church, family, business, or country is difficult to defeat. So how important is unity in God's church? Unity is one of the most imperative and valuable things a church can possess.

    ❧ What are some other practical things the Spartan's teach us about unity?

_____

_____

    ❧ Have you seen the positive effects of unity in a team or church before? Explain.

_____

_____

_____

    ❧ Have you seen the negative effects that accompany a lack of unity before? Explain.

_____

_____

_____

Psalms 133:1 says, *How good and pleasant it is when brothers live together in unity!* The spirit of unity makes all parts of life more pleasant. There is nothing more wonderful than a husband and wife who live in unity. Churches that enjoy a spirit of unity not only are able to do great things to advance God's kingdom but they also have a peace and pleasant excitement that radiates from the group. Unity is a desirable trait and it is spoken of in many different ways throughout the pages of the Bible. For example, look up the following scripture references and write down what they have to say about unity.

    📖 Genesis 13:8-9

_____

_____

    📖 Acts 2:42-47

_____

_____

📖 Acts 4:32

_____

_____

📖 Romans 12:10-16

_____

_____

📖 Philippians 1:27

_____

_____

📖 1 Peter 3:8

_____

_____

Unity is a desirable trait. Sadly, it has become far too uncommon in God's church and among God's people. Over the course of this week we will learn many things about the importance of unity. However, if we fail to practice, work, and spend time developing unity with those around us, we will never see or experience the tremendous benefits of this powerful concept.

Write out your memory verse in the space below. Try to do it completely from memory, then double-check yourself.

TAKE TIME TO PRAY

Unity—Day Two

Memory Verse

Hebrews 10:24

Start today's study by writing out as much of your memory verse as you can in the space below. Then, look up the verse and make any corrections that are needed. Finally, read it three times from your Bible and take just a moment to pray before completing the following lesson.

_____

_____

_____

_____

Everyone seems to agree that unity is a desirable thing, but where does it come from and how do we get it? Many people in the world today have come to believe that unity is a result of nothing more than certain commonalities between people. For example, the local model train club possesses great unity because everyone in the club is passionate about model trains. But if this is where unity comes from, and if it takes nothing more than having things in common, why is there so much division among churches and families? The great majority of people at church love the same things and are passionate about serving Jesus. Most family members share many things in common and long to be united, yet unity seems to escape and remain out of reach despite the commonalities we share.

Still others believe that unity is something we create. Many pastors, for example, go to great lengths to inspire people and promote a positive spirit through programs and Christian initiatives in the hope of creating unity. Parents may plan a family trip or afternoon experience in hopes of increasing the spirit of unity within the family. However successful these things may be, in the short term they usually prove insufficient as time passes. This is not to say that having things in common, inspiring people, formulating programs, or planning family events are useless when it comes to unity. In fact, all of these things can positively affect our efforts to build unity. However, the problem arises when we use these things in an effort to create unity. None of these things, nor any other earthly venture, can create true unity.

📖 Read Ephesians 4:1-6. What are we supposed to do with unity?

_____

_____

🏃 According to this passage, where does true unity come from?

_____

_____

📖 How do verses 4-6 emphasize the concept of unity?

_____

_____

We can all agree that trying to get unity in a small family unit is difficult enough. Trying to achieve unity on a committee at work or on a team at church can at times seem impossible. So how can we then expect to have unity as a church body? In essence, our goal is not so much to create or manufacture unity, but instead, Paul says, it is to keep, or some translations say "maintain," unity. As we learned yesterday, the Spartans had to both create and maintain unity, but Christians must only maintain it, for God himself creates it. We are not unified under a church name, pastor's vision, denominational lines, or a church constitution. Our unity is in Jesus Christ the KING OF KINGS and LORD OF LORDS! Therefore we are to make every effort to keep the unity of the Spirit through the bond of peace.

This is all possible because we are already one body; we have one Spirit, one hope, one Lord, one Faith, one baptism, and one God who is over everything. Our unity as a body of believers comes not from ourselves but from being one with the God of the universe. God has unified us through his one and only Son, Jesus Christ. Our goal is to keep and maintain the unity that we already have in Jesus. This translates to our families as well. Unity for the Christian family is in Christ, not in vacations or family reunions. We cannot create true unity. Instead, we are only called to preserve it.

We find further evidence that we are unable to create or produce unity on our own in Ephesians 4:11-16. This passage describes unity as more than a desirable trait. It describes it as a goal to be reached by all believers. Unity is a mark of maturity and a goal that takes time and effort to attain.

📖 Read Ephesians 4:11-16. According to verses 11-12, why did God give apostles, prophets, evangelists, pastors, and teachers to the church? What is their main role in God's kingdom? 🎬

_____

_____

_____

_____

❧ What other two goals does Paul give, in verse thirteen? ⚒

_____

_____

_____

Is unity a gift created by God for us to maintain, or a goal to be reached? The answer is both. God created unity; in fact, as we learned in Week Twenty, the Godhead is the perfect picture of true unity as the Father, Son, and Spirit all exist in total unity in the form of the Trinity. That can never be replicated, or recreated by individuals, so it is our job to keep the unity that comes through the Spirit. However, because of the sinful world we live in, unity is not easy to keep; therefore it is a goal that all believers should strive to reach. The NIV commentary writes the following on the subject.

> *"The unity of the Spirit" is a gift to be guarded; here "unity in the faith" is a goal to be reached. Such a realization of unity will arise from an increasing knowledge of Christ as the Son of God in corporate as well as in personal experience.*
>
> *In this way the church comes of age; it becomes "mature" (that is, "a perfect, full-grown man"). The singular is employed because the church as a whole is seen as "one new man" in Christ (Eph. 2:15). Individualism is a mark of immaturity. This perfection or completeness is proportionate to the fullness of Christ himself. "Whole measure" or "perfection" can denote age (Matt 6:27; John 9:21) and may well be used here in this sense, since the context has to do with becoming an adult. The meaning would be "attain to the measure of mature age" proper for Christians, who have*

left infancy behind (Eph. 4:14). But the phrase may also refer to spiritual attainment (cf. Luke 2:52). "Fullness" (see comment on Eph. 1:23) is here related to Christ. Just as Christians may be "filled to the measure of all the fullness of God" (Eph. 3:19), so together they are to aspire to "the full measure of perfection found in Christ."[61]

It is clear that we cannot create unity, but how can we get it? The answer in part is found in the other two goals that Paul outlines in Ephesians 4:11-16. Paul's final two goals for believers are that they might become mature through "knowledge of the Son of God," and "attaining to the whole measure of the fullness of Christ." True unity is impossible without an eternal knowledge of Jesus Christ. As the believer matures and discovers the full measure of what it means to live in Christ, true unity is realized as well. Furthermore, as each believer functions in accord with the gifts Christ has given him (verse 7), the body as a whole enjoys unity (cf. verses 3-6) and becomes more spiritually mature (cf. verse 15), more like Jesus Christ in all His fullness (cf. 1:23; 3:19).[62]

Look up the verses that are listed below and decide which of Paul's goals from Ephesians 4:11-16 they correspond to. ✖

1. Ephesians 1:17

   a) Unity

   b) Knowledge of the Son

   c) Fullness of Christ

2. Ephesians 4:5

   a) Unity

   b) Knowledge of the Son

   c) Fullness of Christ

3. Ephesians 4:7; 16

   a) Unity

   b) Knowledge of the Son

   c) Fullness of Christ

Tomorrow, we will examine what Jesus had to say about the importance of unity among believers. Spend some time thinking about the areas of your life that

---

61 Kenneth L. Barker and John R. Kohlenberger, eds., *Zondervan NIV Bible Commentary.* Accordance electronic ed. (Grand Rapids, MI: Zondervan, 1994), n.p.

62 John F. Walvoord and Roy B. Zuck, eds., *The Bible Knowledge Commentary: New Testament.* Accordance electronic ed. (Wheaton, IL: Victor Books, 1983), n.p.

need more unity. Pray about how God might use you to restore or keep the unity at your church, in your home, or at your place of work.

Write out your memory verse in the space below. Try to do it completely from memory, then double-check yourself.

_____

_____

_____

_____

TAKE TIME TO PRAY

Unity—Day Three

Memory Verse

Hebrews 10:24

Start today's study by writing out as much of your memory verse as you can in the space below. Then, look up the verse and make any corrections that are needed. Finally, read it three times from your Bible and take just a moment to pray before completing the following lesson.

So far in our study of unity, we have looked at its importance and its origin. Today we will turn our attention to some specific passages of scripture in which Jesus Christ himself spoke about unity. The scriptures we will look at today all come from the gospel of John. This book in particular gives us incredible insight into some of the most personal and intimate encounters that Christ had with individuals. Therefore it should come as no surprise to find that John's gospel, more than the others, elaborates on the necessity of unity. Start by reading John 17:20-26 and answer the questions below.

❧ Who is this prayer for?

❧ To what does Jesus compare the unity among believers? ✗

_____

_____

_____

❧ What does Jesus say the main purpose for this unity is? ✗

_____

_____

_____

That they may be one as we are one... This is an absolutely astonishing statement included in the prayer of Christ. It seems highly unlikely that Jesus would include such a statement if it were not possible. Therefore, totally unity and oneness should be our goal. This is one of the greatest marks of spiritual maturity in a church, family, or individual believer's life. As we previously learned in the study on the Holy Trinity, the Father, Son, and Spirit exist in complete oneness. While their roles in God's kingdom and divine plan may vary, their unity and oneness are highlighted in their singular mission to redeem humankind and restore the eternal relationship that was damaged by sin's destructive power.

Jesus does not pray that we might be one, like peanut butter and jelly make one sandwich, or like water and ice make one refreshing beverage. His prayer is not that we would just coexist with one another in harmony, but rather that we would be united in love and become one, just as he was one with the Father. The Father did his works through the Son and the Son always did what pleased the Father (John 5:30; 8:29). This spiritual unity is to be patterned in the church.[63] Despite our differences, unity should be the priority among believers. Barnes writes the following on this text in his work *Notes on the New Testament.*

> *There are no ties as tender as those which bind us in the gospel. There is no friendship as pure and enduring as that which results from having the same attachment to the Lord Jesus. Hence Christians, in the New Testament, are represented as being indissolubly united— parts of the same body, and members of the same family, Acts 4:32- 35. 1 Cor. 12:4-31; Eph. 2:20-22; Rom. 12:5. On the ground of this union they are exhorted to love one another, to bear one another's*

---

63   John F. Walvoord and Roy B. Zuck, eds., *The Bible Knowledge Commentary: New Testament.* Accordance electronic ed. (Wheaton, IL: Victor Books, 1983), n.p.

burdens, and to study the things that make for peace, and things wherewith one may edify another, Eph. 4:3; Rom. 12:5-16.[64]

ᵉ❧ Would you describe your church as a place that represents the idea of biblical unity? Why, or why not?

_____

_____

ᵉ❧ Would you describe your family situation with this concept of unity?

_____

_____

ᵉ❧ Would you describe your work environment as a place of unity?

_____

_____

ᵉ❧ In your estimation, what needs to change so that oneness can be achieved in these and other areas of your life? Do you think that unity and oneness is even possible? Why, or why not?

_____

_____

_____

_____

ᵉ❧ How would you describe the concept of oneness to someone else?

_____

_____

_____

_____

Jesus also spoke to the issue of unity in John 6:46-60. Here, Christ emphasized the importance for all believers to remain united or connected to him. It is

64 Albert Barnes, *Barnes' Notes on the New Testament,* Accordance electronic ed. (Altamonte Springs: OakTree Software, 2006), n.p.

not enough for believers to be united only to each other. Our unity comes from and through Christ; therefore, every effort must be made to remain connected to Jesus at all times. Read John 6:46-60 and answer the questions below.

> ⅇ Why was this concept of unity so difficult for the audience to accept? ✖

_____

_____

_____

> ⅇ Which verse speaks primarily to the concept of remaining united to Christ? What does that verse mean to you? ✖

_____

_____

_____

_____

> 📖 The modern church practices communion on a regular basis. In light of this passage, what significance does communion or the Lord's Supper have in the life of a believer?

_____

_____

_____

_____

In John 13:34-35, we read the words of Christ, *A new command I give you: Love one another. As I have loved you, so you must love one another. By this all men will know that you are my disciples, if you love one another.* This was not really a "new" command or a foreign idea for the disciples. However, the command was new in that it defines a special love for other believers based on the sacrificial love of Jesus: *As I have loved you, so you must love one another,* Jesus proclaims. As Jesus was the embodiment of God's love, so now each disciple should embody Christ's love. This love is a sign to the world as well as to every believer (1 John 3:14).[65] While the word "unity" is not used here, it certainly is implied by Christ. This new concept of love for each other was radically different from the selfishness

---

65 John F. Walvoord and Roy B. Zuck, eds., *The Bible Knowledge Commentary: New Testament.* Accordance electronic ed. (Wheaton, IL: Victor Books, 1983), n.p.

and self-absorbed lifestyle of the sinful world. Instead, Christ called all believers to abandon themselves and unite with other believers through love. Unity is more than just a good idea; it's more than just a prayerful request from the savior as well. It is our defining mark as believers. The world will know us by the way we love each other. They will know us by our unity.

Write out your memory verse in the space below. Try to do it completely from memory, then double-check yourself.

TAKE TIME TO PRAY

Unity—Day Four

Memory Verse

Hebrews 10:24

Start today's study by writing out as much of your memory verse as you can in the space below. Then, look up the verse and make any corrections that are needed. Finally, read it three times from your Bible and take just a moment to pray before completing the following lesson.

---

his week, we have examined the importance of unity for all believers. This desirable trait is significant in all areas and levels of our lives. It is critical in our churches, small groups, Bible studies, and mission teams. It is equally valuable in our homes, places of work, and any other location or activity in which the believer is socially involved. We have seen how important the concept of unity is in the Bible and we have examined some of the things that Jesus himself said about unity. But what happens when unity is no longer an option? For our final study on unity, we will attempt to answer this difficult and perplexing dilemma.

All believers should make every effort to keep the unity of the Spirit through the bond of peace, as the Bible commands in Ephesians 4:3. The book of Romans also encourages all Christians to make every effort to do what leads to peace and to mutual edification (Rom. 14:19). But what happens when unity, peace, and mutual edification are no longer an option? This unpleasant and unfortunate circumstance is likely to find us all in some way during our Christian journey. It happened to some of the greatest people in the Bible and it will happen to us as well.

I can recall several instances in my ministry where every effort to keep the unity was made but, for one reason or another, it simply was no longer possible. One situation came about between the church that I pastor and a church plant we had attempted to launch. This plant started like many others, and we had a great deal of success early on. Our core group of fifteen grew to twenty-five within weeks. The crowd that gathered for our monthly service grew from thirty to over one hundred and fifty in less than a year. Everything seemed to be going great until I received a phone call one afternoon from one of the most faithful and dedicated core team members, who informed me she was leaving the new church. When I asked why, she began to tell me several disturbing details about the lay leader of the core group. After weeks of prayer and numerous meetings, it was clear that the core team leader had an incredible need to micro-manage everything. The breaking point for the core team was his unilateral decision to hire a pastor (whom he chose) without consulting the core team, church, or his sponsor church. Around the same time, accusations of embezzlement from his local financial business began to surface and many questions were raised about his involvement at such a high level in the church.

Each time this individual was confronted, he responded in a very Christian and biblical manner, saying things like "I just want to do what's best for the church." He was asked to resign as leader and he willingly turned in his resignation and agreed to turn over the church documents, mailing lists, and other important information within a week. However, the documents never came, and we later learned that on the very night he resigned, he phoned many people in the congregation and started building a resistance to overthrow the core team and regain power. This went on for a period of months behind the scenes, and over time it started to affect the church. The core team was divided and the attendance numbers began to decline. Word also got out about the turmoil that was taking place within the church.

One last attempt was made to keep the unity, and another agreement was reached. Then two weeks later, as this young church prepared for its meeting, someone in the core team came and informed me that this man was meeting across the street and was starting "his own" church. He had a similar name and the same logo, slogan, and mission statement as the church plant. The following week we had our last meeting with this man and it was clear that unity was no longer an option.

Every effort should be made to keep the unity of the Spirit. However, a time may come when it is better for all parties and the kingdom of God for individuals to go their own way. This happened many times in the Bible; however, for the sake of space we will only examine two instances. Start by reading about the situation that came up between Abram and his nephew Lot in Genesis 13.

ᴥ Who offered a solution to the problem? Abram or Lot?

_____

_____

ᴥ What was the solution that was offered?

_____

_____

ᴥ Do you think this speaks to the maturity of Abram? Why, or why not?

_____

_____

ᴥ Honestly, what do you think you would have done in this situation?

_____

_____

ᴥ What other things can we learn from this chapter of scripture?

_____

_____

_____

The quarreling arose between Abram's herdsmen and the herdsmen of Lot. The land they were living in simply was not able to support the increasing size of these men's herds and families. There does not seem to be any outrageous hatred between these two men, but the circumstances provided by the land dictated that they part company. The Hebrew word used to describe the quarreling is "*rib*" (pronounced "reeve"). This small word carries a large meaning. This is more than just a common disagreement about whose cattle will eat what grass. This word means there was a great amount of anger involving bodily struggle one with another; as well as public hostilities.[66] This was not a quiet private dispute between Abram and Lot. This was a community-wide, public argument that could have indeed involved some physical fighting among the herdsmen.

Abram's maturity prevailed and he offered a solution that all could agree on. From this solution, we too can learn several lessons about how to handle situa-

---

66 *BDB A Hebrew and English Lexicon of the Old Testament (Abridged),* (Oxford Clarendon Press,. 1907 OakTree Software, 2001), n.p.

tions that require us to part company with others. First, we clearly see that Abram trusted God fully. By offering Lot the first pick of the land, Abram indicated that he had full confidence in God's ability to continue to bless him and his family despite the land that they might live in.

We also learn that there can be peace even when parting is necessary. Abram and Lot did not burn their bridges as they headed in different directions. In fact, in chapter 14, Abram came to Lot's rescue when he was captured. Despite being able to continue to live with each other in peace, they chose to pursue peace as they lived apart. It is easy in the heat of the moment to say things that we later regret. Sometimes adults say the meanest and most hateful things during the final days of a divorce proceeding, only to realize later that despite parting company, they are still required to communicate and work together for the sake of the children involved. Church splits can include mean, angry, and downright hurtful rhetoric as one group decides to leave. Generally the church members who leave only move a short distance away and it is soon realized that even though they have parted company, it is still necessary for each congregation to work with the other to reach their community for Christ. We should do everything possible to preserve the peace, even when unity is no longer a possibility.

Finally, follow through with the agreement. If you agree to go left, then go left. If you agree to go right, then go right. Don't venture back over into the other's territory. Abram and Lot both did what they said they would do, and this helped preserve the peace even when unity was no longer possible. How do you think the story would have ended if Abram had commanded his herdsmen to graze the flocks and herds in the plain to the east that Lot had chosen? When an agreement is reached, follow through with whatever you have agreed to.

In the book of Acts we find another example of two strong Christians who are unable to preserve and keep the unity of the faith. The Apostle Paul is known to be one of the greatest church planters, and one of the most fearless followers of Christ the world has ever known. However, after many fruitful days of ministry, Barnabas and Paul had a bitter disagreement that led them to the point of going in separate directions. Read about this in Acts 15:30-41, then answer the questions below?

❧ What was the argument about?

_____

_____

❧ Who do you think was right?

_____

_____

❧ Why do you think disagreements like this happen between people who are so committed to Christ?

_____

_____

_____

From this passage, we can conclude that these men also set us a good example of what to do when unity is no longer an option. Paul and Barnabas both trusted that God would bless their ministries as they parted company, and he did. Also like Abram and Lot, they kept the peace even when they separated. Late in Paul's life he actually calls on Timothy to bring Mark to him because he was helpful for Paul's ministry (2 Tim 4:11). So apparently, Paul and Barnabas and those they traveled with kept in touch enough to know what was going on in each other's ministries. These men chose to live in peace with each other even after they separated. We don't see or hear of either man demeaning the other, or attempting to harm the other's ministry. Peace prevailed, even when unity could not. Both men also followed through with the agreement. Paul took his group and went through Syria and Cilicia to build up the churches there. Barnabas took Mark and left for Cyprus. Neither tried to interfere with the other's work.

To close our lesson on unity, remember to do everything possible to keep the unity of the Spirit. We should always do as much as we can to attempt to live in both peace and unity. Every effort should be made to remain united in love despite the circumstances or situations we may face. However, when unity is no longer an option, and going in separate directions is the only possible solution, Christians should trust God, keep the peace, and follow through with the agreement.

❧ Think about personal situations you have faced in the past that required you to part company with someone or some group. Did you do these three things? How might the situation have been different if you had followed these three steps?

_____

_____

_____

_____

_____

_____

Write out your memory verse in the space below. Try to do it completely from memory, then double-check yourself.

TAKE TIME TO PRAY

To review, use the space below to write all the memory verses you have learned so far, including this week's. You can also use this space for personal notes about this lesson.

_____

_____

_____

_____

_____

_____

_____

_____

_____

_____

_____

_____

_____

_____

_____

_____

_____

_____

_____

_____

Victory—Day One

Memory Verse

Psalms 18:35

Start today's study by writing out your memory verse in the space below. Then, read it three times from your Bible and take just a moment to pray before completing the following lesson.

---

*E*veryone knows what it means to be victorious. However, the word or concept of victory can be difficult to understand because it carries so many meanings. The original word comes from the Latin word *victoria*, which applied primarily to defeating an enemy in battle. Today, the term is much broader. For example, our military today celebrates strategic victories and tactical victories. The headline in the paper might read, "Local man wins chess tournament with a stunning victory!" The modern-day concept of victory even allows individuals to experience victory in defeat. The losing team might be viewed as winners based on sportsmanship, or the victory might just be making it to the championship game, or coming from behind and beating all the odds to have a chance to win. You can even experience personal victories when you reach a goal, such as losing twenty pounds, successfully completing a project, or finishing a marathon. In the same way, spiritual victories come in many shapes and sizes. The main goal of this week's study is not to examine all the different possibilities for victory, but rather to learn how we can become victorious in our everyday lives. This starts with sacrifice.

There is no hope of victory without sacrifice. If you truly desire to be victorious in your spiritual walk, you must be willing to sacrifice anything that might hinder your progress or get in your way. The fact that you have completed twenty-one weeks of this study shows that you are one who desires to be victorious and is willing to make whatever sacrifices are necessary to grow closer to Christ. Past generations have understood the significance of sacrifice as it relates to victory. The heroes that fought in the Second World War, for example, were willing to make extreme sacrifices to defeat the evil that faced their generation. Their families back home in the states willingly rose to the challenge as well, and went without many of the luxuries of life in order to assist in the war so that the Allies could be victorious. While there are still people who understand that victory can never be achieved without sacrifice, many today simply want the prize without paying the price.

If you desire to win a gold medal at the Olympics, you must be willing to pay the price. Great sacrifices must be made in order to eat right, train for hours on end, and fight through the pain of injuries that will no doubt happen along the way. Those who desire to start their own business will be forced to make many sacrifices to ensure its success. If you desire to be victorious in your marriage, you may have to sacrifice time at work or be willing to lose a big sale in order to take your wife out on a date. If you desire to be victorious as a parent, it will require sacrifice. If financial victory is something you desire, you must be willing to sacrifice in order to save money. And if spiritual victory is what you desire, it too will require sacrifice. There simply is no victory without sacrifice. Look up the following verses and identify the kinds of sacrifices that were required for victory.

📖 Matthew 4:19-22 ⚒

_____

_____

📖 Luke 5:27-30

_____

_____

📖 Luke 9:57-62

_____

_____

📖 Luke 18:18-30 ✗

_____

_____

📖 Hebrews 9:21-28

_____

_____

📖 1 John 4:10

_____

_____

As we look at the great men and women of the Bible, it is easy to see that they all had at least one thing in common. They were all willing to make many sacrifices to be used by God. Whether it was Abraham, Joseph, Moses, Esther, or Nehemiah from the Old Testament, or Peter, James, Matthew, Mark, Luke, Mary, or Paul from the New Testament, each made tremendous sacrifices and, because they were willing to pay the price, they won some of the most incredible victories the Christian faith has ever known. Jesus Christ himself is the greatest example of this principle. He won the ultimate victory through his death, burial, and resurrection by defeating Satan and overcoming evil once and for all. Yet in doing so, he also made the ultimate sacrifice by giving his life for the victory. It is impossible to speak about victory until we understand that sacrifice will be essential as well.

❧ What have you sacrificed to follow Christ?

_____

_____

❧ What are you currently giving up in order to grow closer to Christ?

_____

_____

❧ What have you refused to give up? Why?

_____

_____

❧ Can you think of any great victory that has been won without sacrifice?

_____

_____

❧ How do you think your life would change if you were willing to sacrifice everything for the sake of Christ?

_____

_____

_____

_____

_____

❧ What would be different in your church if all believers understood the necessity of sacrifice?

_____

_____

_____

_____

_____

❧ How would our world be different?

_____

_____

_____

_____

_____

Conclude today's study by reading the passage of scripture that your memory verse comes from this week. Read Psalms 18:31-50 and make notes about any significant points you would like to share with your small group at the next meeting.

Write out your memory verse in the space below. Try to do it completely from memory, then double-check yourself.

TAKE TIME TO PRAY

Victory—Day Two

Memory Verse

Psalms 18:35

Start today's study by writing out as much of your memory verse as you can in the space below. Then, look up the verse and make any corrections that are needed. Finally, read it three times from your Bible and take just a moment to pray before completing the following lesson.

One Sunday morning I asked a series of strange questions to our congregation. "How many of you want to fail today?" "Raise your hand if you desire to be a loser in life." "If you woke up this morning and thought I hope this is the worst day of my life, would you raise your hand?" There were well over one thousand people in attendance that day and not a single person raised a hand. Was it fear of embarrassment that caused them to sit on their hands? Of course not; the truth is that we all want to be victorious. Each of us has an inner desire to excel and be successful in life. We want to conquer our fears, defeat our enemies, and overcome our temptations. We desire victory, but most people simply don't know how to achieve it.

Like most boys growing up, I dreamed of one day scoring the winning touchdown at the Superbowl or bringing in the winning run at the World Series. There is no telling how many thousands of times I dodged ghost tacklers and dove into the end zone with one second left on the clock, or slapped a baseball out into the pasture where my father's cows were grazing and felt the joy of having my team rush out of the dugout and put me on their shoulders. The desire to be victorious begins at an early age and while I no longer dream of scoring the winning touchdown or RBI, I have no less passion when it comes to victory. Today I dream about celebrating my fiftieth wedding anniversary with my wife and being victorious as a husband. As I tuck my children in at night and close my eyes to pray over their innocent lives, I see myself walking my daughter down the aisle, or celebrating as my son fulfills his great God-given purpose in life. I long for victory as a father. Sometimes as I pray in my study, I imagine myself one day walking down those streets of gold and meeting those who were impacted, touched, discipled, trained, and strengthened through the years I spent in ministry. Personally, I long for the day that I am able to stand face-to-face with Christ and humbly bow at his feet in worship and thank him for the eternal victory he made possible for me. I don't care to be rich or famous. But I wake up each day with victory on my heart and mind. And if you are honest with yourself, you do too.

Yesterday we looked at one of the keys to victory. Sacrifice is essential if we have any hope of victory in our lives. Christ Jesus made the ultimate sacrifice and secured the eternal victory, but as believers we must be willing to sacrifice as well to experience victory. Today we will look at three more keys to victory from the book of Joshua. Read Joshua 6:1-21, then answer the questions below.

- How many days did they march around the city?

  _____

- How many times did they march around the city the first six days?

  _____

- How many times did they march around the city on the seventh day?

  _____

- How many priests carried the trumpets of ram's horns in front of the ark?

  _____

- Is there any common number in the above questions? What is the significance of this number? ✗

  _____

  _____

   ✺ When did Joshua tell the people how many times and how many days they would march around the city?

_____

_____

   ✺ How would you have felt if you were in Joshua's army? What questions would you have asked if given the chance?

_____

_____

_____

If you want to be victorious you must remember who's in charge. Furthermore, you must be willing to submit to that authority. Joshua was leading the army but he was not in charge. The Lord himself was calling the shots; Joshua was in the Lord's army and so are we. While most Christians today would rightly say that God is with us, few are willing to acknowledge that God is leading us through his Holy Spirit. We don't want to follow or do it his way. As a result, we miss out on the joy of victory in our lives. Think for a moment about what might have happened if Joshua had tried to take Jericho on his own, using his own tactics and military skills. Thankfully we don't have to read about that story; instead, we read about the great victory of Jericho as the walls came crashing down. If you desire victory in your marriage, with your children, at work, in business, on the field, at church, or in any other area of life, you must remember who's in charge and do it his way. It will no doubt require obedience and sacrifice, but victory is worth it.

The next key to victory is to expect the unexpected. The Bible says, _Then the LORD said to Joshua, "See, I have delivered Jericho into your hands, along with its king and its fighting men. March around the city once with all the armed men. Do this for six days... When you hear them sound a long blast on the trumpets, have all the people give a loud shout; then the wall of the city will collapse and the people will go up, every man straight in"_ Josh 6:2-5). The Hebrew word for "see" here can mean to view, look, or become visible. Could God have actually shown Joshua the outcome of the battle? Of course! But still this sounds like a crazy plan. Furthermore, as far as scripture is concerned, Joshua never told anyone else what was going to happen. They didn't know if they were going to march for a week, a month, or a year. It is highly probable that many of Joshua's men thought he was crazy because this was unlike any other military strategy of the day. Day after day these men got up, put on their armor, prepared for battle, got mentally prepared for action, then went for a stroll around the city. It would take some imagination to conceive of a more, foolish, ridiculous, crazy plan to invade a well-defended and fortified city. But when God's in charge, you'd better expect the unexpected. Our

God is creative, powerful, and strange when it comes to victory. After all, what kind of imagination would one need to conceive of the redemptive plan of God? That he would send his one and only son to die as a sinless lamb on the cross, for a despicable, fallen race such as ours while we were his enemies? Don't refuse to march just because the plan is not what you expected or you will miss out on the victory.

The final key to victory is to never quit or give up. What would the outcome of the battle have been if the men had refused to march on that seventh day? Or worse yet, what would the result have been if on the seventh day, after marching around the city six times, they said "We've had enough; let's go back to camp." Again, we would not be reading about a victory had they quit one lap short. It's sad to think how many marriages have ended in divorce one lap short of a breakthrough. Or how many friendships have never been restored because we refused to walk that last lap of forgiveness. Or how many churches have split one lap short of victory. I wonder how many times we have stopped praying for and witnessing to our lost friends and family members one lap too soon. Never stop marching, never quit, and never give up unless God says your mission is over. You never know what God will do tomorrow, or if you just make one more lap around those walls, they just might come tumbling down in the most miraculous and victorious way.

& Can you list the four keys to victory?

1. _____

2. _____

3. _____

4. _____

& Which of the four do you find most difficult? Why?

_____

_____

_____

& Do you think achieving victory is more attainable if you do these four things? Explain, using examples from the past if possible.

_____

_____

_____

_____

Write out your memory verse in the space below. Try to do it completely from memory, then double-check yourself.

TAKE TIME TO PRAY

Victory—Day Three

Memory Verse

Psalms 18:35

Start today's study by writing out as much of your memory verse as you can in the space below. Then, look up the verse and make any corrections that are needed. Finally, read it three times from your Bible and take just a moment to pray before completing the following lesson.

---

*U*nderstanding the four keys to victory is extremely important when it comes to our preparation for victory. However, those four keys are not the only critical things to remember. When it comes to victory, preparation is essential for the modern day disciple. It is simply too late to prepare once the enemy has arrived and is threatening to overrun your position. Without preparation, long-term victory is unlikely.

One summer during my college years, while I was working for a local farmer, I learned the value of preparation. I am a task-oriented individual by nature, and doing the small things to prepare for the day seemed pointless to me at the time. For example, the man I worked for would rise each morning at four and perform a series of stretches and exercises to prepare his body for the day. He would then spend an hour studying God's word to prepare his mind and spirit for anything he might encounter. At 6:00, when we arrived for breakfast, this man had already been preparing for the upcoming day for two hours. After breakfast we would be asked to meticulously check the equipment we would be using for the day. One day after I had rushed to be the first on the tractor to get started with the day's work, my boss came over and shared a story about the importance of preparation.

He said there was once a hard-working young man who asked for a job on a logging crew. The foreman asked, "Can you fell a tree?" The young man stepped forward and skillfully felled the great tree in front of him and the foreman put him to work on a crew immediately, with great expectations. Three days later the foreman came to the young man at the end of the shift and said, "You can pick up your check on your way out today." "What do you mean", the young man replied, "we don't get paid till next week." "I know, but you are falling behind, so I am going to have to let you go," said the foreman. The young man objected, saying, "But I'm one of your hardest workers. I arrive first and leave last, and I have even been working through my coffee breaks!" "I know," said the foreman. "I don't understand either but you are just not keeping up." Looking down at the boy's axe, the foreman asked, "Have you been sharpening your axe?" The young man replied, "No, I've been working too hard to take the time."

When my boss had finished the story, he climbed down out of my tractor and left without saying a word. I was confused—was I fired, or was there a lesson I was supposed to learn from that silly story? I drove away and went to work, and thought about the story for the next several hours, then I realized how important preparation was. Each day as we arrived back at the farmer's house, I and many of the other hands were worn out. All we wanted to do was go home and sleep because we knew that at 6:00 tomorrow, we would be required to do it all over again. The farmer, however, was still hard at work each day as we drove away. Generally he was working in the barn, feeding animals around the house, or fixing the equipment we had broken during the day. Despite being nearly three times our age, and working alongside us all day long, when we went home to sleep he was still hard at work. Years of early morning preparation and his great attention to the smallest details about his body, spiritual health, and equipment, made the difference. He was more effective because he took time to sharpen his axe.

It is no different when it comes to victory. Knowing the keys to victory is not enough; we must prepare to be victorious as well. We can learn several lessons about preparing for victory from the life of David. Read the passage in 2 Samuel 5:17-25, then answer the questions below.

⁂ Who was looking for David?

_____

⁂ In this passage, how many times did David "inquire of the Lord?"

_____

❧ Does God answer David with the same answer each time he makes an inquiry? If not, how are his answers different?

_____

_____

_____

_____

The first thing we must do in order to prepare for victory is to always remain vigilant. The text says that "David heard" what was about to happen. This allowed him the time he needed to make the necessary plans to defeat his enemy. Almost all of the things that bring Christians down today could be avoided if we would only learn to look and listen better. When we see the attack from a distance, it gives us time to prepare our strategy and defenses to overcome our adversary. We should always be on the lookout for the attack that is sure to come. David was able to achieve victory because he was vigilant. This gave him time to retreat into the "stronghold" in order to prepare for battle. If we are vigilant, we are less likely to be caught off guard and more likely to experience victory in every area of our life. Look up the following verses and write down what they have to say about being vigilant.

📖 Matthew 24:42-43

_____

_____

📖 Matthew 26:40-41

_____

_____

📖 Romans 16:17 ✗

_____

_____

📖 Galatians 5:15

_____

_____

📖 1 Timothy 4:16

_____

_____

Next, David "asked the Lord" what to do. It seems so obvious but how many times do we fail and fall prey to our enemy simply because we don't ask God what to do. God answers David quickly and gives him specific advice on how to achieve victory over the Philistines. Many times we run to God and ask for advice only when we are on the verge of defeat. At our lowest moment, when our backs are against the wall, we hit our knees in one last desperate attempt to avoid defeat. David, however, did this as part of his preparation for victory and it made all of the difference. We should prepare by remaining in constant communication with God. Look up the following verses that have to do with our communication with God, and make notes that can be used in your next class discussion.

📖 1 Samuel 30:8

_____

_____

📖 James 1:5-8

_____

_____

📖 1 John 5:14-15

_____

_____

Finally, we see through this event in the life of David the importance of following God. This man not only asked God; he obeyed God as well. The first time David inquired of the Lord, God basically said "Go, for I will surely hand the Philistines over to you." But the second time God said, "Do not go straight up..." David had to be willing to listen and change his tactics. It would have been easy to assume that, because God had previously said go straight in for I am handing your enemy to you on a silver platter, David might have adopted this strategy in his next encounter as well. Christians today have a bad habit of assuming many things about God's plans and will. We assume that because he healed our friend, he will heal us as well. Or that the event God blessed last year must certainly be the event we should attempt this year. We assume that the strategy God previously used to deliver victory into our lives will not change at our next encounter with the enemy.

So we fail to look and listen, or ask for God's advice. Instead, we foolishly run into the arms of our enemy and suffer defeat. We must be careful to avoid making assumptions about what God would have us to do, and instead listen, ask, and follow him at each individual obstacle we face.

📖 What assumption was made in John 9:1-7?

_____

_____

📖 Who made the assumption?

_____

_____

📖 What does this teach you?

_____

_____

God alone can bring victory into our lives. David said, *As waters break out, the LORD has broken out against my enemies before me* (2 Sam 5:20). While it is God who overwhelms our enemies, we must do our part to prepare for the battle. God's power brings victory to all situations, circumstances, and even tragedies. However, God chooses to use his people in the process as well. Therefore we must take the time to sharpen our spiritual axe and prepare for victory if we have any hope of achieving it.

Write out your memory verse in the space below. Try to do it completely from memory, then double-check yourself.

_____

_____

_____

_____

TAKE TIME TO PRAY

Victory—Day Four

Memory Verse

Psalms 18:35

Start today's study by writing out as much of your memory verse as you can in the space below. Then, look up the verse and make any corrections that are needed. Finally, read it three times from your Bible and take just a moment to pray before completing the following lesson.

_____

_____

_____

_____

The Greek word for victory is νίκη; in English it is known as Nike. In Greek mythology, Nike was also a goddess who personified victory throughout the time of the ancient Greek culture. She is known as the Winged Goddess of Victory. The Roman equivalent was Victoria. Depending upon the time of various myths, she was described as the daughter of Pallas (Titan) and Styx (Water), and the sister of Kratos (Strength), Bia (Force), and Zelus (Zeal). Nike and her siblings were close companions of Zeus, the dominant deity of the Greek pantheon. Nike assumed the role of the divine charioteer, a role in which she often is portrayed in classical Greek art. Nike flew around battlefields rewarding the victors with glory and fame.[67]

---

67 "Nike (mythology)." Wikipedia, the Free Encyclopedia. http://en.wikipedia.org/wiki/Nike_ (mythology) (accessed June 27, 2010).

Sadly, to many believers in the world today the victorious full and abundant life that is spoken of in the Bible seems like Greek mythology as well. Many fight depression, doubts, anxiety, abuse, divorce, financial struggles, marriage issues, sickness, chronic pain, loneliness, temptation, or addictions, and wonder if there really is such a thing as the victorious life. The answer is YES, and victory can be yours, if you will follow the keys to victory and prepare for it.

The New Testament assures us of the reality of victory in the lives of those who believe. However, we can't create victory ourselves; it is achieved only once we fully submit our lives to Jesus Christ. Read what Paul had to say to the Corinthian church in 1 Corinthians 15:51-58 on the subject of victory, then answer the questions below.

❧ What is the mystery that Paul speaks about in this passage?

_____

_____

❧ What has been "swallowed up in victory?"

_____

_____

❧ Who gives the victory?

_____

_____

So why does the victorious life seem so illusive and hard to attain? Biblical scholar John MacArthur offers the following explanation.

> *Christ's resurrection broke the power of death for those who believe in Him, and death is no longer master over them because "death no longer is master over Him" (Rom 6:9). But death is still the enemy of man. Even for Christians it violates our dominion of God's creation, it breaks love relationships, it disrupts families, and causes great grief in the loss of those dear to us. We no longer need fear death, but it still invades and torments us while we are mortal.*[68]

Despite our current struggles, we will one day enjoy the eternal victory that is promised in God's word. And despite the fact that we have already won the victory through the blood of Jesus, we will still have struggles, temptations,

---

68   John MacArthur, *1 Corinthians,* MacArthur New Testament Commentary. Accordance electronic ed. (Chicago: Moody Press, 1984), 444.

and hardships in this life because of sin. Followers of Christ don't expect to be exempted from the struggle against sin's destructive forces, but we can be certain that victory is ours because of our Lord and Savior Jesus Christ. 1 Peter 1:3-9 elaborates on a similar point. Read the text closely and then answer the following questions.

   ❧ Does this passage look at the trials, temptations, and difficulties we face as being negative or positive? Explain.

_____

_____

_____

   ❧ According to these verses, how secure is our salvation?

_____

_____

_____

Once again, in 1 John 5:1-5, we find that those who have trusted Christ and remain in him will indeed overcome the world and all of its hardships. When we obey and follow Christ, the road will indeed be narrow, uncomfortable, and at times difficult to travel. But victory is still reserved for those who believe. There is nothing in all of creation that can strip believers from the eternal victory that Christ has secured for each of us. Answer the following questions after you have thoroughly read 1 John 5:1-5.

   ❧ What single attribute is equated with loving God in this passage? ⚒

_____

   ❧ Verse 3 says, *and his commands are not* _____
     Do you agree with that statement? Why, or why not?

_____

_____

_____

Verse 5 says, *Who is it that overcomes the world? Only he who believes that Jesus is the Son of God.* The NIV commentary encourages us to observe the progression of John's thought about how victory over the world is gained. It begins with the new birth (verse 4a). It moves on to the believer's experience and act of faith (verse 4b). It culminates in the confession that "Jesus is the Son of God." Victory requires the whole process.[69] Too many people have come to view the victorious life as a single event, when in fact it is a process that takes place over a lifetime. Victories on the field, court, or ice are not won in a single moment but rather through the course of the game. Being victorious at work is about being consistent, dedicated, and committed over a long period of time. The battle for victory in marriage is waged day by day; however, it is achieved over the course of a lifetime. While Christ won the victory once and for all on the cross, redemption was on the heart of God from the fall in the garden. Likewise, we must view victory within the context of eternity rather than the present. Even though today we might find ourselves in what seems to be an endless battle with depression, loneliness, pain, addiction, suffering, temptation, or the most severe trial, we can be certain that victory is indeed ours. When we take this view of the victorious life, it becomes possible to live the full and abundant life that Jesus promises to all who believe.

Write out your memory verse in the space below. Try to do it completely from memory, then double-check yourself.

TAKE TIME TO PRAY

---

69 Kenneth L. Barker and John R. Kohlenberger, eds., *Zondervan NIV Bible Commentary*. Accordance electronic ed. (Grand Rapids, MI: Zondervan, 1994), n.p.

To review, use the space below to write all the memory verses you have learned so far, including this week's. You can also use this space for personal notes about this lesson.

_____

_____

_____

_____

_____

_____

_____

_____

_____

_____

_____

_____

_____

_____

_____

_____

_____

_____

Worthy Walk—Day One

Memory Verse

Philippians 4:8

Start today's study by writing out your memory verse in the space below. Then, read it three times from your Bible and take just a moment to pray before completing the following lesson.

_____

_____

_____

_____

In the fall of my senior year in high school, I set out to become a licensed pilot. Some of my earliest memories as a child are looking up and watching military jets fly in formation over our ranch. My dad seemed to always be yelling at me in an effort to "get my head out of the clouds" and back to the task at hand. My uncle was a fighter pilot in the Navy, as well. As a baby he lifted me up into the cockpit of his fighter when his aircraft carrier was docked here in Texas. While I don't even remember the experience, I suppose it is possible that this was the day that flying became my passion.

My mother was not extremely excited about the idea of her seventeen-year-old son flying airplanes, but she was supportive enough to ride to the San Antonio Airport with me on my first day of flight training. She must have said "Are you sure you want to do this" a thousand times during the hour-long commute. Not only was

I certain that I wanted to be a pilot, I wanted to be the best pilot in the world. I had saved my own money and I was ready to learn to fly.

One day, not long into my flight training, my instructor had a talk with me in the cockpit that I will never forget. He said, "Pete, you are a natural when it comes to flying. You execute the required maneuvers almost perfectly time after time. You are able to hold your altitude and heading better then students who have three times as many hours as you have. And you have learned to land quicker than any student I have ever taught." I was thinking in my head, "Oh yeah, I am the best pilot in the world and I only have 8 hours of flight time!" I am surprised the plane did not crash, as my head was getting larger and larger and larger with each compliment. It was at this point that Richard gave me the "but." He said, "But, you need to relax and understand that it's not all about the mechanics of flying. You need to learn to make the plane a part of who you are, rather than something you are simply flying. You need to look out the window and enjoy the ride as well." He was right. I had memorized the procedures, speeds, proper attitudes, and checklists. I had learned everything I could about the radios, navigation tools, and every other button and switch in the cockpit. And while flying should be approached very seriously, I had taken it too far, and if I had continued with this mindset I would have been a danger to others and myself. In the weeks to come I learned to relax and enjoy the ride. I started to see myself as an extension of the plane when I flew. Gradually everything got easier and smoother, and flying became even more fun. I passed my check ride on the first attempt and received my license. As we taxied into the hanger after making the final landing, the FAA official who was grading my piloting skills commented on how at ease I was during the entire flight.

Sometimes I fear that the disciples of our generation are making the same mistake I made during my flight training. They are so in love with Jesus, they are so grateful for all they have in Christ, and they truly desire to be the best disciples they can be. In their effort to be the best, they memorize scripture, read their Bibles daily, attend church multiple times each week, join every Bible study possible, pray numerous times a day, witness constantly, and courageously confront sin wherever and whenever it might appear. They are technically great Christians, like I was technically a great pilot. However, they are not truly one with Christ in the same way that I was not one with the plane. And while they may have convinced themselves that the ride is enjoyable and fun, there is even more enjoyment to be had.

Because you have made it to week twenty-three of this study, I know that you desire to be the best Christian possible. But despite what many think, this does not happen just because we do the things that, on the outside, make us technically good disciples. Instead, it happens when we learn to walk in a way that is worthy of the Lord. This was a common theme in Paul's letters, as we will discover in this week's lessons. However, before we talk about what it means to live a "worthy life," we must talk about what it does not mean.

Living a life that is worthy of the Lord does not mean that you do things *for* God. The worthy walk is not about a checklist of things you must accomplish each day. It's not about reading your Bible cover-to-cover each year. The worthy walk is not about attending every Bible study or prayer meeting at church. It's not about good deeds, giving generously to the church and those in need, or going on every mission trip possible. While many who live their lives in a way that is worthy of the Lord do these things, the things above do not define the worthy walk.

> ❧ Have you ever done something *for* God that failed? If so, what was it?

_____

_____

It would be impossible to number the things I have attempted with the best intentions *for* God, but that failed miserably. Each time a failure occurred I would find myself in a state of confusion. The thing I attempted was biblical, it was good for the kingdom, and in some cases I had seen, or later saw, God bless other individuals who attempted the same thing—so why not me? Why did this good thing fail when I tried to do it *for* God? Other things I did *for* God were successful, so why not this one?

It took years for me to learn one of the most important lessons any disciple can absorb. Those who desire to live their lives in a way that is worthy of the Lord don't do things *for* God. They do things *with* God. There is a huge difference between the two. I finally understood this when I read these words that Paul wrote to the Thessalonians: *but with the help of our God we dared to tell you his gospel in spite of strong opposition* (1 Thess 2:2). Before arriving in Thessalonica, Paul and Silas had been brutally beaten in Philippi as they attempted to spread the good news of Christ in that city (Acts 16:22-24). I had read this verse as I battled through one of the most difficult times in my ministry, shortly after returning from a mission trip to Africa.

On the last day of that trip I met an African pastor named John. We had just finished checking the water at one of the water wells that our organization (www. operationh2o.org) had dug the year before, and we were preparing to leave this church and spend a few hours shopping for souvenirs before leaving the country later that night. Pastor John asked if we could ride out to his church and assess it as a possible location for another well. It was almost one in the afternoon, and not only was our time schedule tight, we had not eaten lunch yet, and we had failed to pack a lunch because we had not expected to be gone for more than a few hours. Pastor John was insistent and passionate, so I asked him how far it was to his church. He assured me three times that it was just ten minutes down the road. My wife and I agreed to make a quick trip out to his church for a visit. After over an hour of bouncing down a trail that they called a road, I asked John, with dissatisfaction in my voice, "How much farther?" "It's right up here," he said. I had heard that three times before and "right up here" seemed to mean something different in Africa. When we arrived twenty minutes later, I was hungry, drenched in sweat, and covered in red African dirt. To say I was upset would be a huge understatement.

There was something different about this church; it just wasn't like most of the others we had seen in Africa. I could not see many houses around it. We had passed about thirty huts within walking distance up the road and there were another ten here near the church, but where do the people come from, I thought? So I asked, as we evaluated the need for a well at his church, "How many people attend services here each weekend?" Pastor John replied with excitement in his voice, "Last year when I came as pastor we had two women and two children. Last weekend we had five women, five men, and ten children." To confirm I replied, "Pastor John you are doing a great job! Under these conditions, to grow from four to twenty in a year is great." I halfway expected John to correct me, but he said, "Yes, and it is just a joy to serve God."

We had gathered the information we needed and loaded up to leave and Pastor John once again got in the vehicle with us. Hesbon, my driver, said, "We are just going to drop Pastor John off at his house. Don't worry, Wambua (my African name); it's on the way." I had assumed that John lived up the road in the small village we had passed on our way in. But we drove through that village and Hesbon never slowed down. So I asked Pastor John, "Where do you live?" Thinking we might be on another hour-and-a-half rabbit trail, I was certain I would have to kick him to the curb if that was the case. John started to describe where he lived and then I realized that his house was just a few miles from where we had originally picked him up. We must have been at least thirty miles from there. How does this pastor get to his church, I thought? When I asked, he said he rode a bicycle. I learned that Pastor John left his home at midnight twice a week to make this journey in the darkness, through incredibly rough terrain, to minister to twenty people. I looked out the window and heard God say, "Would you do that? If you did not stand in front of thousands to preach, would you still preach?" "Yes God, I would" "Would you ride a bicycle this far for a handful of people like Pastor John does?" Knowing he knew my heart, I was forced to say, "No."

I remember doing my best to keep the tears in, but a few started to find their way down my cheeks anyway. Was I in the ministry for the wrong reasons? Did I really love Christ as much as I claimed to? Was I really the kind of minister people thought I was? Should I even continue to try to be a minister now? I was so convicted and torn that I did not sleep the entire thirty-four hour plane ride home. I know what it must have felt like when Jesus asked the Apostle Peter, "Do you love (agape) me" and all Peter could say was "Yes, I love (phileo) you." It was so humbling to have to honestly admit that my love and devotion was unable to go all the way, unlike Pastor John's.

It was during this time in my ministry, as I searched for the secret of people like the Apostle Paul, who endured so much and yet, despite severe opposition, dared to preach the gospel. Or people like John, who sacrificed so much and found so much joy in having a small part in what God was doing. Where did their passion, dedication, and commitment come from? How did they live lives that were so worthy of the Lord? The answer is that they did things *with* God instead of *for* God. I have done many things *for* God. Some have been great successes, yet many have failed. However, I have never attempted a single thing *with* God that did not succeed.

Would I ride a bicycle thirty miles in the dark to preach to twenty people *for* God? No, and neither would Pastor John. But would I hop in the saddle and peddle the distance for a single soul *with* God? Absolutely! Doing things *for* God is not what life is about, just like flying an airplane is not about gauges, speeds, buttons, and switches. Living a life worthy of the Lord is about walking with God. You should memorize scripture, pray, read your Bible, attend church and Bible studies, share your faith, give, and serve *with* God instead of *for* God. It will make all the difference in the world when it comes to living a life that is indeed worthy of the Lord.

To conclude today's lesson and reinforce this concept, look up the following scriptures and think about the difference between doing things *for* God and *with* God. While the phrase "with God" is found twenty-nine times in the New Testament (NIV), there is only one reference that carries the sense of doing anything "for God." Identify that verse and be prepared to explain its meaning in your next small group meeting.

    Matthew 19:26

_____

_____

    Luke 1:37

_____

_____

    Luke 18:27

_____

_____

    Acts 4:13-20

_____

_____

📖 Galatians 2:19 ⚒

_____

_____

📖 2 Timothy 1:12 ⚒

_____

_____

Write out your memory verse in the space below. Try to do it completely from memory, then double-check yourself.

_____

_____

_____

_____

TAKE TIME TO PRAY

Worthy Walk—Day Two

Memory Verse

Philippians 4:8

Start today's study by writing out as much of your memory verse as you can in the space below. Then, look up the verse and make any corrections that are needed. Finally, read it three times from your Bible and take just a moment to pray before completing the following lesson.

Who have you tried to please today? It would be interesting to carry around a "people-pleaser stopwatch" that could track every second we spend attempting to please another person or group. There is little doubt that if such a gadget existed, most people would be shamefully amazed at the amount of time we spend trying to please other people. As soon as the average Christian opens his eyes in the morning, his efforts to please other people begin. Think about today, for example:

> ❧ Who have you tried to please today in any way?

_____

_____

❧ How much time would you estimate you spent today making an effort to please someone else?

_____

_____

_____

❧ Would you describe yourself as a "people pleaser?"

_____

_____

_____

Some people find resisting the urge to please others impossible. There are several individuals on staff at the church that I pastor who just can never seem to muster the courage, boldness, or confidence to tell others No. They love to "please" people, it brings them joy, and they find fulfillment in making others happy. Then there are people who have no issue with telling people No, and they are not seen as "people pleasers." However, everyone wants to please someone, and even the stiffest, hard, self-sufficient person will attempt to please people in some way. There is nothing wrong with pleasing people. The Bible clearly calls us to serve one another, and when we serve as the Bible calls us to, pleasure is the result. The problem is when we make pleasing others the primary goal of our day or life. When we give priority to pleasing people rather than pleasing God, we miss the worthy walk that we have been called to live. Read Colossians 1:9-14 and answer the following questions.

❧ Does Paul make any mention of "doing things for God" in these verses?

_____

_____

_____

❧ What does he pray God will fill them with? What does that mean?

_____

_____

_____

_____

Almost everyone has seen the classic movie *Alice in Wonderland*. At one point in the film, Alice is walking when she comes to a fork in the road and has an encounter with the Cheshire cat. Alice asks the cat which way she should go. The cat replies by asking, "Where do you want to go?" Alice says, "I don't know." The cat then says, "Well I guess it does not matter then." Many Christians today are like Alice. They have either forgotten what the goal of life is or they never understood what the goal was. Imagine football without a goal line, baseball without a home plate, soccer without the goal, or basketball without the hoop. None of those sports would be much fun without the goal. In fact, they would be so pointless that no one would play them and it is doubtful that any of those sports would even exist without clearly defined goals. Without a goal, life is boring and starts to seem pointless over time. Thankfully however, as believers we do have a goal to reach for and to help guide us each day.

📖 Read Colossians 1:10 again. What do you think our goal is?

_____

_____

_____

The Christian life can seem so complicated and cluttered at times, especially if you don't know what the goal is. Once you understand the goal and learn to reach for it, all other areas of daily life begin to become easier and the full and abundant life that Christ offers will become a reality. The goal for all believers is simply this: "Please Christ in every way." Our goal should be to bring pleasure to the heart of Christ. This is not just the goal for Sunday morning when we go to church; it is the goal for all believers every day. Amazingly, when we strive for this goal and we make it our sole ambition, every other area of life becomes incredibly simple and fulfilling. For example, as a husband there are certain things I do with God that bring him pleasure. Surprisingly, when I commit to doing those things, my wife is satisfied and built-up as well. This also holds true in all other areas of life. As an employer, employee, friend, parent, coach, teacher, or neighbor, when you follow the statutes God has ordained and live with his pleasure as your only goal, you and others will find fulfillment, joy, and pleasure as well. Bill Cosby once said in an interview "I don't know what the key to success is, but the key to failure is trying to please everyone." Make it your goal to please God in every way and you will be amazed how much better life will be.

The devil has hijacked our happiness and stolen our peace and joy because we have foolishly been convinced that the goal in life is to bring pleasure to ourselves and others. While this may satisfy our souls in the short-term, it leaves us spiritually bankrupt in the context of the future. Over time we need more and more pleasure to achieve the same level of satisfaction, much like a drug addict or alcoholic is forced to increase the dose of their drug to achieve the high they long for. Over time the demands that our self-pleasure requires becomes so great that we have little time for God. Further complicating the situation is the pressure we feel to please others. Between self and others, there is simply little if any time left for God's pleasure, and that is exactly the way the devil wants it to be, for it is at this point that doubt, denial, or guilt start to take over in our lives. Some start to doubt that the full and abundant life is even possible; others doubt God's existence—and the devil smiles. Some sink into denial and refuse to admit that they have a problem at all. Over time they simply slip away from the church, and the demons begin to salivate as they see easy prey all alone in the open, away from the flock. Still others feel guilty because they know they should be doing things with God but they don't, because they don't have the time, money, or energy after they have brought pleasure to themselves and others. Here is the secret: make God's pleasure your only goal in life.

- Would your spouse be pleased if you made pleasing God your only goal in life? Why, or why not?

_____

_____

_____

- Would your children be pleased if you made pleasing God your only goal in life? Why, or why not?

_____

_____

_____

- Would your boss be pleased if you made pleasing God your only goal in life? Why, or why not?

_____

_____

_____

- Would your employees or those you work with be pleased if you made pleasing God your only goal in life? Why, or why not?

_____

_____

_____

➳ Would your fellow church members be pleased if you made pleasing God your only goal in life? Why, or why not?

_____

_____

_____

➳ Would your neighbors be pleased if you made pleasing God your only goal in life? Why, or why not?

_____

_____

_____

➳ Would your parents or extended family be pleased if you made pleasing God your only goal in life? Why, or why not?

_____

_____

_____

📖 What did Jesus say about this in John 5:30? ✖

_____

_____

_____

📖 What is significant about God's response in Matthew 3:17? ✖

_____

_____

_____

Tomorrow we will continue looking at Colossians 1:9-14 to discover what the marks of the worthy walk are. Before ending your study today, read those verses again and consider whether you are striving for this goal that is laid out for us in scripture, or are you reaching for something else?

Write out your memory verse in the space below. Try to do it completely from memory, then double-check yourself.

TAKE TIME TO PRAY

Worthy Walk—Day Three

Memory Verse

Philippians 4:8

Start today's study by writing out as much of your memory verse as you can in the space below. Then, look up the verse and make any corrections that are needed. Finally, read it three times from your Bible and take just a moment to pray before completing the following lesson.

_Y_esterday we discovered that the goal for believers is simple: we should strive to please God in all we do. Once again, it is imperative that we don't attempt to do things *for* God but rather that we join God and accomplish his plan for our lives *with* him. When we make his pleasure our only goal in life, we will finally be able to experience the full and abundant life that Jesus offers us in John 10:10. Today we are going to look at the marks of the worthy walk. Read Colossians 1:9-14 and attempt to identify the things that Paul says mark the person who lives a life worthy of the Lord. Then explain each one in your own words. ✗

1. _____

2. _____

3. _____

4. _____

5. _____

6. _____

7. _____

There are signs, signals, and marks for reaching any goal. For example, the official at a football game will raise both arms into the air to signal that a touchdown or field goal has been scored. In baseball the umpire will signal audibly and physically with different motions whether a runner is safe or out. The umpire will also signal or mark each pitch to signal whether it was a strike or a ball. There are signals in basketball, soccer, hockey, rodeo events, rugby, and most other sports as well. When we reach a goal at work, there might be a signal of verbal praise, extra time-off, or even a bonus or pay raise. When a husband and wife finally finish painting a room in their house, they give each other a high-five to mark their achievement. In the same way there are signs, signals, or marks that help us identify our progress as we attempt to live a life that is worthy of the Lord. Paul outlines seven of them in our passage.

First, he says that we will bear fruit in every good work. Doing good works will not get us into heaven. Doing good works will not earn us brownie points with God, either. But good works do show the world that we have been transformed and changed by the power of the cross. When you make pleasing God in every way your sole goal in life, it is inevitable that God will call you to do things that will be rightly seen as good works. Those works will bear fruit and mark your worthy walk with Jesus as you do things with him.

📖 Read Galatians 5:22-26 and then list the fruits of the Spirit. What other fruits of the Spirit you can think of?

_____

_____

_____

📖 What does Ephesians 2:8-10 say about the role of good works in a believer's life?

_____

_____

📖 What does James 2:14-26 say about the role of good works in a believer's life?

_____

_____

The next mark is an ever-increasing knowledge of God. Some scholars have translated this verse _increasing in the knowledge of God_. The idea in the Greek text is that our spiritual maturity is progressive. We must be constantly and consistently moving forward in our faith. Those who live their lives in a way that is worthy of the Lord are never satisfied with standing still in their faith. They desire to grow, learn, and be challenged. In just a few weeks, you will finish this study. Will your spiritual growth stop as well? Will you say, I have learned the basics and that is good enough for me? Or will you press on and increase your knowledge and understanding of God and the Christian faith? Paul says that those who desire to please God in every way and live a life that is worthy of the Lord will be marked by an ever-increasing or progressing spiritual maturity.

Spiritual strength is a third factor that results from knowing God's will and pleasing him. Being strengthened with all power according to his glorious might includes three words for strength: "being strengthened" is δυναμούμενοι (dynamoumenoi); "power" is δυνάμει (dynamei), or spiritual vitality; and "might" is κράτος (kratos) "power that overcomes resistance"; used only of God in the New Testament.[70] The idea behind these three words in this phrase seems to be that believers who walk in a way that is worthy of the Lord have confidence that God is with them in all they do. In other words, they don't fear change or not knowing what will happen tomorrow because they are confident in God's power, and they trust him totally. My friend Bob is a shining example of this trait. No matter what happens, he never loses his confidence in God. It is not a foolish confidence that puts God to the test but rather a confidence that has come from walking with God for over seventy years. Bob has come to understand and trust that, no matter what, if God says it or if God's in it, he can totally trust and depend on God to provide whatever is necessary to complete the task. Those with this mark are full of God's strength because they trust in the Lord totally.

📖 What does 1 Thessalonians 5:24 say about this mark?

_____

_____

_____

---

70   John F. Walvoord and Roy B. Zuck, eds., _The Bible Knowledge Commentary: New Testament._ Accordance electronic ed. (Wheaton, IL: Victor Books, 1983), n.p.

📖 What does Philippians 4:13 say about this mark? ✗

_____

_____

_____

_____

❧ Do you believe the message behind these two verses? Why, or why not?

_____

_____

_____

_____

The next two marks can be dealt with as one. Paul cites endurance and patience as something that those who are living a life worthy of the Lord will possess. The Greek word used for "endurance" simply means the ability to see things through, while patience means that as a believer you are able to keep your cool in spite of injury or insult. Christians should not start things they don't intend to finish. Endurance is necessary in all areas of life, such as marriage, raising children, work, church, and discipleship. In the same spirit, we are to be patient as well. Christians should not seek revenge or be people of wrath, despite the circumstances and situations in which we may find ourselves. Examine the following verses and decide if they speak to endurance, patience, or both. Then identify some key principles contained within the passage.

📖 Luke 6:27-29

_____

_____

📖 Luke 14:28-30

_____

_____

📖 Romans 12:10-13

_____

_____

📖 Romans 15:1-3

_____

_____

📖 Colossians 3:12-14

_____

_____

Paul combines the final two marks of joy and thanksgiving. He states that the disciple who is living a life that is worthy of the Lord will "joyfully give thanks." In Week Ten, we studied joy in great detail; therefore we will only touch on its importance briefly here. Many Christians today possess an attitude of sadness and defeat. Those who are walking with the Lord should possess an attitude of joy. Despite hardship, insults, injury, pain, loneliness, or even the death of a loved one, those walking with God have an unexplainable joy that surrounds them. It is not a fake or manufactured joy, but rather a genuine, sincere joy that cannot be hidden or contained. That joy is often expressed through thanksgiving. A thankful heart is a mark of those who are living a life worthy of the Lord. These people feel that they have far more to be thankful for than they have to be sad or angry about. Joy and thankfulness therefore overflow out of those living a life worthy of the Lord and invade the lives of those around them. See if you can identify what the following verses have to say about joy and thanksgiving.

📖 Acts 13:49-52

_____

_____

📖 Romans 14:17-19

_____

_____

📖 Ephesians 5:3-4

_____

_____

📖 Philippians 4:4-7

_____

_____

📖 1 Timothy 2:1-3

_____

_____

These marks should not be viewed as the "only" marks one will see in the lives of those who are walking in a way that is worthy of the Lord. There are many signs, signals, and marks that identify the lives of those who are following God with all of their hearts in an attempt to live a worthy life. Finally, don't make the mistake of trying to "do" these things, either. The worthy life can't be achieved by doing things; it is simply impossible. Rather we are to reach for the goal of bringing God pleasure by allowing him to direct our lives. We then walk with God to accomplish his will for our lives, and in so doing, these markers and many others will spring up smilingly from nowhere. The worthy walk can't be forced; instead it comes from a natural desire to please God in everything you do.

Write out your memory verse in the space below. Try to do it completely from memory, then double-check yourself.

TAKE TIME TO PRAY

Worthy Walk—Day Four

Memory Verse

Philippians 4:8

Start today's study by writing out as much of your memory verse as you can in the space below. Then, look up the verse and make any corrections that are needed. Finally, read it three times from your Bible and take just a moment to pray before completing the following lesson.

_____

_____

_____

_____

In our first study we learned what the worthy walk was not. Over the past two days we have focused on exploring what the goal of our lives should be, as well as the marks that we will be able to see once we start to walk in a way that is worthy of the Lord. Today we are going to look at what the result will be if we indeed make pleasing God in every way our goal and if we should choose to live a life that is worthy of the Lord. To start today's lesson, look up the following scriptures that also talk about living the worthy life and write down any significant points you feel each passage makes. Be prepared to discuss these in your next small group meeting.

📖 Ephesians 4:1-3

_____

_____

📖 Philippians 1:25-28

_____

_____

📖 1 Thessalonians 2:10-12

_____

_____

📖 2 Thessalonians 1:11-12

_____

_____

If you set out to please God in every way, what will happen? Will you become rich, famous, skinny, or popular? Will you be promoted at work, cheered in your community, and celebrated in history books? After all, remaining focused enough to forsake your own pleasure and the pleasure of others is difficult and demanding, and requires a great deal of discipline. So it is natural to ask, "What's in it for me?" There are at least three positive things that you will receive when you make pleasing God in every way your only goal in life.

The first is that you will live a life of purpose. It has been said that everyone ends up somewhere in life, but a few people end up there on purpose. When you make pleasing God your only goal in life, you will end up where he desires you to be. Have you ever seen an animal with two heads? Personally, I have seen both a baby calf and a full-grown snake with two heads. Life for these animals was confusing, full of hardship, and debilitating to the point that neither could survive without a great deal of assistance from humans. When you live your life trying to please yourself and everyone else, you are like a two-headed snake. Looking at these animals can only be described as a "freak show." Let's face it: life is confusing. You can never seem to figure out which way to go or what to do next. Over time, hardships arise as you are unable to meet your own self-imposed expectations of yourself. Eventually you become debilitated by the constant stress, confusion, and lack of purpose that life seems to have. When we live our lives with multiple goals in an attempt to please multiple people, it becomes a "freak show." When your only goal in life is pleasing God, however, this problem is solved. Every area of life now has purpose. Each decision matters and makes a difference in God's plan for humanity, and your purpose in life begins to become clear.

The Apostle Paul is one of the best-known figures in the New Testament. People look at Paul's life and can't help but see that this man lived a life of great purpose. Did this happen by accident or was it just by chance that his life was used in such a mighty way by God? No, the truth is that Paul's goal was to please God. It was his only goal, and the result of living his life with that sole goal was that his life is easily seen as a life of purpose. Learn more about the life and purpose of Paul by reading the following passages.

📖 Romans 15:17-22

_____

_____

📖 1 Corinthians 1:17

_____

_____

📖 Ephesians 3:7-9

_____

_____

📖 2 Timothy 3:10-11

_____

_____

❧ What would those who know you best say your purpose in life has been up until now? Are you satisfied with that answer?

_____

_____

_____

_____

Not only will your life be one of purpose, it will also be a positive life as well, should you choose to make pleasing God in every way your only goal in life. I certainly don't mean to imply that your life will be easy, or without trouble or pain, if you make God's pleasure your only priority. Paul, for example, certainly had his share of problems, trouble, and pain. However, those who live a life worthy of the Lord will find that their lives, like Paul's and so many others', will have a positive impact on the world. If you want to leave a legacy and make a positive difference, you must learn to walk and live in a way that is worthy of the Lord. Read Acts 11:25-26 and answer the questions below.

> In what city did the word Christian first appear? Do you think that Paul's ministry in this city made a positive impact on the world? Why?

_____

_____

_____

> What other things in Paul's ministry can you think of that would characterize his life as being positive? ✗

_____

_____

_____

The NIV commentary claims that it was "others within the city—evidently the nonbelievers who were more perceptive in this matter than the church itself—nicknamed this group of Jewish and Gentile believers "Christians.""[71] The ministry of Barnabas and Paul had such a positive effect in this city that even nonbelievers noticed the difference in the lives of these new followers of Christ. They began to call them "little Christs." This name remains today, in the form of "Christian" and "Christianity." What a legacy has been left behind by the ministry of these men. Their focus and only goal in life was to please God in every way. The result was a positive life that made a lasting impact.

The final thing that will result when people make God's pleasure their only goal in life is that they will live a productive life. Everyone wants to be able to produce something with the time they are given. As a father, I desire to produce good, well-behaved, honest, obedient, God-fearing children who will grow up to become productive members of God's economy as well. As a husband, I long to do my part in producing a healthy marriage. As a pastor, I want to be used in the process of making disciples. Here is the problem, no matter how great my kids are, or how good my marriage is, or how many disciples I encourage or train. If I have not

---

71 Kenneth L. Barker and John R. Kohlenberger, eds., *Zondervan NIV Bible Commentary*. Accordance electronic ed. (Grand Rapids, MI: Zondervan, 1994), n.p.

lived my life in a way that was worthy of the Lord, I have not produced anything that will last. In the end, only what we produce through our worthy walk with God will endure. You can produce these things and many more without putting forth the effort to live a life that is worthy of the Lord. The only problem is that all you produce will one day disappear and be gone. Only that which is produced as a result of your worthy walk will last for eternity.

📖 Read 1 Corinthians 9:24-27 and identify the parts of this passage that concern the three results we have discussed today. 🎬

1. Purposeful _____

_____

2. Positive _____

_____

3. Productive _____

_____

Living a life that is worthy for the Lord is not about doing things for God; it's about doing things with God. God is not impressed by our efforts. He is impressed when we obey his commands. His divine pleasure should captivate our mind, body, and soul every waking hour. When we desire and long to please him in every way, and the fruits of such a life become visible, we will see the results that have been discussed today as well. This life is not a burden to bear; it is a blessing to receive. It is available to all. However, few will dare to experience the power and freedom of such a life.

Write out your memory verse in the space below. Try to do it completely from memory, then double-check yourself.

_____

_____

_____

_____

TAKE TIME TO PRAY

To review, use the space below to write all the memory verses you have learned so far, including this week's. You can also use this space for personal notes about this lesson.

X-Commandments—Day One

Memory Verse

Ten Commandments

I don't like to be gone from the church I pastor on the weekends. I truly enjoy the fellowship and the way that the Spirit moves in our church so much that it is almost painful to be away. However, for various reasons, I do miss several weekends each year. On one such occasion, while I was spending time with my family on a vacation, I decided to invite a gentleman who came highly recommended by several other ministers to fill the pulpit in my absence. After speaking with him on several occasions, and praying over the matter a great deal, I felt at ease with the decision to bring him in. While I was gone I had no anxiety about what might be happening at our church.

When I returned from vacation on the Monday after he had delivered his message, I was surprised to find that several people had sent me e-mails with a single complaint about his sermon. I reluctantly picked up my phone to check my messages, knowing that surely others had called as well. They all said the same thing in one way or another: "He made us feel so stupid because we did not know the Ten Commandments." During his message, the evangelist asked those who could name all ten of the Ten Commandments to raise their hand. Out of the entire congregation, only the small hand of a ten-year-old child rose from the audience. He called on her and like a champion she rattled off all ten and received great applause from the large crowd. Then the speaker spent several minutes telling everyone in the congregation how important and basic the Ten Commandments are, and if they had not taken the time to learn the most fundamental and basic concepts of their faith, surely they were spiritual babies.

Naturally I was embarrassed, frustrated, and angry. "How could he do that," I thought. "I trusted him with the pulpit in front of a thousand people and he pulls a stunt like that." I said to myself, "He does not even have a church. It's easy for him to travel around and make judgments on other churches because he does not know how hard it is to teach people things like the Ten Commandments." I was ready to pick up the phone and give him a piece of my mind. I reached to grab the receiver and every line in the church was busy. After all, it was a Monday morning. As I waited for a line to clear, I begin to plead my case to God. Through that short time in prayer I realized that the problem was not the messenger who had delivered the message. It was that those who had heard it really were not prepared spiritually in many ways. I could make excuses, or I could do a better job of discipling and teaching the basics of the faith to those I lead.

So I gave myself a test. With a blank sheet of paper I tried to list all ten of the commandments. Honestly, I did fairly well, but even I did not get all ten exactly right, and I was far from perfect when it came to placing them in the right order. So I started learning them myself. Not so that I could stand if he ever came back to our church and show him that I was truly a man of God. Rather, my motive was so that I could teach others. You can't teach others about something you do not know, so I had to begin the process with myself and most likely you will as well.

※ Without looking them up, give yourself a quiz. Try to list the Ten Commandments as accurately as possible and in the correct order in the space below.

1. _____

2. _____

3. _____

4. _____

5. _____

6. _____

7. _____

8. _____

9. _____

10. _____

※ Now read the entire chapter of Exodus 20, and list out the Ten Commandments in order in the space below.

1. _____

2. _____

3. _____

4. _____

5. _____

6. _____

7. _____

8. _____

9. _____

10. _____

❧ Spend some time thinking about each commandment and do the following for each of the Ten Commandments:

A. Define what the commandment means in your own words.

1. _____

_____

2. _____

_____

3. _____

_____

4. _____

_____

5. _____

_____

6. _____

_____

7. _____

_____

8. _____

_____

9. _____

_____

10. _____

_____

B. Explain why the commandment would be important for believers today.

1. _____

_____

2. _____

_____

3. _____

_____

4. _____

_____

5. _____

_____

6. _____

_____

7. _____

_____

8. _____

_____

9. _____

_____

10. _____

_____

C. Explain how the body of Christ and the world as a whole might be different if believers knew and followed these Ten Commandments from God.

_____

_____

_____

_____

Instead of memorizing a passage of scripture this week, the challenge is to memorize the Ten Commandments in order. This is not so that you can stand and prove how spiritual you are. Although it would be a great feeling to know that you could stand if called upon to recite the Ten Commandments, it would be even more amazing if your entire church stood when some evangelist challenged them on these grounds. However, the motivation is much deeper and more significant than this. Knowing these Ten Commandments is fundamental to understanding the Christian faith. While some will argue that these commandments are under the old law and they are useless to believers today under the new law of Christ, this simply is not true. Read Matthew 5:17-48 and answer the questions below.

❧ What are some of the Ten Commandments that Jesus mentions in this passage?

_____

_____

_____

❧ Does he abolish them or expand them? Explain, and list examples of your answer. ✖

_____

_____

It is clear that Jesus did not get rid of the commandments when he brought the "new law." In fact, if anything, the expectations of these commandments Christ mentions in Matthew 5 seem to be even more detailed and strict then those in

Exodus 20. Personally I am of the opinion that all scripture is God-breathed and useful; therefore, it is all worthy of our attention and effort, especially in light of how basic and powerful these Ten Commandments are to the Christian faith. They were important enough for God to pen them with his own hand. Jesus himself thought they were important enough to teach and preach about them. The question is whether the church thinks they are important enough to learn.

Complete today's study by again listing out the Ten Commandments from memory without looking back at your notes. Then check yourself and spend some time learning these commandments.

1. _____

2. _____

3. _____

4. _____

5. _____

6. _____

7. _____

8. _____

9. _____

10. _____

TAKE TIME TO PRAY

X-Commandments—Day Two

Memory Verse

Ten Commandments

Start today's study by writing out the Ten Commandments in order. When you are finished, look them up in Exodus 20 and make corrections to what you wrote. Finally, spend some time reflecting on these commandments as you memorize them and then take a moment to pray about whatever God lays on your heart.

1. _____

2. _____

3. _____

4. _____

5. _____

6. _____

7. _____

8. _____

9. _____

10. _____

Yesterday we talked about the importance of knowing the Ten Commandments, not only because they are at the foundation of our Christian faith, but also because they can guide us through life if we choose to live by these commandments and the others that we have received from God. As recently as a few generations ago, most Christians knew the Ten Commandments by heart. Today, very few know them. This is in part because no one seems to be emphasizing their importance or teaching them to future generations. If you don't know them, chances are your children don't either. If they don't know them, neither will your grandchildren or great-grandchildren. We must learn all we can about our faith and be diligent about passing along what we learn to future generations.

📖 What does Deuteronomy 4:9-10 tell the modern day disciple about passing on our faith to future generations?

____

____

____

📖 Below is how I would recommend you memorize the Ten Commandments. Anything similar to this will do as well if you choose some different wording. The important thing is that you learn them in the order God gave them to his people.

1. Don't place anything before God.
2. Don't worship any idol.
3. Don't misuse the Lord's name.
4. Keep the Sabbath Holy through rest and worship.
5. Honor your parents.
6. Don't murder.
7. Don't commit adultery.
8. Don't steal.
9. Don't lie.
10. Don't covet.

Do you notice anything that the first four commandments have in common? Do you notice anything that the last six have in common? What? ⚒

____

____

____

The Ten Commandments are also at times referred to as the Decalogue. The Hebrew title of the Ten Commandments (Exod 34:28) is usually translated as "The Ten Words." These commands were first given to Moses at Sinai about fifty days after the Israelite people left Egypt (Exod 19:10-25). God wrote these commands down twice for Moses. This took place because Moses destroyed the first set of tablets upon his return from Mount Sinai to the camp of the Israelites. The sight of God's people dancing around a golden calf drove him to destroy the commandments that God had placed in his hands (Exod 32:19). God then re-wrote them for Moses, according to Exodus 34:1. Those tablets were placed in the Ark of the Covenant (Deut 10:5; 1 Kgs 8:9). Little is known about the remaining history of these two stones; however, the significance of the words that God penned on the rocks that Moses chiseled out of the mountain side has stood the test of time, and our churches and culture are desperately in need of rediscovering their significance in our lives.

The Ten Commandments are mentioned five times in the New Testament. Take a few minutes to look up these verses. Write down any significant points that are made about the Ten Commandments in these New Testament passages.

Matthew 5:17-20

_____

_____

Mark 10:17-25; Luke 18:19-27

_____

_____

Romans 7:7-25 ✗

_____

_____

Romans 13:8-10

_____

_____

1 Timothy 1:8-11

_____

_____

  Do you think the Ten Commandments are still useful today even under the new covenant in Christ? Why, or why not?

_____

_____

_____

_____

The Ten Commandments have been categorized and broken down in many different ways from the time of the theologian named Origen to the present day. Many have even speculated about why God did not write all ten on one tablet and which commands were on which tablet. In recent history, the case has been made that perhaps all ten commands were on one stone and that God made two copies of the same ten commands. "Recent knowledge of ancient covenant forms has shown that the stipulations of the covenant—the laws imposed by the covenant-lord— were written in duplicate. The covenant-lord retained one copy and deposited the other in the sanctuary of the god of the people on whom he was imposing his covenant. In the case of the Decalogue, Yahweh is both Covenant-Lord and also God of Israel. He, therefore, takes both copies into his care: the whole care, continuance, and maintenance of the covenant relationship rests with him."[72]

Regardless of how you break the commandments down, it seems obvious that there is a clear distinction between the first four and last six. Each of the first four commands deals with our interaction and relationship with God himself. The last six exclusively deal with interpersonal relationships between humans.

The first commandment states, *You shall have no other gods before me* (Exod 20:3). This can be described as the "rule of religion." The Life Application Commentary points out the following about the very first command that we are called to live by as believers.

> *The Israelites had just come from Egypt, a land of many idols and many gods. Because each god represented a different aspect of life, it was common to worship many gods in order to get the maximum number of blessings. When God told his people to worship and believe in him, that wasn't so hard for them—he was just one more god to add to the list. But when he said, "You must not have any other god but me," that was difficult for the people to accept. But if they didn't learn that the God who led them out of Egypt was the only true God, they could not be his people—no matter how faithfully they kept the other nine commandments. Thus, God made this his first commandment. Today we can allow many things to become gods to us. Money, fame, work, or pleasure can become gods when we concentrate too much*

---

72 *NIV Dictionary*, Accordance electronic ed., n.p.

on them for personal identity, meaning, and security. No one sets out with the intention of worshiping these things. But by the amount of time we devote to them, they can grow into gods that ultimately control our thoughts and energies. Letting God hold the central place in our lives keeps these things from turning into gods.[73]

God's commandment was not "worship me"; it was "worship only me." There is a difference between the two. It is so easy to place other things before God. Many of these things that take priority over God are indeed good things. However, even good things can cause us to break any of the Ten Commandments. We must be careful not to allow anything to take priority over God.

📖 Does what Jesus said in Luke 9:57-62 seem more significant and logical in light of this first command? Why or why not?

_____

_____

_____

❧ What have you placed before God in the past? (List them)

_____

_____

_____

❧ What are you placing before him now? (List them)

_____

_____

_____

❧ Do you plan to do anything about it? Why, or why not? What do you plan to do?

_____

_____

_____

---

73 *Life Application Study Bible,* Accordance electronic ed. (Carol Stream, IL: Tyndale House Publishers, 2004), n.p.

The second command can be viewed as the commandment about worship for God. It says, *You shall not make for yourself an idol in the form of anything in heaven above or on the earth beneath or in the waters below. You shall not bow down to them or worship them* (Exod 20:4-5). The Hebrew word used for idol in verse 4 is "pesel," which refers to something that is "carved," generally from wood or stone. It seems that the Hebrews thought they could get around this command simply by casting their idols from different kinds of metals instead of carving them from wood or stone. In Exodus 34:18, however, this too is forbidden. God is so holy and divinely unique that there is nothing in all of creation that could remotely come close to capturing his greatness in the form of an idol. God therefore forbids his followers from attempting to make idols for that purpose or any other. Our God is a jealous God (Exod 34:14; Deut 5:9; 6:15; 32:16-21) and those who worship him must worship him alone. He does not want us to worship a statue, picture, or anything else that "represents" him. His desire is that we would worship him.

> ❧ Have you ever had a person or thing in your life that you worshiped as an idol, that you willingly placed before God? What was it?

> ❧ Do you have anything today in your life that would be considered such an idol? What do you plan to do with it?

> ❧ Is the fact that the Bible describes God as being a "jealous God" surprising or difficult for you to understand? What do you think this means?

Tomorrow we will look at the next four commandments. As you prepare to end your study today, spend some time thinking about the commands we covered today and the next four as well. All ten of these commands are important and they serve a great purpose in our lives. Therefore, it is important that we do more than just memorize them; we must learn all we can about them as well.

Complete today's study by again listing out the Ten Commandments from memory without looking back at your notes. Then check yourself and spend some time learning these commandments.

1. _____

2. _____

3. _____

4. _____

5. _____

6. _____

7. _____

8. _____

9. _____

10. _____

TAKE TIME TO PRAY

X-Commandments—Day Three

Memory Verse

Ten Commandments

Start today's study by writing out the Ten Commandments in order. When you are finished, look them up in Exodus 20 and make corrections to what you wrote. Finally, spend some time reflecting on these commandments as you memorize them and then take a moment to pray about whatever God lays on your heart.

1. _____
2. _____
3. _____
4. _____
5. _____
6. _____
7. _____
8. _____
9. _____
10. _____

*L*ike the first two commandments that we studied yesterday, the next two concern our relationship with our Creator as well. The third commandment reads, *You shall not misuse the name of the LORD your God, for the LORD will not hold anyone guiltless who misuses his name* (Exod 20:*). This commandment can be described with the word "reverence."

Names are important. When I was growing up in grade school, people made fun of my name. Peter, Peter, Pumpkin Eater was a favorite of both my friends and the bullies at school. Later the tune was changed and included obscenities and vulgar language that does not bear repeating. My mother told me to remember, "Sticks and stones may break my bones, but words will never hurt me." While that rhyme was easy to remember and repeat when needed, it was not true in my life. When my name was being attacked, the words did hurt—many times more than sticks and stones.

Like our names, God's name is important and special as well. How we use God's name tells the world what we think about him. When people misuse or make fun of your name, they convey that they don't take you seriously or respect you. If the attack is strong enough, it may show others that the attacker despises you. When we use God's name in vain, what do we tell the world? What are we really saying when we flippantly throw it around by saying "Oh God..." or "Jesus!"? God's name deserves honor, glory, respect, fame, and praise, for he is our holy Creator, Savior, and Lord. Be careful how you use his name.

📖 In Leviticus 19:12, how does it say we should or should not use God's name?

_____

_____

_____

❦ List some specific ways we tend to use God's name in the wrong way in our culture.

_____

_____

_____

The fourth command also has to do with the relationship between God and humanity. Starting in verse 8, it reads, *Remember the Sabbath day by keeping it holy. Six days you shall labor and do all your work, but the seventh day is a Sabbath to the LORD your God. On it you shall not do any work, neither you, nor your son or daughter, nor your manservant or maidservant, nor your animals, nor the alien within your gates. For in six days the LORD made the heavens and the earth, the sea, and all that is in them, but he rested on the seventh day. There-*

fore the LORD blessed the Sabbath day and made it holy (Exod 20:7-11). Remember that it was God who penned these commandments, and it is amazing that he took so much time to explain this one for us. It is almost as if he knew that this would be a difficult commandment for humans to adhere to, so he explained the commandment about the Sabbath in great detail and at great length, in order to symbolize both its physical importance and its spiritual significance in our lives.

There is a great deal of debate surrounding the issue of the actual day of the Sabbath. Most people cite Saturday or Sunday as being the Sabbath or day of rest. From these verses it does not appear that God is particularly worried about which day we observe as the Sabbath. Rather, his primary concern is that we not work more than six days. He commands us to take the seventh day for rest, and to keep that day holy.

Many people view this as a burden or an unreasonable command in our fast-paced, hectic lives. We simply have no time for rest. Our days of rest are full of chores around the house, running the kids to or from practice, shopping, or changing the oil in the car. We say things like "Well, that's not really work" because it is a different kind of work, but the truth is that these things are indeed work and they too are prohibited in this fourth command. The Sabbath is a day that is set aside for two things: rest and worship. Don't neglect God's wisdom and provision. Observe this commandment and you will see the benefits in all areas of your life.

📖 What does "Remember the Sabbath day by keeping it holy" mean to you?

_____

_____

_____

📖 What does "Six days you shall labor and do all your work, ¹⁰but the seventh day is a Sabbath to the LORD your God. On it you shall not do any work, neither you, nor your son or daughter, nor your manservant or maidservant, nor your animals, nor the alien within your gates" mean to you? Are you doing this? Why, or why not?

_____

_____

_____

_____

_____

_____

📖 What does "For in six days the LORD made the heavens and the earth, the sea, and all that is in them, but he rested on the seventh day, therefore the LORD blessed the Sabbath day and made it holy" mean to you?

_____

_____

_____

_____

❧ How would your life be different if you actually followed this commandment?

_____

_____

❧ What would the benefits be?

_____

_____

❧ What would the negatives be?

_____

_____

❧ What do you need to change to make the Sabbath a regular part of your life?

_____

_____

❧ Will you take the Sabbath challenge? For the next six weeks, set aside one day of each week for nothing other than worship and rest.

   ☐ Yes, I will.

   ☐ No, I won't

The first four commandments focus on our relationship with God. The following six commandments focus primarily on our relationship with one another. They can be seen as the basic moral code that governs all life on planet Earth. The first of these commands reads, _Honor your father and your mother, so that you may live long in the land the LORD your God is giving you_ (Exod 20:12)

One commentary suggests that that this command involves (1) prizing parents highly (cf. Prov 4:8); (2) caring, showing affection for them (Ps 91:15); and (3) showing respect or fear, or revering them (Lev 19:3). Parents are to be shown honor, but nowhere is their word to rival or be a substitute for God's word.[74] All believers should make every effort to honor their parents.

Some have argued that their parents are unworthy of honor. What if your father sexually abused you or your mother disowned you as a child? What if your parents have committed some other grievous or hideous action against you? What if they are not Christians? Are we still called to honor them? The answer is yes. God does not say, "Honor your father and mother if they deserve it." He says instead that we are to honor them. There are no conditions or exemptions for this commandment.

Now, you don't have to condone or accept your parents' sin. You are not commanded to defend your parents or make excuses for them. But you must honor them. This command really has very little to do with our parents; instead, it is about us. It is about our spiritual maturity and ability to place someone else above ourselves and honor them. This does not mean we submit to an abusive father or mother. It does not mean that we are forbidden from telling the proper authorities if our parents are breaking a law. It simply means that we don't run our parents down and we should not intentionally hurt them, even if they hurt us.

   ❧ Is this commandment easy or difficult for you to accept? Why?

   ❧ What are some of the common ways we break this commandment in our society today?

The sixth command simply reads *You shall not murder* (Exod 20:13). This commandment has been interpreted wrongly for generations. The Hebrew

---

74 Kenneth L. Barker and John R. Kohlenberger, eds., *Zondervan NIV Bible Commentary*. Accordance electronic ed. (Grand Rapids, MI: Zondervan, 1994), n.p.

language has seven words that can mean murder. The word used here is *rasah*. Of the seven words, this is the one word that signifies "murder" where premeditation and intentionality are present.[75] In other words, this is not a prohibition against killing; it is a command not to take another's life intentionally or without cause. Some have falsely tried to use this verse as a prohibition against war, capital punishment, and even eating meat. However, the Bible is clear that this commandment concerns one human taking another's life through some premeditated and intentional act of violence.

📖 Look up and carefully read Genesis 1:26-27 and 9:6. Why do you think God prohibits us from murdering each other? ⚒

_____

_____

_____

_____

📖 Read the following verses and identify when the Bible says that Christians are allowed to take a life. ⚒

- Genesis 9:3

_____

_____

- Genesis 9:6

_____

_____

- Exodus 22:2

_____

_____

- Deuteronomy 19:5

_____

_____

---

75 Kenneth L. Barker and John R. Kohlenberger, eds., *Zondervan NIV Bible Commentary*. Accordance electronic ed. (Grand Rapids, MI: Zondervan, 1994), n.p.

Tomorrow's lesson will center on the final four commandments that God gave to his people in Exodus 20. Before you conclude your lesson today, take some time to reflect on the first six commandments that you have studied. Are you following them? Could you explain them to a friend? Do you understand their importance in everyday life? Do you view them as a blessing, or a burden? These questions and others will help you solidify these commandments in both your heart and life.

Close today by again listing out the Ten Commandments from memory without looking back at your notes. Then check yourself and spend some time learning these commandments.

1. _____

2. _____

3. _____

4. _____

5. _____

6. _____

7. _____

8. _____

9. _____

10. _____

TAKE TIME TO PRAY

X-Commandments—Day Four

Memory Verse

Ten Commandments

Start today's study by writing out the Ten Commandments in order. When you are finished, look them up in Exodus 20 and make corrections to what you wrote. Finally, spend some time reflecting on these commandments as you memorize them and then take a moment to pray about whatever God lays on your heart.

1. _____
2. _____
3. _____
4. _____
5. _____
6. _____
7. _____
8. _____
9. _____
10. _____

S o far, we have looked at the first six commandments found in Exodus 20. To-day we will conclude our lesson on the Ten Commandments by looking at the meaning behind the final four commandments.

The seventh commandment says *You shall not commit adultery* (Exod 20:14). The verb "to commit adultery" can be used of either men or women.[76] When Po-tiphar's wife attempted to entice Joseph into sleeping with her, Joseph protested in part by saying *How then could I do such a wicked thing and sin against God?* (Gen 39:9). When either men or women cheat on their spouses, they are indeed sin-ning against God who instituted the sacred union of marriage between a man and a woman. Hebrews 13:4 states that *marriage should be honored by all, and the mar-riage bed kept pure, for God will judge the adulterer and all the sexually immoral.*

   📖 What was the punishment prescribed by God for adultery in Deuteronomy 22:22-29?

_____

_____

_____

   📖 How did Jesus expand on this issue in Matthew 5:27-28?

_____

_____

_____

You shall not steal is the eighth commandment that God gives to his people (Exod 20:15). When someone steals something, they are not only stealing from another individual, they are indeed stealing from God as well. In Psalms 24:1, among other places, we learn that everything in the entire world belongs to God. Therefore, anything we possess has been given to us directly from God. When you take something from someone else, you are stealing the very thing that God has given to them. Stealing comes in many different forms. Look at some of them be-low and write out if you have ever been guilty of steeling any of these things from another person.

   ❧ Money

_____

_____

---

76 Kenneth L. Barker and John R. Kohlenberger, eds., *Zondervan NIV Bible Commentary*. Ac-cordance electronic ed. (Grand Rapids, MI: Zondervan, 1994), n.p.

ॐ Material Possessions

_____

_____

ॐ Time 🎬

_____

_____

ॐ Joy

_____

_____

ॐ Peace

_____

_____

The ninth commandment deals with lying by saying, *You shall not give false testimony against your neighbor* (Exod 20:16). The Life Application Study Bible says that "we should be honest in our private dealings as well as in our public statements. In either situation, we 'testify falsely' by leaving something out of a story, telling a half-truth, twisting the facts, or inventing a falsehood. God warns us against deception. Even though deception is a way of life for many people, God's people must not give in to it!"[77] Truth and trust are crucial to Christianity. At the core of God's character, you will find truth. There is nothing to hide; no reason to lie or twist the truth. When we live our lives in a way that honors and pleases God, there is absolutely no benefit to lying. Only when we are doing things that we should not be, or acting in ways that are unbecoming to Christians, do we find lying, deception, and other such means to be necessary in our lives. These are tools of our enemy, not our Father in heaven.

Personally, I love the story of the resurrection from the gospel of Mark, particularly the passage in Mark 16:6 when the angel of the Lord says. "Don't be alarmed." He said, "You are looking for Jesus the Nazarene, who was crucified. He has risen! He is not here. See the place where they laid him." How different would this account be if this angel had said, "Just trust me, Jesus is not in there, but you can't go in and see..." That would make me examine with a little more

---

77 *Life Application Study Bible,* Accordance electronic ed. (Carol Stream, IL: Tyndale House Publishers, 2004), n.p.

suspicion this whole issue of the resurrection. But the angel says "Go ahead; have a look. He is not in there." Christianity has nothing to hide. We have no reason to lie or be deceitful. However, many believers today choose to live their lives through a series of lies and deceptions, and in so doing, they break one of God's commandments.

    ❧ Do you like it when people lie to you?

_____

_____

    ❧ Do you enjoy lying?

_____

_____

    ❧ Can you think of anything good that has ever come from a lie?

_____

_____

    ❧ What are some specific examples in scripture that deal with lying or telling the truth?

_____

_____

The final commandment says *You shall not covet your neighbor's house. You shall not covet your neighbor's wife, or his manservant or maidservant, his ox or donkey, or anything that belongs to your neighbor* (Exod 20:17). When we covet something that belongs to another, we are earnestly seeking or longing after something that is not ours. This goes beyond simply admiring someone else's possessions, or thinking that "I'd like to have one of those." Coveting includes envy—resenting the fact that others have what you don't.[78] When we fall into this kind of thinking, it is like saying "God you have not given me enough; I want more!" We look like a small child who throws a fit as she watches another child play with a toy. As adults, we realize how foolish the child is acting and how fleeting the pleasure of that toy actually is. However, in the midst of coveting what the other child has, the toddler throwing the tantrum is convinced she needs the toy and she needs it now. We are commanded not to covet what others might have, but instead to learn the secret of being content and happy with what God has placed in our own

---

78 *Ibid.*

hands. Read the following scriptures and write down what they have to say about this commandment.

📖 Deuteronomy 5:21

_____

_____

📖 Philippians 4:10-13

_____

_____

📖 1 Timothy 6:6-12

_____

_____

Now that you have studied and memorized these Ten Commandments that God gave to his people in Exodus 20, we should take just a moment to look at an encounter Jesus had with a man who was considered to be an expert in the Law. This man decided to test Jesus in an attempt to discover which law or commandment was the greatest. Read about this encounter in Matthew 22:34-40.

📖 Write out verses 37-39 in the space below.

_____

_____

_____

_____

_____

_____

_____

_____

_____

_____

📖 Now write out the Ten Commandments from Exodus 20 from memory. Then identify which of Jesus' two commands coincide with each of the Ten Commandments.

1. _____

2. _____

3. _____

4. _____

5. _____

6. _____

7. _____

8. _____

9. _____

10. _____

✌ After studying the Ten Commandments from the Old Testament, does Jesus' teaching about these two commandments make more sense to you? Why do you think Jesus listed these two commandments as the greatest? ✗

_____

_____

_____

_____

The Ten Commandments that God has given us in Exodus 20 along with all of the other commands in the Bible are not intended to be a yoke of slavery or a burden for believers. He has graciously given us these commandments to be a blessing in our lives. When God's people follow these basic commandments and allow them to dictate how they live in relation to God and to other believers, they will learn that these commandments are about God's divine provision in our lives. When we follow them and use them properly (1 Tim 1:8), it is amazing how much better every area of life becomes. Teach these commandments to your children, friends, and everyone else you know so that they might be blessed by them as well.

Close today by again listing out the Ten Commandments from memory without looking back at your notes. Then check yourself and spend some time learning these commandments.

1. _____

2. _____

3. _____

4. _____

5. _____

6. _____

7. _____

8. _____

9. _____

10. _____

TAKE TIME TO PRAY

MEMORY VERSE REVIEW

To review, use the space below to write all the memory verses you have learned so far, including this week's. You can also use this space for personal notes about this lesson.

_____

_____

_____

_____

_____

_____

_____

_____

_____

_____

_____

_____

_____

_____

_____

_____

_____

_____

Yield—Day One

Memory Verse

Luke 10:27

Start today's study by writing out your memory verse in the space below. Then, read it three times from your Bible and take just a moment to pray before completing the following lesson.

```
_____

_____

_____

_____
```

The first person I told about my idea for this Bible study curriculum was my friend Chris. We met in college, and while we got along, I would not describe Chris as being my "best friend" or even my "second-best friend" through my college years. Shortly after we graduated, Chris, along with all of my other friends, moved to other parts of Texas to pursue their careers. Chris later moved to Florida, which means we rarely get to see each other in person. Despite the distance and time that has passed, today Chris is indeed one of my closest and most trusted friends. There are many things I love about Chris. He is honest, sincere, and a man who desires to please God above all else. But Chris is also a great encourager. When I started to explain my ideas for this workbook, Chris encouraged me to step out and go to work on the content. It was actually Chris who came up with the name *The Absolute Basics of Christianity*, as I bounced ideas off of him for each letter of the alphabet. However, after several months of planning and outlining, Chris said, "I just don't know what you are going to do about the letters X, Y, and Z." God revealed his plan for X, and Z, to me while I was on a mission trip to Central America. Chris continued to pray with me about what to do with the Y, when finally one morning God confirmed in my heart that the subject for this week was to be "yielding." I opened my email to send Chris the good news, only to find a message in my inbox from him that had arrived twenty minutes earlier. His message simply said, "yielding." It was great confirmation not only for this week's study, but also that God had his hand on this entire work. I am thankful for friends like Chris who prayed for and participated in different aspects of the completion of this study. I am even more thankful that God placed him in my life. He truly is a great example of what it means to have a yielding spirit.

The word yield is generally used Biblically to describe the "yield" that a crop produces. However, this is not the kind of yield that the modern day disciple must, and needs to, understand. Instead, we must learn once again what it means to yield our lives to God. We must be able to comprehend what it means to yield all we are, all we have, and all we desire, so that we can receive something greater in our lives.

    ❧ When you see a yield sign while driving, what do you do?

_____

_____

    ❧ What are some other words that might be synonyms for the word "yield"? ✗

_____

_____

    📖 Read Galatians 2:5 and Acts 27:15, and write a basic definition for the word yield in the space below.

_____

_____

_____

Two Greek words contained in these verses give us a clear picture of what it means to yield our lives. In fact several translations actually use the word yield in the text. Louw and Nida give the following definition for the words used in these two passages, "to give in to a superior power or force—'to give in to, or to surrender." [79] Yielding, surrender, giving in, deferring, and giving way are not popular concepts in the world today. Sadly, many see the idea of yielding as a sign of weakness. As a result we have become so conditioned to resist yielding, submitting, or surrendering that we have foolishly been trying to rule our own lives, without realizing that it is impossible to be a disciple of Christ, find the full and abundant life, or please God without freely yielding our lives to his divine will.

The fact that you have completed twenty-four weeks of this study proves that you are dedicated to growing as a believer. However, dedication is not what God desires. Dedication without a yielding and submissive spirit will prove to have little effect for the long race you are running. For the remainder of today's study you should look up the following scripture passages. In each, you will find an example of someone who possessed a yielding spirit and as a result was used by God. Make notes about each and be prepared to discuss these different biblical figures, as well as concepts of yielding, in your next small group time.

📖 Genesis 22:1-18

_____

_____

📖 Exodus 3:1—4:18

_____

_____

📖 Jonah chapter 1—3:5

_____

_____

📖 Matthew 4:17-22

_____

_____

📖 Matthew 26:36-39

_____

_____

---

79 Johannes P. Louw and Eugene A. Nida, *Greek–English Lexicon of the New Testament Based on Semantic Domains,* (New York: United Bible Societies), n.p.

    😊 What do these people have in common?

_____

_____

    😊 What do you have in common with them?

_____

_____

    😊 What keeps you from being as submissive as those you have just read about?

_____

_____

Write out your memory verse in the space below. Try to do it completely from memory, then double-check yourself.

_____

_____

_____

_____

TAKE TIME TO PRAY

Yield—Day Two

Memory Verse

Luke 10:27

Start today's study by writing out as much of your memory verse as you can in the space below. Then, look up the verse and make any corrections that are needed. Finally, read it three times from your Bible and take just a moment to pray before completing the following lesson.

---

*I*n yesterday's lesson, one of the last questions you were asked to answer was, "What do these people have in common?" Of course the simple answer is that they were all people who yielded to God's will. The Bible is full of men and women who chose to submit and surrender all that they were to God. This is what made them usable as God's vessels. It was their willingness to yield, submit, and surrender that allowed them to be used by God to change the world. God continues to search for men and women like these to this very day. Read Matthew 1:18-23, and Luke 1:26-38 and answer the questions below.

❧ Which verses in these two passages point to a yielding attitude in the lives of Joseph and Mary?

_____

_____

_____

❧ Honestly, how do you think you might have responded to this situation?

_____

_____

_____

❧ Read Luke 1:28-30 again, What do these verses tell you about yielding?

_____

_____

_____

Joseph and Mary were pledged to be married. They had entered the one-year waiting period before the actual marriage ceremony would be performed and they would officially be seen as husband and wife. It is impossible to know exactly what was going on in their lives during this time, for the Bible does not provide the exact details. However, one can imagine that this couple was most probably doing what young couples, both then and now, do in preparation for marriage. Of course, there was a wedding to be planned. Joseph might have been working on building a house, saving money, and building his carpentry business to support his new family. Perhaps they talked together about their hopes and dreams. Surely at times their imaginations would have drifted into the future as they envisioned what the perfect marriage and life might look like. Everything was right on track until the angel showed up.

The pregnancy changed everything. Joseph was embarrassed, humiliated, and no doubt upset when he learned of Mary's pregnancy. Mary was troubled and shocked when she found out that she was pregnant. She must have thought, "How am I going to explain this to Joseph and my parents?" Their plans for a perfect wedding ceremony were derailed. Their hopes and dreams of a perfect family and wonderful life were now in jeopardy. This pregnancy changed everything.

Joseph had every right to demand that Mary be killed for her unfaithfulness. But he was a righteous man and decided to do all he could to keep the matter quiet and just divorce her. However, when the angel of God appeared to Joseph, he relented and decided to take Mary as his wife. Joseph willingly laid aside his reputation, his dreams, and his desires in order to follow God's plan. Mary was no different; she said, "I am the Lords servant." The Greek word translated "servant" is *doule*, which can also be translated as "bond slave."

There were many ways that slaves could be acquired during the biblical period. They could be captured and forced into slavery as prisoners of war (Num 31:7-9). They could be purchased (Lev 25:44), given as a gift (Gen 29:24), or acquired as payment for a debt that was owed (Lev 25:39). Some were born as slaves (Exod 21:4) and still others were made slaves after being arrested if they had no means to pay for something they had stolen (Exod 22:2-3). Mary, however, had not been captured, purchased, or gifted; she wasn't sold as payment for a debt, born as a slave, or arrested with no means to pay for her crime. She was not forced into slavery at all. Instead, she said she was a "bond slave" or "bondservant" to God. Read about this in Exodus 21:5-6.

    ❧ How is this different from the other forms of slavery?

_____

_____

    ❧ Who decides that a person will be a "bondservant?"

_____

_____

    ❧ How long does this servant hood last?

_____

_____

Being a bondservant required complete submission, and a full yielding of one's life to another. By becoming a bondservant, you were giving someone else total control over your life. It was voluntary slavery. What would make anyone want to do such a thing? Only the grace and goodness of the master would lead any individual to voluntarily become a slave. Individuals who desired to be bondservants trusted their masters so much that they felt their life would ultimately be better in service to those masters rather than in service to themselves. Mary believed that despite this unexplainable situation that God had placed her in, she was better off as his slave then as a slave to the world. So she submitted her life and yielded all of who she was to God, the Master. And because of her willingness to do so, along with Joseph, God brought his one and only Son into the world to redeem all of humanity from the forced slavery of sin.

ᘓ Do you feel like you have been forced into slavery for God?

_____

_____

ᘓ Do you consider yourself to be a bondservant, or are you simply free to do what you want? Do you think this is the best way to live life?

_____

_____

_____

ᘓ Does your life match up with the answer as stated above?

_____

_____

Finish today's lesson by looking up the following passages and considering what they teach you about yielding your life to God.

📖 Acts 2:42-47 ✗

_____

_____

📖 Acts 4:13-31

_____

_____

📖 Acts 5:1-11

_____

_____

📖 Acts 10:1-48 ✗

_____

_____

Write out your memory verse in the space below. Try to do it completely from memory, then double-check yourself.

TAKE TIME TO PRAY

Yield—Day Three

Memory Verse

Luke 10:27

Start today's study by writing out as much of your memory verse as you can in the space below. Then, look up the verse and make any corrections that are needed. Finally, read it three times from your Bible and take just a moment to pray before completing the following lesson.

_____

_____

_____

_____

The concept of surrender, or yielding, is foreign to most people in America because it is simply an unacceptable outcome to anything in our lives. What we have failed to understand is that God does not want us to roll over and give up. He just wants us to give up trying to do everything on our own. His desire is that we would yield and allow him to have the right-of-way in our lives. In the process of yielding and surrendering to his divine plan, we will find the simple, sweet, satisfying life that we have been searching for. We do not need to create or manufacture the perfect life; God has already done that for us. We just need to surrender to his plans and purposes and receive the full and abundant life that he has offered.

The problem for many people comes from a lack of trust. While they may say that they fully trust God, in reality they live their lives expressing the opposite.

Worry, anxiety, stress, and a seemingly endless sense of disillusionment surround their lives. For example, there is a woman I have known for years who is always saying things like "I just have to trust God. I just don't know where our next meal is going to come from. I just hope we can eat this month. I just have to trust that God will provide for me and my family." She is always anxious, worried, and scared that she will not be able to eat. She is constantly touting how much she must trust God for her next meal. The only problem is that she is a millionaire thirty times over. Yet she is legitimately worried that she won't be able to eat tonight. Despite claiming to trust God for her next meal, the fact of the matter is that despite having an abundance of God's provision in her life, she still refuses to trust God.

There is another lady I have known for many years who is raising her five children alone after losing her husband. They live in a small run-down house, they shop at Goodwill (I do too, by the way), and the only time they eat out is when someone sends them a gift card. Yet this woman is never worried about her next meal; she trusts God completely. Several years ago, while on a trip to Africa, I was invited into the home of an African pastor. There were several other Americans on the team with me, and nearly fifteen other African pastors in the small hut that night. We laughed and shared stories as the ladies prepared dinner. When it came time to eat, a small plate of rice and chicken was served to me and the other Americans. We prayed and then we were directed to start eating. "I will wait till you all have your food," I said. "There was not enough," replied the host. "This is all we have but we know God will provide for our needs." Some might be tempted to think that this was a trick to get the Americans to pull out their checkbooks. However, the look in the man's eyes, and the absence of the single chicken which was in the yard when we arrived, confirmed in my heart that these people had given all they had to give that night. They had learned the secret of being able to fully surrender and trust God. Have you? Read the following verses and determine if God is trustworthy enough to surrender your life to.

📖 Genesis 1:1-31

_____

_____

📖 Psalms 139:13

_____

_____

📖 Isaiah 45:18

_____

_____

📖 Jeremiah 29:11

_____

_____

📖 Romans 8:28

_____

_____

📖 Philippians 1:3-6

_____

_____

📖 1 Thessalonians 5:23-24

_____

_____

  ❧ Do you think your life would be better or worse if you yielded totally to God's will? Why?

_____

_____

Despite knowing that life would be better through surrender, some people still insist on doing it their own way. Jonah was such a man. The text says in Jonah 1:1-3, *The word of the LORD came to Jonah son of Amittai:* ²*"Go to the great city of Nineveh and preach against it, because its wickedness has come up before me."* ³*But Jonah ran away from the LORD and headed for Tarshish. He went down to Joppa, where he found a ship bound for that port. After paying the fare, he went aboard and sailed for Tarshish to flee from the LORD.* Jonah did not think he was supposed to go to Nineveh; he did not have to guess what God desired for this portion of his life. The Bible says that God came and told him exactly what to do. But Jonah refused to yield. He would not surrender his pride, time, and stubborn attitude, so instead of yielding he ran away from God. Read the full account of this portion of his life from Jonah 1—3:5 again and answer the questions below.

  ❧ What were the results of refusing to yield? Be specific.

_____

_____

❧ Was he better off when he ran from God or when he yielded his life to God? Why? Be specific.

_____

_____

❧ Have you ever felt like you were in the belly of a great fish? When was it? Did it happen because you ran or because you yielded?

_____

_____

❧ What other biblical examples can you think of when it comes to refusing to yield or surrender to God's will? How did it work out for them?

_____

_____

❧ Do you trust God enough today to say that you will totally surrender your life to his control? If not, what needs to happen so this can take place?

_____

_____

_____

_____

Write out your memory verse in the space below. Try to do it completely from memory, then double-check yourself.

_____

_____

_____

_____

TAKE TIME TO PRAY

Yield—Day Four

Memory Verse

Luke 10:27

Start today's study by writing out as much of your memory verse as you can in the space below. Then, look up the verse and make any corrections that are needed. Finally, read it three times from your Bible and take just a moment to pray before completing the following lesson.

_____

_____

_____

_____

The only person to ever live a perfect life was Jesus Christ. He was fully human, yet he was able to lead a sinless life. This not only made Jesus the perfect sacrifice that God needed to redeem humanity. It also makes him the perfect model for all believers to look to when determining how we live our lives today. What was it that enabled Christ to live this perfect life and become a perfect example for each of us? It was his willingness to yield and surrender everything to his Father. Look up the following verses and write down the different ways that Christ exhibited a yielding spirit.

📖 Matthew 26:36-44

_____

_____

📖 Luke 4:1-15 ⚒

_____

_____

📖 John 5:16-30

_____

_____

📖 John 8:27-30

_____

_____

📖 John 10:17-18

_____

_____

📖 John 12:23-28

_____

_____

📖 John 14:9-14

_____

_____

📖 John 14:30-31

_____

_____

📖 John 18:10-11

_____

_____

There are many other scriptures that show how submissive Christ was to his Father. We must learn to live such a life ourselves. Not only are we challenged and commanded to live our lives in the same way our Savior did, but this is also where you will find fulfillment, peace, joy, comfort, and the full and abundant life we all desire to have. These things escape us in part because we are unwilling to surrender to the Father. Even in Christ's death, we see a calm, a peace, a sense of trust. Why? Because he had completely yielded his life to the will of his Father. When you live such a life, even the most difficult circumstances and trials become bearable.

This week you have looked at the lives of people such as Abraham, Moses, Jonah, Joseph, Mary, and Peter. These people represent a small portion of those throughout history who have chosen a life of surrender and been used by God in amazing ways. We could look at Esther, Nehemiah, David, Daniel, Jeremiah, John, Paul, Barnabas, Timothy, and many others as well. As you think about these and all the others who yielded their lives to Christ, it is important to remember that none were forced to surrender. God did not make any of these men or women yield. Even Jesus Christ himself could have chosen to disobey the Father. So why did they do it? Why did they give up everything to live a life of total surrender? The answer is simple: when you have a personal encounter with the God of the universe who knit you together in your mother's womb and saved your soul, any response short of total surrender is unthinkable. God's plans for your life are so much better than your own. Learn to yield all that you are and you will discover all that you were created to be. You will never really be free until you learn to surrender.

Write out your memory verse in the space below. Try to do it completely from memory, then double-check yourself.

TAKE TIME TO PRAY

To review, use the space below to write all the memory verses you have learned so far, including this week's. You can also use this space for personal notes about this lesson.

_____

_____

_____

_____

_____

_____

_____

_____

_____

_____

_____

_____

_____

_____

_____

_____

_____

Zelotes—Day One

Memory Verse

Psalm 25:10

Start today's study by writing out your memory verse in the space below. Then, read it three times from your Bible and take just a moment to pray before completing the following lesson.

*Z*elotes is the Greek word that we translate in English as zealous. Over the years this word has gained a bad reputation in both the world and the church. To be zealous is considered undesirable in any society that relishes living in the grey areas of life, refusing to take sides and stand for truth. There should, however, be no shame, guilt, or hesitation in the life of a believer when it comes to being zealous for God.

The actual definition for this word by one source reads "zealot, enthusiast, adherent, one who has the feelings or attitudes of deep commitment to a person or cause; in the New Testament this can technically refer to a person who belonged to a nationalist Jewish group that sought independence from Rome.[80] For the sake

---

80 *Greek to English Dictionary and Index to the NIV New Testament, from the Zondervan NIV Exhaustive Concordance,* s.v. "n.p.

of this study we will not examine the origin or political movement of Jews who became known as zealots due to their desire for independence from Rome. However, we will focus on the spiritual implications of what it means to be zealous for God. By completing this twenty-six week study, you have proven that you are zealous for the Lord. However, take a moment to quickly answer the questions below.

- Are you enthusiastic when it comes to your faith?

  ____

  ____

- Do you adhere to the commands of Christ?

  ____

  ____

- Do you have strong feelings about your faith?

  ____

  ____

- Do you have a deep commitment to Christ?

  ____

  ____

- Are you fully devoted to advancing God's kingdom through the gospel of Christ?

  ____

  ____

- Are you zealous?

  ____

  ____

To be zealous was not automatically a bad thing during the New Testament period. One of Christ's disciples was referred to as a zealot on several occasions. It is not entirely clear if this was due to his involvement in the political group or if this was some sort of nickname to distinguish him from another disciple with the same name. In either case, this example among others proves that being zealous for Christ is not undesirable. Look up the following positive examples of those who were zealous for God. Answer the questions below and make notes to refer to in your next small group time.

    📖 Look up and read Matthew 10:2-4, Mark 3:16-19, Luke 6:13-16, and Acts 1:11-14. Who did this zealot share a name with?

_____

_____

    📖 Romans 12:11

_____

_____

    📖 2 Corinthians 8:21-23

_____

_____

    📖 Galatians 4:17-19

_____

_____

While being zealous for God is a desirable trait, if we fail to remain committed to Christ and begin to become zealous for ourselves in the name of Christ, it turns into one of the most horrific, divisive, and destructive impurities that can come from humanity. Many people through the centuries have claimed to be zealous for God, but in reality they were selfishly attempting to advance their own kingdom rather than God's. Examine the following scriptures that identify the negative aspects of being zealous. Be sure to write notes to be used in your next small group session.

    📖 Matthew 23:23-28

_____

_____

    📖 Acts 22:3-5

_____

_____

📖 Galatians 1:13-16

_____

_____

📖 Philippians 3:4-8

_____

_____

❧ What are some of the things that are different between the right kind of zealousness and the wrong kind?

_____

_____

_____

_____

_____

❧ What is the right motive to be zealous for the things of God?

_____

_____

_____

_____

_____

❧ Do you think doing things for God pleases him? What does God want from us? How does that relate to being zealous?

_____

_____

_____

_____

_____

Your commitment to this study and the Word of God over the past twenty-six weeks speaks volumes about your desire to be used by God and to honor him with your life. Do not fear being seen as one who is zealous for Christ. The world needs more men and women of all ages, backgrounds, and ethnicities to take a stand for Christ and be zealous in a God-honoring way. May you be one who is counted among the great saints of old who dared to be zealous for the KING OF KINGS and LORD of LORDS.

The remaining three days of this course will be spent reviewing all twenty-six studies that you have completed. Finish strong by completing all three days and seriously considering the questions and challenges that are contained in the following three studies.

Finish today's study by writing out all of your twenty-six memory verses from memory on another sheet of paper, along with the Ten Commandments. Take your time and study the verses as you write them out.

Write out your memory verse in the space below. Try to do it completely from memory, then double-check yourself.

TAKE TIME TO PRAY

Zelotes—Day Two

Memory Verse

Psalms 25:10

Start today's study by writing out as much of your memory verse as you can in the space below. Then, look up the verse and make any corrections that are needed. Finally, read it three times from your Bible and take just a moment to pray before completing the following lesson.

*B*ased on what you have learned over the past twenty-six weeks, answer the questions below. Take your time and seriously consider each question. Doing this exercise will allow you to review all twenty-six lessons from *The Absolute Basics of Christianity*. You will be amazed at how much you have learned about your faith in such a short time. Your dedication to God's word and your efforts to become the best disciple possible will be highlighted over the final three lessons in this workbook, and will show just how zealous you have been. Start today's study by writing out all of your twenty-six memory verses from memory on another sheet of paper, along with the Ten Commandments. Take your time and study the verses as you write them out.

❧ Is your salvation secure? How do you know? What scripture backs that up?

_____

_____

❧ How would you explain the assurance of salvation to someone else?

_____

_____

❧ List any of your memory verses that deal with salvation.

_____

_____

❧ Have you been baptized by immersion? If not, why?

_____

_____

❧ How would you explain the importance of baptism to someone else?

_____

_____

❧ Do you think everyone should be baptized? Why, or why not?

_____

_____

❧ List any memory verses that deal with baptism.

_____

_____

❧ Do you regularly attend church? Why, or why not?

_____

_____

❧ Do you think church is important? Why, or why not?

_____

_____

❧ Who benefits when you go to church? Explain.

_____

_____

❧ Are you a member of your church? Why, or why not?

_____

_____

❧ How would you explain the importance of church to someone that does not attend regularly?

_____

_____

❧ List any memory verses you can think of that deal with church.

_____

_____

❧ What does it mean to be a disciple of Christ? Do you consider yourself to be a disciple? Why, or why not?

_____

_____

❧ Who is your Barnabas?

_____

_____

❧ Who is your Timothy?

_____

_____

❧ List any memory verses you can recall that deal with discipleship.

_____

_____

❧ What is the four-step plan you learned in Week Five about sharing your testimony?

_____

_____

❧ Do you actively share your faith? Why, or why not?

_____

_____

❧ Do you consider yourself to be a minister or missionary? Why, or why not?

_____

_____

❧ List any memory verses that deal with evangelism.

_____

_____

❧ Are you withholding forgiveness from anyone at the present time? If so, why?

_____

_____

❧ How would you explain the importance of forgiveness to someone who refused to practice it?

_____

_____

❧ List any memory verses that deal with forgiveness.

_____

_____

❧ What are your three main spiritual gifts?

_____

_____

❧ Why did God give you those gifts?

_____

_____

❧ Are you using them? If so, how? If not, why?

_____

_____

❧ Are you abusing your gifts?

_____

_____

❧ List any of your memory verses that deal with gifts.

_____

_____

❧ How would you explain heaven to a nonbeliever?

_____

_____

❧ How would you explain hell to a nonbeliever?

_____

_____

❧ List any of your memory verses that deal with heaven or hell.

_____

_____

Before closing your study today, write this week's memory verse in the space below and then review all twenty five memory verses and the Ten Commandments one more time before praying.

Write out your memory verse in the space below. Try to do it completely from memory, then double-check yourself.

_____

_____

_____

_____

TAKE TIME TO PRAY

Zelotes—Day Three

Memory Verse

Psalms 25:10

Start today's study by writing out as much of your memory verse as you can in the space below. Then, look up the verse and make any corrections that are needed. Finally, read it three times from your Bible and take just a moment to pray before completing the following lesson.

```




```

Based on what you have learned over the past twenty-six weeks, answer the questions below. Take your time and seriously consider each question. Start today's study by writing out all of your twenty-six memory verses from memory on another sheet of paper, along with the Ten Commandments. Take your time and study the verses as you write them out.

   ❧ What did God mean when he said, "I AM that I AM?"

❧ List some of God's character traits.

_____

_____

❧ List some of Jesus Christ's traits.

_____

_____

❧ List any memory verses that deal with God or Jesus.

_____

_____

❧ What is real joy to you?

_____

_____

❧ Do you have real joy today? If so, where does it come from? If not, explain why you think joy is eluding you.

_____

_____

❧ List any memory verses that relate to joy.

_____

_____

❧ What is the kingdom of God?

_____

_____

❧ How would you explain it to a nonbeliever?

_____

_____

_____

❧ Who will enter the kingdom of God?

_____

_____

❧ List any memory verse that deals with God's kingdom.

_____

_____

❧ What are the different types of love in the New Testament? Give examples of each.

_____

_____

❧ How would you explain God's love to a nonbeliever?

_____

_____

❧ What is the greatest thing about love to you?

_____

_____

❧ List any of your memory verses that highlight God's love.

_____

_____

❧ What are the three things you can do with money?

_____

_____

❧ What order should we do those three things in? Are you practicing this in your life?

_____

_____

❧ What is the definition of a tithe?

_____

_____

❧ How would you explain the importance of tithing and giving to another church member who says it's not important?

_____

_____

❧ List any of your memory verses that deal with money.

_____

_____

❧ How do we receive new life?

_____

_____

❧ How can a man or woman be born again when they are old?

_____

_____

❧ How would you tell a nonbeliever that they can receive new life?

_____

_____

❧ List any memory verses that deal with new life.

_____

_____

❧ Which is more important, sacrifice or obedience? Why?

_____

_____

_____

෨ What does it mean to be obedient to God?

_____

_____

෨ Why should we be obedient?

_____

_____

෨ List and write out any of your memory verses that deal with obedience.

_____

_____

෨ When should a Christian pray?

_____

_____

෨ Why should a Christian pray?

_____

_____

෨ How would you explain the ACTS model of prayer to someone else?

_____

_____

෨ List and write out any of your memory verses that deal with prayer.

_____

_____

෨ Why is it important to spend time alone in the stillness with God every day?

_____

_____

⅋ Are you currently spending time with God each day? Why or why not?

_____

_____

⅋ List any of your memory verse that deal with having a quiet time with God.

_____

_____

Before closing your study today, write this week's memory verse in the space below and then review all twenty-five memory verses and the Ten Commandments one more time before praying.

Write out your memory verse in the space below. Try to do it completely from memory, then double-check yourself.

_____

_____

_____

_____

TAKE TIME TO PRAY

Zelotes—Day Four

Memory Verse

Psalm 25:10

Start today's study by writing out as much of your memory verse as you can in the space below. Then, look up the verse and make any corrections that are needed. Finally, read it three times from your Bible and take just a moment to pray before completing the following lesson.

*B*ased on what you have learned over the past twenty-six weeks answer the questions below. Take your time and seriously consider each question. Start today's study by writing out all of your twenty-six memory verses from memory on another sheet of paper, along with the Ten Commandments. Take your time and study the verses as you write them out.

    ❧ Why is reading the Bible on a regular basis important in a believer's life?

❧ Do you think the Bible is trustworthy? Why, or why not?

_____

_____

❧ What are some different ways we experience the word of God?

_____

_____

❧ List any of your memory verses that deal with the importance of God's word in a believer's life.

_____

_____

❧ How would you explain who the Holy Spirit is to a nonbeliever?

_____

_____

❧ What are some of the roles the Spirit plays in our lives today?

_____

_____

❧ Have you seen the Holy Spirit at work in your life recently? When, how, where?

_____

_____

❧ List and write out any verses that deal with the Holy Spirit.

_____

_____

_____

❧ Who are the three persons of the Holy Trinity?

_____

_____

❧ How would you explain the Holy Trinity to someone?

_____

_____

❧ Are the three persons of the Holy Trinity individuals or united as one? Explain.

_____

_____

❧ List any of your memory verses that deal with the Holy Trinity.

_____

_____

❧ Why is unity important?

_____

_____

❧ Why does the devil hate unity?

_____

_____

❧ List all of the memory verses you can think of that deal with unity.

_____

_____

_____

❧ Can there be victory without sacrifice? Explain.

_____

_____

❧ What are some of the keys to victory in our lives?

_____

_____

❧ Who achieved the victory for us? When did it happen?

_____

_____

❧ List all of the memory verses you can think of that deal with victory.

_____

_____

❧ What is the "worthy walk?" How would you explain it to someone else?

_____

_____

❧ What is the difference between doing something for God and doing something with God?

_____

_____

❧ Do you feel like you are living a life that is worthy of the Lord? Why, or why not?

_____

_____

_____

❧ List all of the memory verses you can think of that deal with the worthy walk.

_____

_____

❧ List and briefly explain all of the Ten Commandments in order.

1. _____

_____

2. _____

_____

3. _____

_____

4. _____

_____

5. _____

_____

6. _____

_____

7. _____

_____

8. _____

_____

9. _____

_____

10. _____

_____

ⅉ How did Jesus enhance these commandments?

_____

_____

ⅉ What two commandments did Jesus say summed up the entire law?

_____

_____

_____

_____

ⅉ List any of your memory verses that deal with the Ten Commandments.

_____

_____

ⅉ Is being zealous good or bad? Explain?

_____

_____

ⅉ Are you zealous? In what way?

_____

_____

ⅉ List any of your memory verses that have to do with being zealous.

_____

_____

Congratulations! You have completed this study. In the back of this workbook you will find a form that can be filled out and mailed in. When you do this, I will personally sign and send you a certificate that marks your accomplishment of completing *The Absolute Basics of Christianity*. Your spiritual journey is not over, God has great plans for your life!

PASTOR PETE

Write out your memory verse in the space below. Try to do it completely from memory, then double-check yourself.

TAKE TIME TO PRAY

To review, use the space below to write all the memory verses you have learned so far, including this week's. You can also use this space for personal notes about this lesson.

Congratulations!

You have just finished *The Absolute Basics of Christianity*. I would love to send you a certificate in recognition of your completion of this study. Each certificate is personalized with your name, date of completion, and my personal signature. Take just a few minutes to fill out the form on the following page and mail it in to receive your certificate. Once again congratulations on completing this study. Please remember to check **www.pastorpete.org** often for more resources, and books that will help you continue to grow.

PASTOR PETE PAWELEK

To receive your personalized completion certificate mail the following completed form along with $2.00 to:

Cowboy Fellowship
Attn. Absolute Basics
PO Box 68
Pleasanton Tx. 78064

THE ABSOLUTE BASICS OF CHRISTIANITY

Name (as you want it to appear): _____

Date: _____

Return Address: _____

Email: _____

Church Name: _____

Church Address: _____

Pastors Name: _____

I certify that I have completed all of the lessons in *The Absolute Basics of Christianity* to the best of my ability.

Student Signature _____

Pastor/Group Leader Signature _____

Memory Verse System

*T*here are many different ways to memorize scripture. This is the method I developed years ago to memorize Greek and Hebrew vocabulary during seminary. It is not a fancy system or very complicated but I have found it to be extremely effective.

To use this system you will need to have some index cards, and three rings that are used to hold index cards. These rings can generally be found in the same area as the index cards at most stores. The three rings should be different colors, if at all possible. For example, my rings are red, orange, and green. Here is how I use the rings.

My red ring is what I call the "hot ring." I keep five memory verses on this ring and I review them multiple times throughout the day. This ring and these five cards are never far away and whenever I have a few seconds or minutes I flip through the cards. When I get ready to add my sixth card, I then take off the first card and move it to the orange ring.

The orange ring can contain as many cards as needed. I review these cards on average once a day, five days a week. Once I feel that I have a great handle on the particular verse, I move it to my green ring.

My green ring is my 'go' ring. Cards on this ring are ones that I have fully and totally memorized and I no longer have any trouble at all with them. I review this ring about two or three times a week. If I find a verse that I can no longer remember, I move it back to my orange ring until I have again mastered it. I have included a chart that should guide you as to which ring each verse should be on as you work your way through this study.

KEYS TO MEMORIZATION

Personally, I have never been good at memorizing things. I had trouble remembering my phone number and address in grade school, and still to this day I struggle with simple things like names, dates, numbers, and many other things that require memorization. However, I have been able to memorize verses using the following principles and I hope they will benefit you as well.

1. Practice makes perfect- you have to practice, practice, practice! You must review your verses everyday for the rest of your life. If you stop, you will lose all that you worked so hard to learn.

2. Get organized. Sure, you can just write your verses down on a piece of paper, but for long-term success you need to have an organized plan of attack. Use the index cards and rings to keep your verses well organized.

3. Don't just memorize, study. It is a mistake to try to memorize anything just to have it in your memory. If you want to remember something, you need to study it and learn all you can about it. As you memorize these verses, think about them, examine them, and study them. This will help you remember them.

4. Pray. Ask God to help you in your effort to memorize scripture. When we ask, we are sure to receive.

MEMORY VERSE CHART VOLUMES ONE & TWO

Week	Red	Orange	Green
1	Romans 10:9		
2	Matthew 28:19-20 Romans 10:9		
3	1 Cor. 12:27 Matthew 28:19-20 Romans 10:9		
4	1 John 2:6 1 Cor. 12:27 Matthew 28:19-20 Romans 10:9		
5	Mark 16:15 1 John 2:6 1 Cor. 12:27 Matthew 28:19-20 Romans 10:9		

6	Matthew 19:26 Mark 16:15 1 John 2:6 1 Cor. 12:27 Matthew 28:19-20	Romans 10:9	
7	Romans 12:1 Matthew 19:26 Mark 16:15 1 John 2:6 1 Cor. 12:27	Matthew 28:19-20 Romans 10:9	
8	John 14:6 Romans 12:1 Matthew 19:26 Mark 16:15 1 John 2:6	1 Cor. 12:27 Matthew 28:19-20 Romans 10:9	
9	1 Peter 15-16 John 14:6 Romans 12:1 Matthew 19:26 Mark 16:15	1 John 2:6 1 Cor. 12:27 Matthew 28:19-20 Romans 10:9	
10	Philippians. 4:4 1 Peter 15-16 John 14:6 Romans 12:1 Matthew 19:26	Mark 16:15 1 John 2:6 1 Cor. 12:27 Matthew 28:19-20 Romans 10:9	
11	Matthew 6:33 Philippians. 4:4 1 Peter 15-16 John 14:6 Romans 12:1	Matthew 19:26 Mark 16:15 1 John 2:6 1 Cor. 12:27 Matthew 28:19-20	Romans 10:9
12	John 3:16-17 Matthew 6:33 Philippians. 4:4 1 Peter 15-16 John 14:6	Romans 12:1 Matthew 19:26 Mark 16:15 1 John 2:6 1 Cor. 12:27	Matthew 28:19-20 Romans 10:9

13	John 1:16 John 3:16-17 Matthew 6:33 Philippians. 4:4 1 Peter 15-16	John 14:6 Romans 12:1 Matthew 19:26 Mark 16:15 1 John 2:6	1 Cor. 12:27 Matthew 28:19-20 Romans 10:9
14	John 10:10 John 1:16 John 3:16-17 Matthew 6:33 Philippians. 4:4	1 Peter 15-16 John 14:6 Romans 12:1 Matthew 19:26 Mark 16:15	1 John 2:6 1 Cor. 12:27 Matthew 28:19-20 Romans 10:9
15	1 John 2:5-6 John 10:10 John 1:16 John 3:16-17 Matthew 6:33	Philippians. 4:4 1 Peter 15-16 John 14:6 Romans 12:1 Matthew 19:26	Mark 16:15 1 John 2:6 1 Cor. 12:27 Matthew 28:19-20 Romans 10:9
16	1 Thessalonians 5:16-18 1 John 2:5-6 John 10:10 John 1:16 John 3:16-17	Matthew 6:33 Philippians. 4:4 1 Peter 15-16 John 14:6 Romans 12:1	Matthew 19:26 Mark 16:15 1 John 2:6 1 Cor. 12:27 Matthew 28:19-20 Romans 10:9
17	Psalms 23:1-3 1 Thessalonians 5:16-18 1 John 2:5-6 John 10:10 John 1:16	John 3:16-17 Matthew 6:33 Philippians. 4:4 1 Peter 15-16 John 14:6	Romans 12:1 Matthew 19:26 Mark 16:15 1 John 2:6 1 Cor. 12:27 Matthew 28:19-20 Romans 10:9
18	2 Timothy 3:16-17 Psalms 23:1-3 1 Thessalonians 5:16-18 1 John 2:5-6 John 10:10	John 1:16 John 3:16-17 Matthew 6:33 Philippians. 4:4 1 Peter 15-16	John 14:6 Romans 12:1 Matthew 19:26 Mark 16:15 1 John 2:6 1 Cor. 12:27 Matthew 28:19-20 Romans 10:9

19	John 15:4 2 Timothy 3:16-17 Psalms 23:1-3 1 Thessalonians 5:16-18 1 John 2:5-6	John 10:10 John 1:16 John 3:16-17 Matthew 6:33 Philippians. 4:4	1 Peter 15-16 John 14:6 Romans 12:1 Matthew 19:26 Mark 16:15 1 John 2:6 1 Cor. 12:27 Matthew 28:19-20 Romans 10:9
20	John 14:23 John 15:4 2 Timothy 3:16-17 Psalms 23:1-3 1 Thessalonians 5:16-18	1 John 2:5-6 John 10:10 John 1:16 John 3:16-17 Matthew 6:33	Philippians. 4:4 1 Peter 15-16 John 14:6 Romans 12:1 Matthew 19:26 Mark 16:15 1 John 2:6 1 Cor. 12:27 Matthew 28:19-20 Romans 10:9
21	Hebrews 10:24 John 14:23 John 15:4 2 Timothy 3:16-17 Psalms 23:1-3	1 Thessalonians 5:16-18 1 John 2:5-6 John 10:10 John 1:16 John 3:16-17	Matthew 6:33 Philippians. 4:4 1 Peter 15-16 John 14:6 Romans 12:1 Matthew 19:26 Mark 16:15 1 John 2:6 1 Cor. 12:27 Matthew 28:19-20 Romans 10:9
22	Psalms 18:35 Hebrews 10:24 John 14:23 John 15:4 2 Timothy 3:16-17	Psalms 23:1-3 1 Thessalonians 5:16-18 1 John 2:5-6 John 10:10 John 1:16	John 3:16-17 Matthew 6:33 Philippians. 4:4 1 Peter 15-16 John 14:6 Romans 12:1 Matthew 19:26

			Mark 16:15 1 John 2:6 1 Cor. 12:27 Matthew 28:19-20 Romans 10:9
23	Philippians 4:8 Psalms 18:35 Hebrews 10:24 John 14:23 John 15:4	2 Timothy 3:16-17 Psalms 23:1-3 1 Thessalonians 5:16-18 1 John 2:5-6 John 10:10	John 1:16 John 3:16-17 Matthew 6:33 Philippians. 4:4 1 Peter 15-16 John 14:6 Romans 12:1 Matthew 19:26 Mark 16:15 1 John 2:6 1 Cor. 12:27 Matthew 28:19-20 Romans 10:9
24	Ten Commandments Philippians 4:8 Psalms 18:35 Hebrews 10:24 John 14:23	John 15:4 2 Timothy 3:16-17 Psalms 23:1-3 1 Thessalonians 5:16-18 1 John 2:5-6	John 10:10 John 1:16 John 3:16-17 Matthew 6:33 Philippians. 4:4 1 Peter 15-16 John 14:6 Romans 12:1 Matthew 19:26 Mark 16:15 1 John 2:6 1 Cor. 12:27 Matthew 28:19-20 Romans 10:9
25	Luke 10:27 Ten Commandments Philippians 4:8 Psalms 18:35 Hebrews 10:24	John 14:23 John 15:4 2 Timothy 3:16-17 Psalms 23:1-3 1 Thessalonians 5:16-18	1 John 2:5-6 John 10:10 John 1:16 John 3:16-17 Matthew 6:33 Philippians. 4:4 1 Peter 15-16 John 14:6

			Romans 12:1 Matthew 19:26 Mark 16:15 1 John 2:6 1 Cor. 12:27 Matthew 28:19-20 Romans 10:9
26	Psalms 25:10 Luke 10:27 Ten Commandments Philippians 4:8 Psalms 18:35	Hebrews 10:24 John 14:23 John 15:4 2 Timothy 3:16-17 Psalms 23:1-3	1 Thessalonians 5:16-18 1 John 2:5-6 John 10:10 John 1:16 John 3:16-17 Matthew 6:33 Philippians. 4:4 1 Peter 15-16 John 14:6 Romans 12:1 Matthew 19:26 Mark 16:15 1 John 2:6 1 Cor. 12:27 Matthew 28:19-20 Romans 10:9

Spiritual Gifts Test

Spiritual Gifts Test[81]

*R*ead each statement below then mark an answer using a 0-5 scale. Don't answer according to what you "wish" the answer was; be as honest as you can, and go with the first thing that comes to your mind.

0 = not at all like me	1 = a little like me	2 = a little more like me
3 = somewhat like me	4 = mostly like me	5 = definitely me

_____ 1. Discerning the character and motives of people is easy for me.

_____ 2. Remembering the specific likes and dislikes of people comes easily for me.

_____ 3. I see truth from the Bible as something you really have to dig for if you want quality.

_____ 4. I like to associate and make plans with "action-oriented" people.

_____ 5. I absolutely enjoy seeing a gift of mine being an answer to someone's specific prayer.

_____ 6. I am able to recognize what responsibilities can or cannot be delegated.

_____ 7. I feel especially comfortable when I'm around individuals who are very sensitive to the feelings of others.

---

81 This spiritual gifts test was given to the church I attended in college. I do not know if our pastor made this up himself or collected the questions from other spiritual gifts tests. I have changed the wording slightly on some of the questions to make their intended purpose clearer.

_____ 8. Speaking or declaring my position on matters is always important to me.

_____ 9. Although like everyone else, I thrive on sincere appreciation for my work, I seem to be able to detect insincerity in the praise of others.

_____ 10. To be honest, I enjoy doing the research behind a lesson I may prepare, more than the actual presenting of it.

_____ 11. I have a hard time staying interested even in a beautiful church service if I can't find several practical applications.

_____ 12. I'm good at handling money and making wise investments.

_____ 13. I like to get things done as fast as possible, and sometimes I'll sacrifice neatness for speed.

_____ 14. The emotional atmosphere with an individual or in a group is something I readily and easily sense.

_____ 15. My commitment to the sovereignty of God is quite possibly my strongest tool for influencing other Christians.

_____ 16. I find much more enjoyment in reaching short-term goals than in attempting to reach long range ones.

_____ 17. When I hear a significant new idea, I often remember it or write it down and compare it later with other truths I know from scripture.

_____ 18. Finding concepts in the scriptures that parallel everyday human experiences is something I enjoy doing and it seems to come relatively easy to me.

_____ 19. I almost always seek counsel before making a special financial gift above my routine tithe.

_____ 20. When a job is done, my first thought is to look for a new challenge to get involved with and keep myself busy.

_____ 21. When I am told of a difficult situation, my first impulse is to remove hurt and bring emotional healing to the people involved.

_____ 22. When I speak in public I am often frank and direct; sometimes my speech is seen as being harsh.

_____ 23. When a project I am working on gets stalled, I feel I should use my personal time, energy, and money if necessary, to assure that it stays on schedule.

_____ 24. I cringe with disapproval when I hear a biblical illustration not used exactly in its proper doctrinal context.

_____ 25. Teaching without practical steps to applications seems to upset me more than it does most of my friends.

_____ 26. My giving is frequently a tool I use specifically to motivate others to support the Lord's work financially.

_____ 27. Seeing all the pieces of a project come together and work smoothly is a source of great fulfillment to me. I like to be a project coordinator.

_____ 28. In a group setting, I seem to be the one who feels the most responsible for making sure that everyone feels accepted.

_____ 29. When I see others violate the truth of scripture, it causes me personally the most intense form of inner pain.

_____ 30. I often wait to get involved in activities until I see a need that no one else is meeting and then I usually am strongly drawn to meet that need.

_____ 31. I would be quite willing to change church memberships in order to sit under the instruction of accurate doctrinal teaching, even if I felt less "warmth" in the new fellowship.

_____ 32. I like to be involved in projects where specific goals are targeted for action and precise scriptural steps are given to fulfill those goals.

_____ 33. I enjoy finding a need and meeting it without anyone even knowing I was responsible.

_____ 34. People seek my counsel when they need an overall practical picture of a situation, especially when long-term goals need to be clarified.

_____ 35. People in distress seem drawn to me and sometimes readily share deeply personal aspects of their problems with me.

_____ 36. A person may claim inward conviction, but I will often demand outward evidence of change before I will embrace that person in fellowship.

_____ 37. I have a hard time saying no when asked to do things and therefore get involved in a large variety of activities.

_____ 38. I am one who places great emphasis on the accuracy of the words a person uses.

_____ 39. When I am speaking or sharing with others, I seem to be intensely aware of visible signs of the acceptance or rejection of what I am communicating.

_____ 40. When I see a need to be met in others, I may wait on meeting that need simply in order to be able to give a more quality gift.

_____ 41. I am not excessively bothered by negative criticism from co-workers if it is required in order to accomplish the ultimate task.

_____ 42. I have noticed that I often feel strained and uncomfortable around individuals who are not very sensitive to the needs of others.

_____ 43. I insist on validating my decisions, often even small ones, by direct scriptural passages.

_____ 44. When everyone is tired on a work project, I seem to be able to maintain the stamina necessary to keep working on the task, and I find myself often using my energy to meet the needs of my co-workers who are feeling worn out.

_____ 45. I enjoy the challenge of doing research to validate a biblical truth.

_____ 46. In the midst of serious problems and trials in someone's life, it is relatively easy for me to see how such difficulties can produce a new level of Christian maturity in that person's life.

_____ 47. I tend to see needs that others have, especially financial or practical ones, which might otherwise go unnoticed by some church members.

_____ 48. If there is no structured leadership in a situation, I am often the one who assumes responsibility for getting things organized.

_____ 49. Being firm with someone is usually my last recourse when dealing with a touchy situation.

_____ 50. I am interested to have others point out my blind spots, especially in areas of biblical truth.

_____ 51. When I hear that a job is going to require extra work and long hours, it seems to make me want to get involved all the more.

_____ 52. I think the most important function of the pastor is to systematically saturate his congregation with detailed biblical truths from his personal research and study. (If it takes you more than five minutes to answer this question, mark it with an "X".)

_____ 53. I enjoy getting together with other Christians one-on-one or in small groups to work out new solutions to scriptural problems.

_____ 54. Public acknowledgement of my giving makes me uncomfortable. I would rather give quietly to worthwhile projects.

_____ 55. I seem to be able to lay my hands quickly on the resources necessary to accomplish even difficult tasks, and others have asked me to help organize projects in the past.

_____ 56. I am quite sensitive to an action that will hurt the feelings of other people.

_____ 57. When considering an action, my first thoughts are about what kind of impact it will have on God's reputation in the community and his holiness.

_____ 58. Although I may be patient in certain areas, when it comes to meeting needs in other people, I become frustrated if I can't act quickly to meet those needs.

_____ 59. When exposed to a new biblical truth, I feel obligated to challenge the knowledge of those teaching (not necessarily in a negative way, but just to be sure that their biblical background is sound.)

_____ 60. I appear to disregard the feelings of those I'm counseling at times because I place such a high emphasis on taking action steps to solve problems.

_____ 61. When I make a contribution to a ministry, I develop a feeling of strong responsibility to the Lord for the quality and integrity of that ministry, even if I am not personally involved in its day-to-day operations.

_____ 62. I don't really feel comfortable beginning a day unless I've taken some time to organize the activities I need to accomplish. I usually try to keep a list of things I need to get done.

_____ 63. When I am around other Christians who are suffering, I quickly sense their mental distress and often suffer emotionally along with them.

_____ 64. Identifying and defining sin with a strong ability to hate evil is one of my most pronounced qualities.

_____ 65. I relish getting involved in projects, especially when the objective is to meet a practical need.

_____ 66. I feel that a working understanding of the Greek and Hebrew languages in which the original Bible manuscripts were written is necessary for someone to be a Bible scholar.

_____ 67. When I use a passage of scripture for practical applications, it may appear that I am taking it out of context to some extent.

_____ 68. Knowing the worth of a project and understanding fully the intentions of its sponsors is my primary consideration when giving money to a project.

_____ 69. When facing a job, I am quite conscious of the amount of time I have to accomplish it, and I am frustrated when personal problems slow down efficiency.

_____ 70. Often I will avoid firmness in trying to spare the feelings of others, even if I appear weak or indecisive because of it.

SCORING

☙ Look back at your answers and add them up according to the score sheet below:

1. Prophet =   # 1, 8, 15, 22, 29, 36, 43, 50, 57, 64   = _____

2. Service =   # 2, 9, 16, 23, 30, 37, 44, 51, 58, 65   = _____

3. Teaching =   # 3, 10, 17, 24, 31, 38, 45, 52, 59, 66   = _____

4. Encouragement =   # 4, 11, 18, 25, 32, 39, 46, 53, 60, 67   = _____

5. Giving =   # 5, 12, 19, 26, 33, 40, 47, 54, 61, 68   = _____

6. Leadership =   # 6, 13, 20, 27, 34, 41, 48, 55, 62, 69   = _____

7. Mercy =   # 7, 14, 21, 28, 35, 42, 49, 56, 63, 70   = _____

☙ List your gifts in order from the highest to the lowest score

     1. _____

     2. _____

     3. _____

     4. _____

     5. _____

     6. _____

     7. _____

☙ Did your gifts inventory match your desire, opportunity, and evidence from Day Four? If not, what was different, and why do you think they might be different?

_____

_____

_____

_____

❧ How do you plan to use your gifts in your church? Be specific; name a ministry or mission team, etc.

_____

_____

_____

_____

PRAYER JOURNAL

Today I prayed:

- A _____

- C _____

- T _____

- S _____

God has answered the following prayers:

_____

_____

As I silenced my thoughts and mind, I heard or sensed God saying:

_____

_____

After praying I feel like I need to take the following specific action:

_____

_____

Before I prayed I was feeling...

_____

_____

After praying I feel...

_____

_____

Other notes or thoughts about today:

_____

_____

---

82 This resource may be copied or reproduced for personal use but may not be re-sold.

SCRIPTURE JOURNAL

Book Name: _____ Chapter: _____ Date: _____

Cross References	*How do these verses apply to your life today?*
	What promises are in these verses?
Key Verses	*What commands are in these verses for you to follow?*
	After reading these verses what do you most need to work on or change?
Key Words/Concepts	*Other notes, thoughts or ideas...*

Made in the USA
Lexington, KY
11 April 2012